The Theatrical Career of Samuel Morgan Smith

The Theatrical Career of
Samuel Morgan Smith

Bernth Lindfors

AFRICA WORLD PRESS

TRENTON | LONDON | CAPE TOWN | NAIROBI | ADDIS ABABA | ASMARA | IBADAN | NEW DELHI

AFRICA WORLD PRESS
541 West Ingham Avenue | Suite B
Trenton, New Jersey 08638

Book design: Dawid Kahts
Cover design: Ashraful Haque
Cover: Photo of Morgan Smith held in the William H. Dorsey Manuscript
Collection, No. 51. Reproduced with permission from the Cheyney University
Archives, Pennsylvania.

Library of Congress Cataloging-in-Publication Data

Names: Lindfors, Bernth, author.
Title: The theatrical career of Samuel Morgan Smith / Bernth Lindfors.
Description: Trenton : Africa World Press, [2018]. | Includes bibliographical
    references and index.
Identifiers: LCCN 2017051396| ISBN 9781569025444 (hb : alk. paper) |
ISBN
    9781569025451 (pb : alk. paper)
Subjects: LCSH: Smith, S. Morgan (Samuel Morgan) | African American
    actors--Biography. | Actors--Great Britain--Biography. | Shakespearean
    actors and actresses--Biography.
Classification: LCC PN2287.S6128 L56 2018 | DDC 792.02/8092 [B] --dc23
LC record available at https://lccn.loc.gov/2017051396

Contents

Illustrations

Contents

Acknowledgments

I wish to thank the numerous librarians and archivists in Philadelphia and the British Isles who assisted me in this project. I have also had strategic help from librarians at the University of Texas at Austin, especially those at the Harry Ransom Center, the Fine Arts Library, and the interlibrary loans office at the Perry Castañeda Library. Thanks too to my daughter Susan Taylor for preparing the index. My biggest debts, though, have been to Michael A. Morrison and Martin Hoyles, who read and commented insightfully on what I have written in this book. Of course, whatever errors and omissions remain are entirely my own responsibility.

1
Philadelphia

L ittle is known about Samuel Morgan Smith's background and upbringing. His passport, issued in Boston on April 12, 1866 as he was preparing to travel to England, records that he was born in the City of Philadelphia on June 20, 1832.[1] It has not been possible to discover exactly where in Philadelphia he was born, who his parents were, how many siblings he had, and where in the city his family originally lived.[2] Part of the problem may derive from the possibility that his surname was recorded in official records simply as Smith without any reference to a middle name or conjoined surname. From the 1830s to 1860s there were many Sam or Samuel Smiths living in the Philadelphia area, and it has proven difficult to pick him out from the crowd.

It has also not been possible to determine the facts of Morgan Smith's early education. At the time, Philadelphia had a number of elementary schools for black children. One can find in Benjamin C. Bacon's *Statistics of the Colored People of Philadelphia* a list of three public schools, two private schools, two charity schools, and one orphan's shelter that had been established for colored children before 1837, when five-year-old Morgan Smith presumably would have been old enough to attend.[3] However, the first high school for such students, the Institute for Colored Youth, was not established until 1852, by which time he would have been twenty years old.[4] There is a possibility, even a likelihood, that he went elsewhere for advanced education, but we know too little about the circumstances of his family life to know where to look.

It was not until 1851 that a Philadelphia city directory eventually identified a "Samuel M. Smith, japanner," living at "Franklin above Crown,"[5] near Franklin Square. According to the *Oxford English Dictionary*, a japanner was "one who follows the trade of varnishing with japan," a lacquer that "gives a hard black gloss." It also used to be a humorous term applied to someone who shined shoes—i.e., a "shoe black."[6] In any case, japanning does not appear to have been a lucrative line of work, for there is no reference in subsequent Philadelphia city directories to Samuel M. Smith continuing in this trade during the next two years.

What he did to support himself during this entire period is unknown, but it appears that at some point he found employment as an apprentice in a barber shop, a job that enabled him to gain valuable experience in cutting hair and shaving beards. By 1854 he had managed to establish his own business as a "hair dresser" at 8 Sansom Street, an address he shared with Charles H. Beeler, an engraver, Eric Stephens, a designer, and the office of Peter S. Smith, a lawyer and counselor.[7]

In Philadelphia hair-dressing was an occupation dominated by blacks in the first half of the nineteenth century. A *Register of Trades of the Colored People in the City of Philadelphia and Districts*, published in 1838, lists more hair-dressers and hair-workers (119) than men employed in other skilled trades such as boot and shoemakers (96), carpenters and cabinet makers (61), tanners (37), and blacksmiths (28).[8] Moreover, nearly all the hair-dressers and hair-workers had their own shops, while many of those engaged in other trades worked as journeymen for others. Census records show that there were 137 black barbers in Philadelphia in 1850 and only 36 white barbers, a difference of nearly 80 percent.[9] A statistical study by Benjamin C. Bacon reports that by 1856, the number of black barbers there had risen to 248[10], and the 1860 census figures for Philadelphia show a further increase to 315. However, that same census reveals that there were now 358 white barbers in the city, more than two-thirds of whom were foreign-born, most of them immigrants from Germany.[11] So there was now some competition in the hair-dressing profession, though there is evidence that the German barbers "appear to have had trouble breaking into the higher end of barbering."[12]

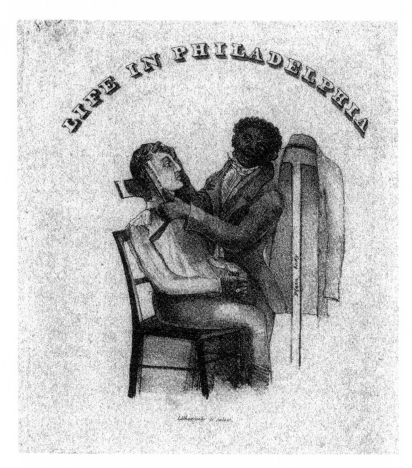

Figure 1. "Life in Philadelphia" lithograph by Anthony Imbert, HSP graphics collection [V66]. Reproduced with permission from the Historical Society of Pennsylvania.

The most prosperous black barbers in Philadelphia were those who catered to white customers exclusively. The same was true in other American cities. In a book written by a mixed-race barber on *The Colored Aristocracy of St. Louis*, Cyprian Clamorgan claimed that

> A majority of our colored aristocracy belong to the tonsorial profession; a mulatto takes to razor and soap as naturally as a young duck to a pool of water, or a strapped Frenchman to dancing; they certainly make the best barbers in the world, and were doubtless intended by nature for the art. In its exercise, they take white men by the nose without giving offense, and without an effusion of blood.[13]

One historian of the trade notes that

> Most black barbers, regardless of where they were geographically, came from the small group of slaves freed selectively with the help of their master. These men were most likely to be light-skinned. In turn, skin color may have helped bridge the social divide with white customers and convince them to feel comfortable entering their barbershops in the first place. Whatever the causes for their success, black barbers certainly found more opportunities to work than did other free black men, even other skilled workers.[14]

Of course, it was not necessary to be light-skinned or of mixed race to be a successful barber. What mattered most was the relationship such enterprising entrepreneurs managed to establish with their white customers. This required some sensitivity to prevailing social norms. A black barber had to show considerable respect and deference to the white men he served. Only by doing so could he earn a measure of their respect, confidence, and trust. He also had to display great skill with a comb and scissors as well as exceptional care when wielding a razor. And most of all, to ensure that he would continue to prosper by attracting the highest paying clientele, a black barber would have to deny to serve men of his own race. This was the only way he could run a first-class establishment.[15]

There were black leaders who deplored this kind of discrimination in black-owned businesses. They felt that such barbers were degrading their race through abject subservience, thereby reinforcing notions of white superiority. Frederick Douglass was one of the most vocal critics. In an article published in his newspaper he urged parents to "Make Your Sons Mechanics and Farmers—not Waiters, Porters, and Barbers."[16] Historian Leslie M. Harris has pointed out that Douglass was responding to a series of articles that had appeared in his own paper written by James McCune Smith, a prominent black intellectual who had "attempted to bring dignity to all types of manual labor and warned against the confusion of individual wealth and character."[17] Douglass, in contrast, argued that menial occupations like barbering "beget, in those engaged in them, improvidence, wastefulness, [and] a fondness for dress and display. Catering to the pride and vanity of others, they become themselves proud, vain and fopish [*sic*]." Further, such workers inevitably lose respectability, no matter how much they might happen to earn by playing such a servile role. "To shave a half dozen faces in the morning, and sleep or play the guitar in the afternoon—all this might be easy; but is it noble, is it manly, and does it improve and elevate us?"[18]

Douglass wasn't the only black leader to condemn black barbers. Those attending the Ohio Colored Convention in Cincinnati in 1852 had gone a step further in asserting that a "colored [barber] who refuses to shave a colored man because he is colored, is much worse than a white man who refuses to eat, drink, ride, walk, or be educated with a colored man…for the former is a party *de facto* to riveting chains around his own neck and the necks of his much injured race."[19]

Black barbers were quick to respond to these charges. Men like Uriah Boston from Poughkeepsie and Lewis Woodson from Pittsburgh defended themselves and others engaged in their occupation by asserting that "they are, in every way, as intelligent and respectable as any other class of businessmen and much more so than some others," that barbering indeed provided "an easy, practical, and certain means" of bettering the condition of their race, especially considering that "our efforts to obtain wealth have not been equal to our efforts to obtain knowledge."[20] Handicapped by their inability to acquire advanced education, men who succeeded in a profitable business such as barbering could not only claim status in their community but could also adequately support a family. Martin Delany had entered the debate earlier by noting that "Until colored men, attain to a position above permitting their mothers, sisters, wives, and daughters, to do the drudgery and menial offices of other men's wives and daughters, it is useless, it is nonsense, it is pitiable mockery, to talk about equality and elevation."[21] Harris, in her book aptly entitled *In the Shadow of Slavery,* observes that black barbers "at their best were independent businessmen, owning their shops and tools," and as such "potentially exemplified an alternate model of independent manhood," but "they were in a bind. No doubt if they chose to integrate their shops, most whites would take their business to other segregated shops."[22] Most black workers simply could not afford the high prices charged in first-class barber shops.

Morgan Smith, in setting up his shop at a time when this debate was going on in the black community, had to decide whether he would serve customers of his own race or deal exclusively with a white clientele. He appears to have chosen the latter. There is evidence that white men of some social standing patronized his establishment and did him favors later on when he needed their help. He could rely on them because he had earned their friendship while attending to their cosmetic needs.

The Reverend Bayard R. Hall, in *Frank Freeman's Barber Shop,* a novel he published in 1852 that told the story of a slave who won freedom and achieved business success as a barber, praised the ambience of a first-class black barber shop, emphasizing the comforts it offered its customers:

> Of all lounging places in Philadelphia, Frank Freeman's Barber Shop was the place. His rooms were large, convenient, and airy. There was for everything a place, and everything was in its place; for everything a time, and everything in time. Order reigned, all was neat, clean, comfortable. It was cool in summer and warm in winter. The paraphernalia were pre-eminently barbarish [sic]. There also you found the best newspapers and the best company.
>
> When you went in you felt at once homeish, and did not want to go out again—you had half a notion to stay and learn barbering; and on taking the chair to be beautified, the handling was so artistic, so tasteful, so gentlemanly, you wished to be shaved all day; or secretly hoped your hair would grow up as fast as it was cut off! Frank was just the dandy!
>
> Freeman's customers were all white folks.[23]

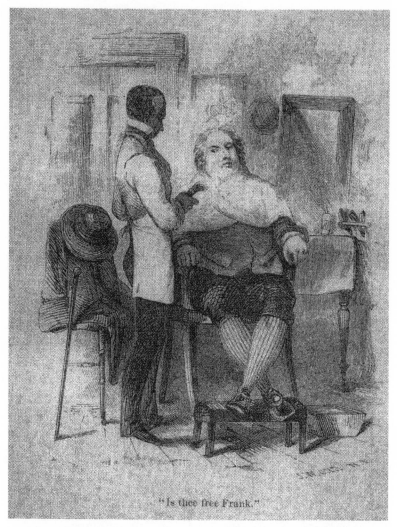

Figure 2. Frontispiece of Baynard Rush Hall's *Frank Freeman's Barber Shop* (1852). Reproduced with permission from the Harry Ransom Center, University of Texas at Austin.

This more than likely was the kind of work place Morgan Smith wished to establish.

His shop may have become popular among actors and theatre managers, for by 1858 it was strategically located at 609 Sansom

Street in a fine neighborhood close to Independence Square and right at the center of the theatre district in the city: only a block from the Chestnut Street Theater, three blocks from the Walnut Street Theatre, and four blocks from the Arch Street Theatre.[24] Even a smaller performance venue such as the Wheatley Dramatic Hall at Fifth and Gaskill Street was not far away. Also, Morgan Smith may have been unusual among black barbers, for a friend familiar with his background revealed he had somehow "managed to get some money and a decidedly good education. He was at an early age fond of reading Shakspeare, and fond too...of imagining the looks and behavior of his leading characters."[25] It is conceivable that he may have entertained some of the performers he served by reciting or enacting passages from Shakespeare while shaving them or trimming their hair. To feed this dramatic interest, he had resolved to attend shows at local theatres even though this required that he, like others of his race, had to sit on a "shelf near the roof, where, surrounded by yelling, whistling and ever-fighting boys, he studied the performances on the stage."[26]

Within a few years, as his business grew, Morgan Smith began to gain more visibility in the black community by displaying his talents as a public lecturer and entertainer. His first appearance in this double role may have been at a musical and literary entertainment sponsored by the Philadelphia Library Company of Colored Persons on November 2, 1858, where he gave an address on the subject of "Woman," followed by recitations and vocal as well as instrumental music in which he took part.[27] A year later, on December 13, he lectured again before the same society on "Friendship," a performance hailed in the black press as having been "well written, well-delivered and well applauded."[28]

The Philadelphia Library Company of Coloured Persons, founded 1833, had been established to serve the black community by providing a place of learning and exchange, much as the Library Company of Philadelphia served the white community. It helped to promote literacy and public speaking among its members through a number of activities, including readings, debates, and weekly lectures.[29] According to an early report in an abolitionist newspaper, debates there

> were conducted with a degree of spirit and propriety and

displayed a cogency and acuteness of reasoning, and an elevation and elegance of language...The subjects of discussion generally relate to [members'] own rights and interests and frequently result in decisions from which the prejudiced mind of the white man would startle and shrink with apprehension.[30]

Morgan Smith became a very active participant in these debates, and at a meeting on February 7, 1860 to appoint officers, he was elected as an Assistant Secretary of this society.[31]

He played a prominent role in other public gatherings as well, especially those that addressed salient political issues. On January 30, 1860 he served as Vice-President of a meeting of "colored citizens" at the Philadelphia Institute that had been convened to petition the Governor of Virginia concerning the fate of two black prisoners who had been condemned to death for their participation in John Brown's raid on Harper's Ferry a few months earlier. On that occasion he gave an eloquent speech and helped to draft for publication the resolutions adopted at the gathering.[32] Then at a subsequent meeting on March 30, he spoke out on behalf of men who had been arrested and imprisoned for attempting to free a fugitive slave who had been seized in Pennsylvania and returned to servitude in Virginia. He also co-authored the resolution produced at this assembly and served as chairman on a committee to raise money for the prisoners.[33] At the beginning of May he participated in a debate held at Israel Church about another black prisoner, William Still, who had perjured himself by agreeing to plead guilty to a charge of libel but had been released from confinement early, prompting a controversy in the press.[34]

What is remarkable about all these proceedings is how many black barbers were involved in them. Isaiah C. Wears, James Douglass, Charles Jones, and Frederick C. Revels were also elected officials of the Philadelphia Library Company of Colored Persons and regularly attended the weekly events there. Two of Philadelphia's wealthiest barbers, Jacob C. White and Joshua P.B. Eddy, are on record as having taken part in debates at such public meetings.[35] All of them were members of an intellectual elite in the black community.

It is clear that Morgan Smith's interests extended beyond theatre and politics to other realms as well. He was also an enthusiastic musician who displayed talent both as a lyricist and as a performer.

The Historical Society of Pennsylvania in Philadelphia holds the manuscript of a song he was commissioned to compose for a gathering early in 1860. In a letter accompanying the verses, he wrote

> My Dr Sir
>
> You will plainly see that I have strictly followed yr instructions— "Not to hurry my-Self"—though you may rest assured that while I always take pleasure in following the desires of my friends yet in this case this "Observance" has only been consequent upon forgetfulness. In singing this Song the first 2 lines in each verse are re-sung after having gone through with the whole 4 after which the Chorus follows.
>
> I avail my-self of this opportunity of reassuring you of my fr[ien]dly regard.
>
> S. M. Smith
>
> Jan 23/60

The song itself was a plea for tolerance:

> Let us speak of a man as we find him and censure alone what we see
>
> And should a man blame let's remind him that from faults we are none of us free
>
> If the veil from the heart could be torn and the mind could be read on the brow
>
> There are many we pass by with scorn whom we're loading with high honors now
>
> Let us speak of a man as we find him & heed not what others may say
>
> If he's frail then a kind word will bind him where coldness would turn him away
>
> For the heart must be barren indeed where no bud of repentance may bloom
>
> Then pause ere you cause it to bleed on a smile or frown hangs it[s] doom

Chorus
Let us speak of a man Let us speak of a man Let us speak of a
man as we find him[36]

This song may have been intended as an effort to cool tempers
that may have been inflamed during some of the debates at public
meetings.

**Figure 3. Program of a Grand Complimentary Concert at
Sansom Street Hall, 30 May 1860, Leon Gardiner collection
of American Negro Historical Society records [0008].
Reproduced with permission from the Historical Society of
Pennsylvania.**

Even more remarkable than this manuscript is a printed program, also preserved in a file at the Historical Society of Pennsylvania, giving details of a Grand Complimentary Concert to honor Madame Mary L. Brown that was held at the Samson Street Hall on Wednesday evening, May 30, 1860. The featured performers were Madame Brown herself as well as "the renowned Vocalist, Miss E.T. Greenfield, the Black Swan...[who] having in the kindest manner volunteered her highly valuable services" and Mr. S. Morgan Smith, "who has kindly consented to sing for this occasion." In the first part of the concert, after a piano forte solo by Professor Koenig, Morgan Smith sang an aria, "Brighter than the stars soft gleaming" from Verdi's opera *Il Trovatore*, followed by Madame Brown who sang "Oh love for me thy power" from Bellini's *Somnambula*, and then the Black Swan who rendered "Oh! My Fernand" from Donizetti's *La Favourita*. Next came a duet by Madame Brown and Morgan Smith who performed "Thus to die thy love possessing" from Verdi's opera *Ernani*. This part of the concert concluded with Professor Koenig playing a Schottische Brilliante on the piano. The second part had the Swan and Madame Brown teaming up to sing Donizetti's "Maria Padilla," Morgan Smith offering F. Kücken's ballad "Good Night, Farewell," and the Swan warbling Rondinella's "See the pale and silvery moon." Then the three artists together sang the "Celebrated Terzetto" from Verdi's *Attilla*, after which Madame Brown gave a final solo, "Dear friends of youth" from Verdi's *Sicilian Vespers*. Professor Koenig rounded off the evening by playing another piece on the piano.[37]

Elizabeth Taylor Greenfield, born a slave in Mississippi in 1824, had been freed and raised by a Quaker woman in Philadelphia who, along with others, encouraged the remarkable natural talent this young girl had for singing. Her voice was said to have "a full round sound...of immense compass and depth" and could range over three and a half octaves.[38]

> Refused by a professor of music, on account of her color, to be included in the list of his pupils, she worked hard to overcome the difficulties surrounding her, and with marked success. Her improvement was rapid; she received invitations to entertain private parties, and frequently volunteered to aid various charities. The first occasion on which she sang in public

was before the Buffalo Musical Association [in 1851]. Her subsequent success was rapid. She visited Europe [in 1853-54] and sang before the various crowned heads [including Queen Victoria], receiving lavish praise and innumerable presents.[39]

While abroad, she received professional training from Sir George Smart, Queen Victoria's organist and composer. Among her patrons in England were four duchesses as well as other nobility and Mrs. Harriet Beecher Stowe.[40] When she returned to the United States, she received a warm welcome and resettled in Philadelphia, where she gave frequent concerts, sometimes with singers she had taught. Madame Mary L. Brown, who became known as the American Nightingale, was one of her protégées.[41]

The fact that Morgan Smith was invited to appear in a concert with the Black Swan and the American Nightingale raises further questions about his education. Where did he get his training as an operatic singer? Was he one of Greenfield's pupils, or did he happen to have a natural gift that enabled him to appear in public without embarrassment alongside professional vocalists? This, like his fondness for Shakespeare, is another of his personal peculiarities that is very difficult to explain. One wishes to know how he managed to acquire such remarkable interests and abilities, especially since there was not even a high school for black students in Philadelphia while Morgan Smith was growing up.[42]

Before this year ended, Morgan Smith added one more new experience to his list of accomplishments: On November 11, 1860 he married Mary Eliza Taylor, the eighteen-year-old daughter of Ann Taylor, a widowed or divorced colored laundress.[43] Mary had been born in Virginia, but her family had been living in Philadelphia for at least the previous decade.[44] For the first two years of their marriage the couple lived at 704 Steward Street in a mixed working class neighborhood.[45]

In January 1861 seven Southern slave states seceded from the United States and formed the Confederate States of America, and by April the civil war had begun. Morgan Smith continued running his barber shop for the next few years, but he became increasingly involved in civic affairs. In February of 1861 he was appointed to a committee of the Athenian Lodge of Masons and the following

December he was elected as a correspondent of the Right Worshipful Grand Lodge of Pennsylvania, another Masonic organization in Philadelphia.[46] He and Mary's first child, Edwin Smith, was born on August 24, 1861, but the boy died a year later on August 30, 1862.[47] The following November Morgan Smith was elected to serve on the Executive Committee of the Social, Civil and Statistical Association of the Colored People of Pennsylvania,[48] an organization with seventy-five members that had "for its objects mutual protection, the general recognition of the civil and social rights of the colored people, and the improvement of 'the condition of the colored race by every means calculated to exalt their common humanity, and to raise them to the God ordained level of the great brotherhood of man.'"[49] In December he gave an address at an event celebrating the 29th anniversary of the Philadelphia Library Company of Colored Persons.[50]

Meanwhile, the civil war was raging on. Philadelphia, at that time the second largest city in the country and the closest urban center to the warfront,[51] was also home to the largest free black community in the North, comprising 4 percent of the city's total population.[52] As such, it was a center of abolition and a destination for fugitive slaves escaping on the Underground Railroad.[53] After President Lincoln issued the Emancipation Proclamation on January 1, 1863, the War Department authorized the recruitment of Negro soldiers in a number of Northern states,[54] and by the middle of the year Philadelphia was supporting the effort with a strong publicity campaign.

Morgan Smith had joined with other civic leaders, white and black, to promote colored enlistment in the Union Army. Confederate forces had entered Pennsylvania and were engaging Union troops at Gettysburg at the beginning of July, and there were fears that they might advance toward the capital afterwards.[55] A Supervisory Committee on recruitment in Philadelphia was urging colored residents to come forward and defend the city: "We need the aid of every Man who can shoulder a musket or handle a pick."[56] On July 6th a mass meeting was held downtown at which Frederick Douglass and other prominent abolitionists spoke, calling upon every Able-Bodied Colored Man to enter the Army for the THREE YEARS' SERVICE, and join in fighting the Battles of Liberty and the Union. A new era is open to us. For generations we have suffered under the horrors of slavery, outrage and wrong; our manhood has been denied, our citizenship blotted out, our souls seared and burned, our spirits cowed and crushed, and the hopes of the future of our race involved in doubts and darkness. But now the whole aspect of our relations to the white race is changed. Now therefore is our most precious moment. Let us Rush to Arms! **Fail Now and our Race is Doomed.**[57]

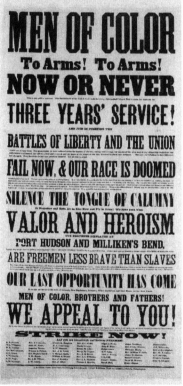

Morgan Smith was one of more than fifty distinguished citizens who signed this call to arms. He also contributed funds for a flag that was presented on August 31st to the 6th Regiment of Colored Troops stationed and being trained at Camp William Penn.[58]

One wonders if perhaps Morgan Smith answered the call himself. In December he was re-elected to his position on the Committee of Correspondence at the Right Worshipful Grand Lodge of Pennsylvania,[59] but there is no record of him attending meetings of this or any other society for the whole of 1864. His barber shop, now located at NW 6th and Walnut Street, and his home, now at 1311 Lombard Street, continued to be listed in *McElroy's Philadelphia City Directory for 1864*, but this still leaves open the possibility that he could have enlisted in a

Figure 4. Broadside of a mass meeting held in Philadelphia, July 6, 1863. (Rare (4)5777.F.55). Reproduced with permission from the Library Company of Philadelphia.

colored regiment for all or a portion of this year. A search through the lists of colored recruits recorded in Samuel P. Bates's *History of Pennsylvania Volunteers, 1861-5* yields five men named Samuel Smith, but only two of them could possibly be the man we are looking for, and both turned out to be unreliable soldiers. The first, a private in Company C of the 22nd Colored Regiment, was mustered in on December 17, 1863 and deserted on February 9, 1864.[60] The other, a private in Company K of the 43rd Colored Regiment, was mustered in on March 27, 1864 but never joined the company.[61] The remaining Samuel Smiths, also mustered in on various dates in 1864, were not mustered out or discharged until several months after the war ended in April 1865, at which time Morgan Smith was quite busy in Philadelphia.[62] There is also an intriguing reference to a black barber named Samuel Smith who enlisted in Philadelphia as a sailor on June 23, 1864, but he too continued serving on vessels beyond the conclusion of the war. If further disqualifying proof were needed, it could be found in the fact that this sailor stood only five feet two inches tall,[63] whereas Morgan Smith, according to his 1866 passport, measured a full five feet six and a half inches.

Whether or not Morgan Smith actually joined a colored regiment and fought in the war, there can be no doubt about his views on slavery, for these were published a few years earlier, probably in 1860, in a pamphlet entitled *A Critical Review of the Late Speech of Charles O'Conor, "Negro Slavery not Unjust."* O'Conor, a former U.S. District Attorney for New York[64] who sympathized with the Southern states and wanted them to remain as part of a united nation, had delivered a speech at a Union meeting in New York on December 19, 1859 criticizing abolitionists and members of Congress in the North "who declare themselves to be enlisted in a crusade against slavery."[65]

> We are told that slavery is unjust; we are told that it is a matter of conscience to put it down, and that whatever treaties, or compacts, or laws, or constitutions, have been made to sanction and uphold it, it is still unholy, and that we are bound to trample upon treaties, compacts, laws, and constitutions, and to stand

by what these men arrogantly tell us is the law of God and a fundamental principle of natural justice.[66]

In response to such arguments, O'Conor insisted that

> negro slavery is not unjust...that it is benign in its influences upon the white man, and upon the black...I maintain that it is ordained by nature; that it is a necessity of both races...[The negro] has ample strength and is competent to labor, but nature denies to him either the intellect to govern or the willingness to work. Both were denied him. That same power which deprived him of the will to labor, gave him, in our country, as a recompense, a master to coerce that duty, and convert him into a useful and valuable servant...I hold that the negro is decreed by nature to a state of pupilage under the dominion of the wiser white man...The negro, to be sure, is a bondman for life.[67]

O'Conor ended by demanding that

> We must no longer favor political leaders who talk about negro slavery being an evil [but should instead] secure in the councils of the nation men who are true to the Constitution, who are lovers of the Union, men who cannot be induced by considerations of imaginary benevolence for a people who really do not desire their aid, to sacrifice or to jeopard in any degree the blessings we enjoy under this Union. May it be perpetual.[68]

In his reply to O'Conor's speech, Morgan Smith began by admitting that he initially sought to publish his rebuttal under a pseudonym in a letter to the editor of a New York newspaper, but, having received no acknowledgment or response from that paper, had decided to issue a lengthier riposte in Philadelphia in a pamphlet bearing his own name. He promised to "show the sophistry of [O'Conor's] logic, and the total untruthfulness of his statement of facts [for] he utterly fails to produce any arguments, any references, any data, any quotation or authority to support him in the advancement of such monstrously revolting, uncivilized, unchristian and inhuman assertions, affecting a portion of God's humanity."[69] All this "very bad lawyer" offers are simple assertions.

First, "it is pretended that God made the black man to be a slave

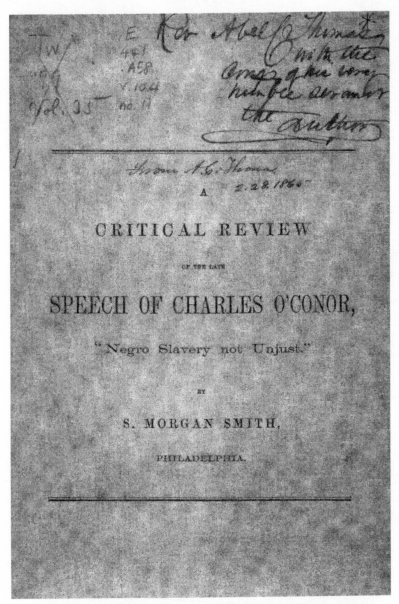

Figure 5. Cover of S. Morgan Smith's *A Critical Review of the Late Speech of Charles O'Conor: "Negro Slavery Not Unjust,"* 1860. Reproduced with permission from the Historical Society of Pennsylvania.

wherever he has placed him," but Morgan Smith could find nothing in the Bible where "God at any one time expresses a determination to exalt one man above another, from complexion, or draws a line of distinction between men in consequence of inferior capacities, birth, or dissimilarity in that which constitutes their respective due. And why? Because God created men equal."[70]

And this God-given equality of men made it illogical for O'Conor to claim that "the negro, to be sure, is to be a bondman for life" and that white men had "an unquestionable Divine right to hold him in slavery."[71] Morgan Smith did not rely solely on scripture to make his points; at strategic moments he inserted relevant quotations from John Wesley, Frederick Douglass, Martin Robison Delaney, and Henry Highland Garnet for support.

O'Conor believed that negroes "are of some other creation than the human family, that 'intellect has been denied them,' that they have been created without any natural desire to work, that they are extremely 'lazy and stupid,' that their only thriving state is slavery, and that of course must be perpetual, that they can only thrive and live in hot climates...[that] they in short are barbarians." Morgan Smith condemned all such claims as "*lies, base, false, villainous lies*, sufficient in gravity to assign [O'Conor] to the lowest possible depth of humanity...I think that to any man of any reflective, unbiased mind, but one conclusion will follow, and that is that none other than a man knowingly crazy, or amazingly ignorant, would pile together such an accumulation of ridiculous, nonsensical reasonings."[72]

This angry, articulate essay was the vigorous response of a young, well-educated black man to the blithe, unsupported racial assumptions of a white lawyer twice his age. It was Morgan Smith's first public intervention in the racial politics of his day.

One of the prominent public figures who proved influential in Morgan Smith's life in the years preceding and during the civil war was James E. Murdoch, a man he had first met in 1852-53 when training as a barber. Murdoch, born in Philadelphia in 1811, was by then a famous actor who had launched his career locally at the Arch Street and Chestnut Street theatres and had subsequently moved on to performing leading roles in New York, California, and at the Haymarket Theatre in London. When he was in his thirties, he had taken some time off to study the science of elocution and thereafter he often gave dramatic readings applying the principles he had learned.[73] In 1845 he had co-authored with William Russell a volume entitled *Orthophony: or Vocal Culture in Elocution*[74] that included exercises on breathing, enunciation, tone, and other techniques of effective utterance.

In 1861, shortly after the war broke out, he learned that his younger son had enlisted in a regiment in Washington, and he rushed to find him. Asked to give a speech by his son's comrades, he "not only animated the regiment, but he also convinced himself as to the line of duty which he was called upon to pursue. He at once abandoned his theatrical career, resolving to devote all his time, talent, and energy to the cause of his country, and not to reappear upon the stage until that cause should be triumphant."[75]

William Norris reports that

> Between 1861 to 1865 Murdoch crisscrossed the country many times, refusing to accept any payment other than that for his expenses. It is estimated that he raised at least $250,000 for various Soldiers Aid Societies and related causes. His patriotism won high praise and recognition from Lincoln himself, who attended several of Murdoch's readings in the Senate Chamber, and it won the lasting gratitude and friendship of a host of civic, political, and military figures. Murdoch was, in effect, a one-man USO, even spending considerable time with several armies in the field, and on two occasions actually participating in minor military operations.[76]

It was on one of Murdoch's return visits to Philadelphia between 1863 and 1865 that Morgan Smith had occasion to write to him to beg a special favor. The letter was written on the stationery of S. Morgan Smith's Saloon, N.W. Corner Walnut and Sixth Street, Philadelphia, which advertised "SMITH's Celebrated Hair Tonic, for the Growth, Preservation, Strength and Beauty of the Hair. Also the finest article of genuine imported Bay Rum. N.B.—All articles necessary for Gentleman's Toilet furnished at the shortest notice: also, a fine stock of *Gentlemen's Furnishing Goods*, with the very best articles of imported *Segars, Tobacco, Umbrellas, &c., c.,* always on hand."

The letter read as follows:

J.E. Murdoch, Esq.

My Dr Sir

Your writer indulges the hope that when you shall have read his note it will alter what might otherwise be deemed presum[p]tion.

Being a great lover of the poets & with others esteeming at all times yr performances a rare pleasure I have resorted to the ordinary medium to obtain admission to the Readings you have been recently giving but having the misfortune to have placed on me—though not through my own *Agency* a *"Colored Skin"* I am debar[r]ed from what would be to me & my Lady a great delight.

I am thus compelled to throw myself on the slightest claim of an old acquaintance with attention given you professionally long since.

Yr writer having during his apprenticeship dressed yr toilet whenever you appeared at the old Chestnut St Theatre at that period familiarly known as *"Sam"* now asks of you the favor that you will grant him & his Lady such permission as will enable him to obtain admittance to yr Reading on tomorrow night as his Business would preclude availing himself—though offered—the one for Saturday night. He might add that persons of color have been admitted though he ow[e]s it to truth to state that he has not the fortune to be as *fair skinned*. In conclusion yr writer cannot withhold the remarks that the sincerity of his desire to attend this reading can be tested by the earnest of his perfect willingness to that purchase which enables others but he has been forced as a last effort to obtain this long desired pleasure to thus apply.

With his sincere [?] hopes for yr good health & continued prosperity

He is yr humble & obdt. Servt

S. Morgan Smith

P.S. having for quite a period been conducting Business as Principal I shall be very happy to see you at any time when I shall exert myself to reciprocate for the favor now asked.[77]

Figure 6. Frontispiece of James E. Murdoch's *The Stage, or Recollections of Actors and Acting* (1880).

This letter confirms that Morgan Smith had found work as an apprentice barber, and since Murdoch had performed at the Chestnut Street Theatre for several weeks in 1852 and again for several weeks in 1853, we may assume that it was in one or both of these periods that Morgan Smith had served him.[78] A handwritten note by Murdoch confirms that "Mr. Morgan Smith was my hairdresser at the Phila theatres for several years," and an additional handwritten note by someone else reports that in response to Morgan Smith's request, "Mr Murdoch invited Mr Smith and his Lady to his withdrawing room which opened on to the stage, and leaving the door partially open they were enabled to enjoy the Reading."[79]

Murdoch was back in Philadelphia in February and March of 1865 giving readings in support of charities aiding victims of the war. The program for his appearance at the Concert Hall on February 10th included selections from Shakespeare's *Othello* and Dickens's *Pickwick Papers* as well as heroic and patriotic poems by Henry Wadsworth Longfellow, Robert Browning, Thomas Buchanan Read, George Henry Boker, Francis De Haes Janvier, and others. The following night he read extracts from Shakespeare's *King Henry VIII*, verse by John Greenleaf Whittier, Oliver Wendell Holmes, Jean Ingelow, and more war poems by Read, Boker, and Janvier.[80] Some of these selections can be found in *Patriotism in Poetry and Prose: Selected Passages from Lectures and Patriotic Readings by James E. Murdoch*, published a year after the war ended.[81]

On March 3rd and 4th Murdoch was scheduled to give a second series of "Patriotic and Scriptural Readings" at the Concert Hall.[82] This prompted Morgan Smith to send him another letter, this time inviting him to a reading that he himself was about to give a few days later, on March 10th, at the same venue:

J.E. Murdoch Esq

My dr Sir

Noticing yr announcement for tonight I was happy of the opportunity it afforded to transmit you a ticket for admission to the *Effort* I mentioned when last I saw you. I shall be truly happy if yr stay will admit of yr attendance for though I full well know that you could derive no profit--& possibly hardly entertainment still I believe I shall have yr sympathy & good feeling for my success & should be proud to know my Reading was attended by one so distinguished in the Art.

You will perceive that my personal regard & respect for yr ability & judgement had led me to adopt your selections as my Guide.

With the renewal of my earnest desire for yr presence if in the city

I am yr very obdt servant

S Morgan Smith[83]

Advertisements for the reading he alluded to had been placed in several local papers, stating that

> Mr. S. Morgan Smith, a colored resident of this city, one well known, is about entering on the now popular entertainment of the day, "Public Readings." The novelty of this entertainment for one of his people, is the dramatic selections made. The gentleman is entering on a wide and dangerous field, as it will of course lay him open in comparison with the greatest of histrionic fame. His friends, however, claim for him all its requirements. His selections will prove his merit. Let the public give him a fair hearing. This entertainment will take place at CONCERT HALL, Friday evening, March 10th.[84]

The program for Morgan Smith's "Select Readings and Recitations" revealed that he had indeed used Murdoch as a guide. He opened Part One with excerpts from *King Henry VIII*, following this with Whittier's "Barbara Frietchie," a ballad hailing the gumption of an elderly woman who had defied Confederate troops by insisting on flying the U.S. flag during their invasion of Frederick, Maryland ("'Shoot, if you must, this old gray head,/But spare your country's flag,' she said."). He concluded this section of the program with a selection from Book 2 of William Cowper's *The Task*, an eighteenth-century poem in blank verse that, amidst a variety of moral concerns, condemned slavery as "human nature's broadest, foulest blot."

In Part Two, as a change of pace, Morgan Smith started with "Drifting," a rhyming nonpolitical poem by Thomas Buchanan Read that recalled idyllic sailing off the coast of Naples where "No more, no more/The worldly shore/Upbraids me with its loud uproar!" Next came selections from Shakespeare's *Hamlet*, and finally a poem by George Henry Boker, "The Second Louisiana," that celebrated a black regiment's brave assault on Confederate forces at Port Hudson, Louisiana on May 27, 1863, a bold attack in which, according to a newspaper report of the day, this "negro regiment distinguished itself...especially in charging upon the enemy's siege guns, losing killed and wounded 600."[85] A more recent historical account credits the fearless advance of this regiment as having done much to dissipate the belief that black troops were unreliable under fire and to encourage abolitionist efforts to recruit more blacks for service in the Union army.[86] Most of these selections, like those of

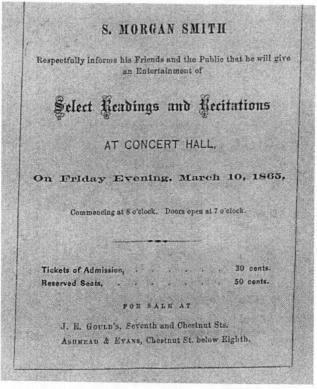

Figure 7. Program of S. Morgan Smith's readings and recitations in Philadelphia, March 10, 1865. Picture Credit: Princeton University Library. Correspondence Scrapbooks; James Edward Murdoch Collection, C0516. Reproduced with permission from the Manuscripts Division, Department of Rare Books and Special Collections, Princeton University Library.

Murdoch a few weeks earlier, were meant to stir patriotic feelings. Morgan Smith's observation that public readings were now the popular entertainment of the day is borne out by the fact that two other readings had taken place during this same period. On February 17th the veteran actor James B. Roberts had read *Hamlet* at the Music Fund Hall,[87] and on March 7th several lady pupils trained by Philip Lawrence had read and recited a selection of literary works. Lawrence also announced to the "Elocutionists of New York, Boston, etc" that he "cordially invites any Teacher of Elocution in America, to produce three pupils to recite against his, at the Academy of Music, for the proud title of 'Youthful Champion Readers of America.' The trial pieces to be 'The Famine,' by Longfellow; 'Alexander's Feast,' by Dryden; and 'Eugene Aram's Dream,' by Hood, three of the most difficult Poems in the English Language. The Judge, on the occasion, to be the Greatest Actor or Best Elocutionist in America."[88]

Encouraged by the response to his first performance as a reader, Morgan Smith decided to try again a month later:

S. MORGAN SMITH respectfully announces to his friends and the public that at the request of many friends, he will give a Second Entertainment of SELECT READINGS AND RECITATIONS at CONCERT HALL, on TUESDAY EVENING, April 11, 1865.

Reading commencing at 8 o'clock. Doors open at 7.

Tickets 50 cents: Reserved Seat Tickets 60 cents.

Tickets for Reserved Seats can be had at Ashmead & Evans', Chestnut street below Eighth; Mr. Tramper's Music Store, Seventh and Chestnut streets.

PROGRAMME

PART FIRST

1. Selections from Shakespeare's Tragedy of "Hamlet," embracing the celebrated soliloquy on "Death," and "Closet Scene."

2. An incident of the Rebellion—"My Eyes are Closing, Mary."

3. "How they brought Good News from Ghent to Aix." Robert Browning.

4. Poem—"Snow."

5. "Barbara Frietchie." (By request.) J.G. Whittier.

PART SECOND

1. "The Charge of the Light Brigade." Alfred Tennyson.

2. "Mr. Pickwick Journeys to Ipswich, and meets with a Romantic Adventure with a middle-aged Lady in Yellow Curl Papers." Charles Dickens.

3. "Sheridan's Ride." T. Buchanan Read.

4. "The Second Louisiana." (By request.) George H. Boker.[89]

This time a review of his performance appeared in one of the Philadelphia papers;

> MR. SMITH'S READINGS.—Last evening Mr. S. Morgan Smith, an intelligent and refined colored citizen of Philadelphia, gave a literary entertainment at Concert Hall, consisting of dramatic, poetical, and prose readings. His selections exhibited excellent taste, and the greater part of them were very well read. A beautiful little poem entitled "Snow" was perhaps his best effort, and "The Charge of the Light Brigade" was also well delivered. Mr. Smith's elocution partakes, however, rather too much of the style taught by those professors of the art who walk in the old beaten track, and the emphasis is placed too exclusively on certain words and passages to the detriment of others equally important. The selections from "Hamlet" were decidedly faulty in this respect, as was also the poem "My Eyes are Closing, Mary." Although the use of proper emphasis is highly important in rendering elocution effective, a speaker should not forget that his audience desires a sufficiently distinct enunciation of every word. Mr. Smith, however, has improved considerably since his last public appearance and gives evidence of fine appreciation of the authors from whose works he selects his programmes.[90]

This reading was delivered two days after General Robert E. Lee had surrendered to General Ulysses S. Grant at Appomattox on April 9th, ending the civil war. And three days later, on April 14th, Abraham Lincoln was shot by John Wilkes Booth at Ford's Theatre.

During the first three months of 1865 Morgan Smith had remained active on the Executive Committee of the Social, Civil and Statistical Association of the Colored People of Pennsylvania in efforts to promote a series of six anti-slavery lectures at the Concert Hall in Philadelphia. The proceeds from these lectures were to be "used by the Executive Committee towards procuring the rights of colored people on the city passenger rail-ways, for the benefit of the freedmen, and to aid sick and wounded soldiers."[91] The first speaker was the famous abolitionist William Lloyd Garrison, who lectured on "The Guilt, Punishment and Redemption of our Country" on January 16, 1865.[92] He was followed on January 25th by Reverend J. Sella Martin, who spoke on "The Friends of the Union in England." Miss E.T. Greenfield, the Black Swan, also sang on this occasion. The remaining lectures in the series were delivered by Frederick Douglass on "Equality before the Law" on February 16th, Mrs. Frances Ellen Watkins Harper on "The Causes and Effects of the War" on February 27th, John Mercer Langston on "The War Our Emancipator" on March 9th; and William D. Kelley on "The War and the Rights of Humanity" on March 22nd. The Black Swan sang after each speech.[93]

Kelley was invited back to Philadelphia on June 22nd to speak on "The Safeguards of Personal Liberty: Reconstruction without Slavery." The invitation came from the Publishing Committee of the Social, Civil and Statistical Association of the Colored People of Pennsylvania who were intent on bringing out "a series of pamphlets on the important subject of suffrage" for "gratuitous circulation." Morgan Smith, who had served as Recording Secretary of the original course of lectures, was one of the three members of this Publishing Committee.[94]

On July 17th the Association convened another public meeting in Philadelphia the object of which "was to take measures for advocating the right of the colored people of this State, and of the whole country, to the elective franchise." After several speeches were given, "Morgan Smith also spoke…with good effect." A series of resolutions was then adopted at this meeting, one of which had been offered by Morgan Smith: "That in view of the influence and aims of this Association we take this occasion to extend to the

Convention, to be assembled at Harrisburg, our cordial co-operation on all measures tending to the securance of our rights."[95]

Nine days later, on July 26th, Morgan Smith gave an "Afternoon Matinee of SELECT READINGS AND RECITATIONS from the most distinguished American and English Authors at the Church on FRANKLIN Street, opposite the Tremont House...commencing at 4 o'clock."[96] The following day he joined an excursion party of more than three hundred Philadelphians who traveled by boat to Cape May, New Jersey, where, the *Christian Recorder* noted, he gave a "'Reading' in the A.M.E. Church, consisting of choice selections from Shakespeare's tragedy of *Hamlet*, the great masterpiece of the prophetic Bard of Avon, and quotations from the gifted Longfellow and others. The reading proved very interesting, and we enjoyed it very much. Great ability and appreciation marked the eloquent rendition, and we regret very much that so few persons were present upon this occasion."[97]

By this time, reading to small audiences in Philadelphia and beyond no longer continued to satisfy Morgan Smith's growing ambition as a public performer. What he wanted now was a chance to act in plays staged at established theatres, but, like Ira Aldridge before him, this kind of opportunity was denied him because of his race. In an article published in the *Philadelphia Times* some years later, the story of how he set out to fulfill his dream was told in some detail:

> When the late Charles W. Brooke resided in Philadelphia he had, at one time, his law offices on Sixth street, above Walnut. At the northwest corner of those two thoroughfares was a barber shop managed by a colored man rejoicing in the mellifluous name of J. [*sic*] Morgan Smith. He had a lingual development worthy of his occupation and delighted most in talking of theatrical matters. His favorite subject of conversation was the wonderful success achieved in Europe by Ira Aldridge. One day after he had given Charles W. Brooke's ambrosial locks that fascinating curl that tortured many a tender heart, he said to the eloquent barrister: "Mr. Brooke, I think I can act as well as that fellow Aldridge. They tell me that you know some of those elocution men, and if you will take me to one of them I will show him

what I can do." Mr. Brooke had his early elocutionary training from Professor White, and later had become a student of James B. Roberts who is still giving vocal instructions in this city. This veteran actor, though very short of stature, has a voice that rivals the thunder that once rumbled from Forrest's lips. He is very emphatic in gesture and in accentuation, and when he enters heart and soul into the delivery of a recitation his eyes glare with a fierceness that is at times absolutely terrifying. He is the kindest and best of men, but he is apt at times to adopt a severity of demeanor that is rather appalling to those unacquainted with his goodness of heart. Into his presence Mr. Brooke escorted J. Morgan Smith and stated the object of his errand. The old-time actor, without saying a word, placed a copy of Shakespeare in the barber's hands, and directing his attention to a dialogue between Rosencrans [*sic*] and Guilderstern [*sic*] in "Hamlet," bade him read. When the negro had concluded Mr. Roberts, in his thunderous tones, each word being rolled off by itself, as is his wont, said: 'That—is—about—as—blankety—blank badly done—as—anything—I—ever—listened to." Then, snatching the book from the hands of the would-be tragedian, he read the lines with strong emphasis and accompanied them with gestures peculiar to himself.

When he finished he bade J. Morgan Smith try again. The man did so, and this time, without meaning to give offense, he followed Mr. Roberts so closely that he imitated to the life every gesture and every peculiarity of emphasis of the instructor. The veteran actor could scarcely conceal his anger. When the negro had finished Mr. Roberts said, biting off each word: "That—is—all—very—well—but—you—need—not—be—a blankety—blank—parrot."

But J. Morgan Smith stood to his determination to be an actor. He appeared first as Othello in Wheatley Dramatic Hall, Fifth and Gaskill streets. He gave such promise of success that he went to Europe, and half a dozen years ago he was performing tragic parts in Edinburgh, Scotland, and was making piles of money.[98]

**Figure 8. Print of James B. Roberts. Reproduced with
permission from the Houghton Library, Harvard University.**

It has not been possible to trace the exact date of Morgan Smith's
alleged debut at the Wheatley Dramatic Hall, but if it happened
at all, it probably took place late in 1865 or early in 1866 when
performances were held there in a large room over 232-234 South
Second Street rather than in a separate building.[99] However, the rest
of this interesting account may be true.[100]

In September 1865 James B. Roberts, at 250 North Ninth Street
in Philadelphia, was advertising "Instruction in Elocution, Action

31

and Stage Business."[101] Born in 1818, he was an actor who had started his career at age eighteen at the Walnut Street Theatre, and at age thirty-nine he had toured for nearly a year in about thirty cities and towns in England, Ireland, and Scotland, including performing leading roles in two of London's most prestigious theatres—Drury Lane and the Lyceum. He returned to Philadelphia in 1858 and continued to play there and to travel extensively as a star.[102] In 1867 he became the lead actor, director and stage manager of the Arch Street Theatre, where he had debuted three decades earlier.[103]

Roberts played a great variety of roles, including such iconic Shakespearean characters as Richard III, Iago, Hamlet, Macbeth, Shylock, Romeo, and King Lear.[104] In 1859 and through the war years he had his greatest success playing Mephistopheles in *Faust and Marguerite*, a retelling of the Faust legend.[105] Morgan Smith would have had an opportunity to see Roberts in many of these roles as well as in others that he chose to add to his own repertoire when touring England.

But Morgan Smith also had plenty of other models to draw upon, for Philadelphia theatres were visited by some of the leading thespians of the day. To mention only the noted Shakespeareans who regularly appeared there between 1859 and 1866, he would have been able to witness performances by James E. Murdoch, Edwin Booth, Barry Sullivan, James W. Wallack, Jr., E. L. Davenport, Edwin Forrest, Charles Dillon, John Wilkes Booth, McKean Buchanan, Junius Brutus Booth, Jr., and Charles Kean. Some of these celebrities secured engagements as visiting stars in Philadelphia for a few weeks each year. A barber with a love for Shakespeare would not have wanted to miss any of them.

Whether Morgan Smith took further instruction from Roberts after his first meeting with him is unclear, but there is evidence that he did seek out others to help in training him for the stage. But first he had to commit himself wholeheartedly to the endeavor.

On November 1, 1865 he gave his last "Entertainments of Select Readings and Recitations" at the Concert Hall on Chestnut street, publicizing the program in the press:

PART I.

1st. Selections from Shakspeare's Tragedy of Macbeth, including the Soliloquies on the "Assassination" and "Dagger."

2^d. "On Board the Cumberland." George H. Boker.

3^d. "Catawba Wine." H. W. Longfellow

4th. "Sheridan's Ride." T. Buchanan Read.

PART II.

1st. Lines on the Receipt of my "Mother's Picture." William Cowper.

2^d. "Snow"

3^d. Poe's celebrated Poem of "The Raven."[106]

On the same date in November, *The Press* published an announcement about Morgan Smith's barber shop:

A CARD.—The undersigned takes pleasure in recommending to his old patrons and the public, his recent Foreman, Mr. FREDERICK C. REVELS, who succeeds to his old business. The thorough knowledge of the business, with the gentlemanly and urbane character of Mr. Revels is the most certain guarantee that all will be pleased to favor him with their patronage.

In retiring from a business association of seventeen years, the undersigned avails himself of this opportunity of returning to his old friends and patrons, for the many acts of kindness bestowed, his sincere acknowledgment.

Respectfully,

S. MORGAN SMITH

All persons having claims against S. MORGAN SMITH can present the same, at 524 Walnut Street, and all persons indebted to S. MORGAN SMITH will pay the same to my successor, Mr. F. C. Revels, who is hereby empowered to give receipt for the same, and a book recording the amount of the debt will be kept on the premises. S.M.S.[107]

In addition to housing Morgan Smith's barber shop, 524 Walnut Street was the address of the Consulate of France, the Antiquarian Society of Philadelphia, the Provident Life Insurance Company, two law offices, a real estate office, and separate offices occupied by a sculptor, an artist, and several clerks. Clearly Morgan Smith had thrived in such an upper-class setting. He could afford to sell his business to an old friend who had also been active in the Philadelphia Library Company of Colored Persons and could now move on toward the objective he had set for himself. His wife had given birth to their second child, also named Samuel Morgan Smith, six months earlier, on May 10th,[108] and he left them in Philadelphia and went to Boston, where, according to a friend,

> he staid in an orthodox hotel on Washington Street, where he was compelled to eat his meals in his room, and piously charged extra for the enforced luxury; but he found in one of the best actors of Boston a man who was able to recognize dramatic genius under a black skin, and who consented to undertake his training. With W. H. Smith, and afterwards with an actor of New York, this man studied. It was necessary that, now that he had resolved to devote himself to the dramatic art, he should be able to visit the stage and the various arrangements behind it. But nothing could induce the managers of any theatre in Boston, New York, or Philadelphia, to permit him at any time of the night or day to examine these stage properties and arrangements. At length having thoroughly mastered the leading characters of the Shaksperian plays, and seeing that there was no possible door to the stage in America, this man started with his wife and child for England.[109]

Born in North Wales in 1806, William Henry Sedley had changed his surname to Smith when as a teenager he left home and decided to try to earn a living as an actor. He showed some promise in juvenile parts, and by the time he was twenty-one, he had become a popular star in provincial theatres in England and Scotland. In 1827 he came to the United States and performed with success in Philadelphia, Baltimore, and Washington. This led to an engagement at the Tremont Theatre in Boston the following year, after which he became the theatre manager there for eight years and subsequently served as an actor-manager at several other major theatres—Boston's National Theatre, Philadelphia's Arch Street Theatre, and the Boston Museum.[110] A profile on him published in 1857 stated, "Of late years he has been induced to give instructions to those who have determined to make the stage their profession."[111] By 1860 he had given up managing theatres and returned to itinerant acting. Morgan Smith may have seen him perform light comedy roles when the Chestnut Street Theatre opened its fall season in August-September 1865, and he may have made arrangements at that time to study under him after selling his barber shop.

Figure 9. Print of William H. Sedley Smith from
Ballou's Pictorial Drawing-Rom Companion,
January 1857. Reproduced with permission from
Houghton Library, Harvard University.

Morgan Smith's training in Boston must have been intensive, even though he evidently had no opportunity to try out roles at any of the theatres there. Before working with Sedley Smith, he may have already memorized the leading roles in several entire Shakespearean plays, particularly the two from which he had made selections for his public readings—*Hamlet* and *Macbeth*—and more than likely he may have rehearsed *Othello* thoroughly as well. But he went well beyond these staples in order to prepare himself for the challenge of presenting a more diversified repertoire when he arrived in England. He threw himself wholeheartedly into this kind of mental toil during the early months of 1866. Had he been able to attend theatres in Boston regularly during this period, he might have benefitted from seeing more than twenty productions of Shakespearean plays featuring such stars as Frank Mayo, Charles Dillon, L.R. Shewell, and Charles Kean, as well as witnessing performances of a few other plays that were about to become part of his own repertoire, but he may not have had frequent opportunities to do so. In any case, he appears to have been content to watch the plays he attended from the gallery, as he had done in Philadelphia.[112]

It may be significant that, just a week before Morgan Smith departed for England, Aaron Molyneaux Hewlett, a black teacher of gymnastics and physical training at Harvard University, had been refused admission to the dress circle of the Boston Theatre, and had been sent to sit in the gallery. He and other black citizens protested this to the Senate and House of Representatives of the Commonwealth of Massachusetts, pointing out that an Act passed by the legislature the previous year provided that no such discrimination should be permitted by any licensed theatre in Boston. They further claimed to have been "informed that the Boston Theatre, Continental Theatre, Howard Athenaeum, particularly, in the city of Boston, are daily excluding proper persons from their exhibitions, invidiously discriminating against them solely on account of their color."[113]

This was not a new issue in Boston. Some years earlier, in 1853, a group of three blacks who had purchased tickets in the family circle for an opera at the Howard Athenaeum had been forcibly removed from that theatre when they declined to accept seats in the gallery instead. The complainants, one of whom was injured, brought charges of assault and battery against the agent of the opera company and the officer who had been ordered to expel them, Testimony given at the trial by witnesses, black theatergoers, a rival manager, and even an usher at the Athenæum affirmed that blacks at other theatrical and musical entertainments at the Athenæum and at the Boston Museum had been able to sit wherever they pleased. The judge also noted that the opera company had never publicly advertised their claim to have the right to exclude certain classes of citizens from certain seats. The case was decided in favor of the plaintiffs and the defendants were fined.[114] This may have been the precedent that enabled Aaron Molyneaux Hewlett and others to press their argument for open seating for all at Boston theatres.

While in Philadelphia Morgan Smith had spent a good deal of time as a community leader dedicated to liberating his people from the shackles of slavery. Now he sought to free himself to pursue the kind of artistic career he craved. Since he could not do so anywhere in the United States, he chose to follow in Ira Aldridge's footsteps and try his luck in a part of the world where his color would no longer be a hindrance. After submitting to the ritual of swearing an oath of allegiance to support, protect, and defend the Constitution and Government of the United States, against all enemies, whether foreign or domestic, he obtained his passport and left Boston with his wife and infant son on April 25th aboard the ship Asia bound for Liverpool.

Endnotes

1 National Archives and Records Administration (NARA); Washington, D.C.: NARA Series: Passport Applications, 1795-1905; Volume #:Role 138 – 01 Apr 1866-30 Apr 1866. Accessed through Ancestry.com. Attempts to search for additional details about his birth and early life using conventional genealogical tools have yielded no further reliable information.

2 There is a record in the 1860 census of a mulatto, Saml. M. Smith, age 26, living with his mother, Mary A. Smith, 50, and two sisters, Talitha Smith, 22, and Emma Smith, 19, in the 3rd Ward, West of 5th Street in Philadelphia (see the "United States Census, 1860 database, *FamilySearch* (https://familysearch. org/ark:/61903/1:1:MXR8-VTQ: accessed 2 December 2015), but Morgan Smith would have been 28 years old by then and, according to *McElroy's Philadelphia Directory*, was living at 704 Steward Street (now Delhi Street

between Montrose and Fitzwater just east of 9th Street). I am grateful to David Ninemire, Head of the Social Science and History Department at the Parkway Central Library branch of the Free Library of Philadelphia, for tracking down the name change of this street. Also, the only sister Morgan Smith is known to have had was identified as Thabertha Smith by his "old friend" Dr. William Henry Johnson, who encountered her some years later in New York City; see *The Autobiography of Dr. William Henry Johnson* (Albany: Argus Company, 1900), 114.

3   Benjamin C. Bacon, *Statistics of the Colored People of Philadelphia* (Philadelphia: T. Ellwood Chapman, 1856), 4-8.

4   C. G. Woodson, *The Education of the Negro Prior to 1861* (New York: Arno Press and the New York Times, 1968), 270. See also *the U.S. Office of Education's History of Schools for the Colored Population* (New York: Arno Press and the New York Times, 1969), 380.

5   *McElroy's Philadelphia Directory for 1851* (Philadelphia: Edward C. and John Biddle, 1851), 397.

6   *The Compact Edition of the Oxford English Dictionary*, 1 (Oxford, U.K.: Oxford University Press, 1980), 1501.

7   For details, see *McElroy's Philadelphia Directory for 1854* (Philadelphia: Edward C. and John Biddle, 1854). It would be interesting to know if the latter was Peter Skenandoah Smith, elder brother of the noted abolitionist Gerrit Smith. General Peter Sken Smith, as he was then usually identified in the press, had been active in Philadelphia politics for more than a decade, having joined with others to form the Native American Party, which opposed immigration of Irish and German Catholics. He was editor of the *Native Eagle and American Advocate*, a weekly magazine published locally, and often spoke at public rallies. He had earlier made and lost a fortune in real estate in St. Augustine, Florida, forcing him to flee north. Even in his younger years as a merchant in Utica, New York, he had gone bankrupt after accumulating large debts. Peter Sken has been described by biographers of his brother as a family "ne'er-do-well" who was a chronic inebriate and in his last days undeniably insane. He may have left Philadelphia in 1855 and is known to have died in a lunatic asylum in Springfield, Massachusetts in 1858. For remarks on him, see Ralph Volney Harlow, *Gerrit Smith: Philanthropist and Reformer* (New York: Henry Holt and Company, 1939) and John Stauffer, *The Black Hearts of Men: Radical Abolitionists and the Transformation of Race* (Cambridge, MA: Harvard University Press, 2002). For information on his life in St. Augustine, see Frank Marotti, Jr., *Heaven's Soldiers: Free People of Color and the Spanish Legacy in Antebellum Florida* (Tuscaloosa: University of Alabama Press, 2013). A very positive obituary appeared in *The Opal, a Monthly Periodical of the State Lunatic Asylum edited by the Patients*, 8, no. 6 (1858): 141-42, claiming he was "a man in every sense of the word....If he had had more prudence perhaps he would have been almost perfect."

8   Anon. *Register of Trades of the Colored People in the City of Philadelphia and*

Districts (Merrihew and Gunn, 1838). According to this report, there were 130 women employed as dressmakers, milliners, and tailoresses.

9   Douglas Walter Bristol, Jr., *Knights of the Razor: Black Barbers in Slavery and Freedom* (Baltimore: Johns Hopkins University Press, 2009), 104.

10 Benjamin C. Bacon, *Statistics of the Colored People of Philadelphia* (1856. Philadelphia: Board of Education, 2nd ed., 1859).

11 Bristol, *Knights of the Razor*, 104.

12 Ibid., 106.

13 Cyprian Clamorgan, *The Colored Aristocracy of St. Louis*, ed. Julie Winch (Columbia: University of Missouri Press, 1999), 46, 52. Quoted in Quincy T. Mills, *Cutting Across the Color Line: Black Barbers and Barber Shops in America* (Philadelphia: University of Pennsylvania Press, 2013), 29.

14 Bristol, *Knights of the Razor*, 88.

15 Even W. E. B. Du Bois, writing on the situation of black barbers at the end of the nineteenth century in *The Philadelphia Negro: A Social Study* (1899. Oxford: Oxford University Press, 2007), 81, observed that "No first-class Negro barber would dare to shave his own brother in his shop in Philadelphia on account of the color prejudice [of his white customers]."

16 [Frederick Douglass], "Make Your Sons Mechanics and Farmers—not Waiters, Porters, and Barbers," *Frederick Douglass' Newspaper*, March 18, 1853.

17 Leslie M. Harris, *In the Shadow of Slavery: African Americans in New York City, 1626-1863* (Chicago: University of Chicago Press, 2003), 240. James McCune Smith had been a former schoolmate and lifelong friend of the famous actor Ira Aldridge. He was a practicing physician in New York who had been trained at the University of Glasgow.

18 [Douglass], "Make Your Sons Mechanics and Farmers."

19 "Proceedings of the Convention, of the Colored Freemen of Ohio, Held in Cincinnati, January 14, 15, 16, 17, and 19, 1852," in Philip S. Foner and George E. Walker, eds., *Proceedings of the Black State Conventions, 1840-1865* (Philadelphia: Temple University Press, 1979), 1: 277.

20 Uriah Boston, "Mr. F. Douglass Sir," *Frederick Douglass' Paper*, April 22, 1853, and quoted in Bristol, *Knights of the Razor*, 117; Lewis Woodson, "Doing Something," *Frederick Douglass' Paper*, October 28, 1853, and quoted in Mills, *Cutting Along the Color Line*, 118. Bristol and Mills are the leading authorities on the history of black barbers in America.

21 Martin Robison Delany, *The Condition, Elevation, Emigration, and Destiny of the Colored People of the United States* (1852; reprint, New York: Arno Press, 1968), 43. Delaney, however, had a low opinion of blacks who worked as barbers, citing the James M. Whitfield, "one of the purest poets in America," as being nonetheless "somewhat reprehensible" for occupying such a "humble position," 132. For more on reactions to Whitfield's occupation, see Mills,

Cutting Along the Color Line, 51-53.

22 Harris, *In the Shadow of Slavery*, 234.

23 Rev. Bayard R. Hall, D.D., *Frank Freeman's Barber Shop* (New York: Charles Scribner, 1852), 320-21. In his preface, Hall claimed that "the essence of our tale is truth... *nearly every* leading incident, *separate* from its place in the story, is a fact; that not a few of these passed under the eyes of the author; and that, in several scenes, he was a *quoram pars*—an actor," v. For more on this novel, see Bristol, *Knights of the Razor*, 56-58, who notes that Hall "employed romanticized stereotypes of African Americans to show his readers they could admire a black barber without foregoing their sense of racial superiority."

24 City directories show that in 1860 he moved his shop to 611 Sansom Street.

25 Moncure D. Conway, "The Negro as Artist: Morgan Smith," *The Radical*, 2 (September 1866): 39.

26 Ibid.

27 Handbill at the Historical Society of Philadelphia.

28 *Weekly Anglo-African*, December 24, 1859.

29 Aslaku Behanu, "Philadelphia Library Company of Colored People," diglib@ temple.edu.

30 *Genius of Universal Emancipation*, 3rd series, 3 (1833): 90. Quoted in Dorothy B. Porter, "The Organized Educational Activities of Negro Literary Societies, 1828-1846," *Journal of Negro Education*, 5, no. 4 (October 1936): 561.

31 *Weekly Anglo-African*, February 18, 1860.

32 "Meeting of Colored Citizens in Philadelphia," *Frederick Douglass' Paper*, February 17, 1860.

33 *Weekly Anglo-African*, April 7, 1860, and April 14, 1860.

34 For further details, see Philadelphia's *The Press*, April 23, 1860, and the *Weekly Anglo-African*, May 12, 1860, May 19, 1860, and June 30, 1860.

35 See the *Weekly Anglo-African*, April 7, 1860 and May 12, 1860. Bristol, *Knights of the Razor*, identifies White as "a leading black barber in Philadelphia" who placed large orders for "cologne water by the pint and cigars by the thousand" as well as a wide range of "personal care products such as hair oil, toothbrushes, and cold cream," 61-63. Bristol also reports that Eddy, though born a slave in Virginia, "became one of the wealthiest black barbers in America," 65. Having acquired his freedom, Eddy "moved to Philadelphia in the 1820s, established his own barbershop, and married the daughter of the most prominent black leader in the city, Richard Allen. He died in 1882, leaving an estate worth $100,000," 87. Bristol, 65-66, notes that Eddy and another wealthy black barber, James M. Auter, owned shops at 415 and 317 Chestnut Street, in an upscale neighborhood only a few blocks away from Morgan Smith's shop. All three evidently prospered in this location.

36 Leon Gardiner's American Negro Collection, Historical Society Records Box 2G file 14.

37 Historical Society of Pennsylvania, MSS No. 8, Box 13G, file 1a.

38 *The Black Swan at Home and Abroad; or, a Biographical Sketch of Miss Elizabeth Taylor Greenfield, the American Vocalist* (Philadelphia: Wm. S. Young, 1855), 5.

39 Obituary in the *New York Times*, April 2, 1876, 2.

40 *The Black Swan at Home and Abroad*, 63-64.

41 Ella Forbes, *African American Women During the Civil War* (New York: Garland, 1998), 205.

42 Russell F. Weigley, ed. *Philadelphia: A 300-Year History* (New York: W.W. Norton. 1982), 354. However, Heather S. Nathans, "'A course of learning and indigenous studies': Shakespearean Education and Theater in Antebellum America," in *Shakespearean Educations: Power, Citizenship, and Performance*, ed. Coppélia Kahn, Heather S. Nathans, and Mimi Godfrey (Newark: University of Delaware Press, 2011), 58-59, claims that "By the 1850s, knowledge of Shakespeare had become an important part of the black educational experience in America—whether it was in the playhouse, the classroom, or the privacy of a select reading club." Lawrence W. Levine, in *Highbrow/Lowbrow: The Emergence of Cultural Hierarch in America* (Cambridge, MA: Harvard University Press, 1988), 37, also reports that "Shakespeare was taught in nineteenth-century schools and colleges as declamation or rhetoric, not literature. For many youngsters Shakespeare was first encountered in schoolbooks as texts to be recited aloud and memorized." Henry W. Simon, *The Reading of Shakespeare in American Schools and Colleges: An Historical Survey* (New York: Simon and Schuster, 1932) gives examples of schoolbooks in which excerpts from Shakespeare's plays were used to teach elocution in nineteenth-century classrooms.

43 *The Press*, November 12, 1860. *McElroy's Philadelphia City Directory for 1860* (Philadelphia: E.C. and J. Biddle, 1860), 977.

44 United States Federal Census records for Philadelphia, 1850 and 1860.

45 For details on their neighbors, see the *McElroy's Philadelphia City Directory* volumes for 1860 and 1861.

46 *Weekly Anglo-African*, February 16, 1861; *Christian Recorder*, January 11, 1862.

47 Database of Philadelphia City Births, 1860-1906, and Philadelphia Death Certificates Index, 1803-1915.

48 *Christian Recorder*, November 8, 1862.

49 *The Press*, November 29, 1962.

50 *Christian Recorder*, December 6, 1862.

41

51 Anthony Waskie, *Philadelphia and the Civil War* (Charleston, SC: History Press, 2011), 13.

52 Ibid., 29. Weigley, *Philadelphia: A 300-Year History*, 385.

53 Ibid., 13-14.

54 James M. McPherson, *The Negro's Civil War: How American Negroes Felt and Acted during the War for the Union* (New York: Vintage, 1965), 173.

55 Winnifred K. MacKay, "Philadelphia during the Civil War, 1861-1865," *Pennsylvania Magazine of History and Biography*, 70, no. 1 (January 1946): 32.

56 Broadside, June 27, 1863, held at the Historical Society of Pennsylvania, 10G, Folder 15

57 Broadside, July 6, 1863, held at the Historical Society of Pennsylvania, Box 16, Folder 17.

58 *Christian Recorder*, September 12, 1863. For information on this camp, see Jeffry D. Wert, "Camp William Penn and the Black Soldier," *Pennsylvania History: A Journal of Mid-Atlantic Studies*, 46, no. 4 (October 1959): 335-346. Wert reports that between June 1863 and May 1865 "nearly 400 white officers and 10,940 enlisted blacks learned the basic art of soldiering within its confines," 335.

59 *Christian Recorder*, January 9, 1864. The Dinte Nightingale Overell Masters McFarlane file at Ancestry.com records the birth of a daughter this year to Samuel and Mary Eliza Morgan Smith, but when the girl died on July 19 and was buried two days later, she is described as having been white and dying at 1324 Wood Street in Philadelphia's 14th Ward, so this record must be inaccurate.

60 Samuel P. Bates, *History of Pennsylvania Volunteers, 1861-5* (Wilmington, NC: Broadfoot Publishing, 1993), 10: 997.

61 Ibid., 10: 1110.

62 Ibid. For details on these men see 10: 1060, 1074, 1104.

63 US, African American Civil War Sailor Index, 1861-1865. Ancestry.com.

64 "O'Conor, Charles," *Encyclopedia Britannica*, 11th edition. (New York: Encyclopedia Britannica, 1910-11), 19: 992.

65 Charles O'Conor, *Speech of Charles O'Conor, Esq., at the Union Meeting at the Academy of Music, New York City, December 19, 1959* (New York: Van Evrie, Horton & Co., [1860], 6.

66 Ibid., 8

67 Ibid., 10-13.

68 Ibid., 11-13.

69 S. Morgan Smith, *A Critical Review of the Late Speech of Charles O'Conor,*

'*Negro Slavery not Unjust*' (Philadelphia: n.p., [1860]), 4-5.

70   Ibid., 8-9.

71   Ibid., 9.

72   Ibid., 12-14.

73   T. Allston Brown, "Murdoch, James E." in *History of the American Stage* (New York: Dick & Fitzgerald, 1870), 254-55.

74   *Orthophony: or Vocal Culture in Elocution* (Boston: William D. Tichnor, 1845). The subtitle of the book was *A Manual of Elementary Exercises Adapted to Dr. Rush's "Philosophy of the Human Voice," and Designed as an Introduction to Russell's "American Elocutionist."* The book was reprinted in a revised edition in 1882.

75   Anon., "Preface," in James E. Murdoch, *Patriotism in Poetry and Prose: Being Passages from Lectures and Patriotic Readings by James E. Murdoch* (Philadelphia: J.B. Lippincott), 9. The preface went on to state, 11-12, that "Various sums of money have been received as subscriptions to the Ladies' Societies in aid of soldiers' families, sick and wounded soldiers, etc. A copy of the book is to be presented to each subscriber....The entire profits from the publication will be given to [such] charities."

76   William Norris, "New Light on the Career of S. Morgan Smith," *Black American Literature Forum*, 18, no. 3 (Autumn 1984): 117.

77   Murdoch Collection, Box 1, Scrapbook II, Department of Rare Books and Special Collections, Princeton University Library. Norris, ibid., believes that this letter was "probably" written in 1863, arguing that that year "suggests itself due to the letter's location among the Murdoch papers, and due to the address given on Smith's letterhead." It is true that Murdoch gave a reading of Robert Browning's "How They Brought the Good News from Ghent to Aix" at Philadelphia's Academy of Music on February 9, 1863 and also gave a "Great Patriotic Address! For the Benefit of the Sick & Wounded Soldiers and Their Families" at the Academy of Music on August 13, 1863, but he had also given a number of public readings in Philadelphia's Concert Hall on May 22, 1862, and there again on several occasions in February and March 1865. For details see *The Press*, February 9, 1863; a handbill at the Philadelphia Library Company dated August 13, 1863 (sm#AM 1863 Acad. Mus.), and notices in the *Philadelphia Inquirer*, February 10, 1865, and the *Public Ledger*, March 3, 9, and 14, 1865.

78   Arthur Herman Wilson's doctoral dissertation *A History of the Philadelphia Theatre 1835 to 1855* (Philadelphia: University of Philadelphia Press, 1935), 700, records that J. E. Murdoch appeared at the Chestnut Street Theatre for twenty nights in April-May 1852 and for ten nights in February and another ten nights in June in 1853.

79   Both notes are preserved in the Murdoch Collection, Box 1, Scrapbook II, Department of Rare Books and Special Collections, Princeton University

Library.

80   *Philadelphia Inquirer*, February 10, 1865.

81   The subtitle of this book, published in Philadelphia by J.B. Lippincott in 1866, was *Also, Poems by Thomas Buchanan Read, George H. Boker, Francis De Haes Janvier, and Other American Authors, Commemorative of the Gallant Deeds of our Noble Defenders on Land and Sea.*

82   *Public Ledger*, March 3, 1865.

83   This letter is also held in the Murdoch Collection, Box 1, Scrapbook II, Department of Rare Books and Special Collections, Princeton University Library.

84   *Philadelphia Inquirer*, March 2, 1865. Some of the later announcements in the *Sunday Dispatch,* March 5; *The Press*, March 7 and 8, and the *Public Ledger*, March 10, gave details on the selections scheduled to be read.

85   *Boston Evening Transcript*, June 6, 1863.

86   Lawrence Lee Hewitt, *Port Hudson, Confederate Bastion on the Mississippi* (Baton Rouge: Louisiana State University Press, 1987), 140-49, 177-78.

87   *Public Ledger*, February 17, 1865.

88   *Philadelphia Inquirer*, March 6, 1865. This "Trial of Skill in Declamation" took place on November 14, 1865, when the pupils of J. B. Brown of New York challenged those of Philip Lawrence by reading a number of pieces, two of which—"Barbara Frietchie" and "Sheridan's Ride—were among the selections that had been performed by Morgan Smith on April 11, 1865. See the *Philadelphia Inquirer*, November 14, 1865 for further details on this contest. At his final reading on November 1, 1865, Morgan Smith repeated "Sheridan's Ride" and added to his program Edgar Allan Poe's "The Raven," another piece that was included in the competition between pupils two weeks later. See *The Press*, November 1, 1865; *Public Ledger*, November 1, 1865.

89   *Sunday Dispatch*, April 9, 1865; *The Press*, April 10 and 11, 1865; *Public Ledger*, April 10, 1865.

90   *The Press*, April 12, 1865.

91   *Christian Recorder*, January 7, 1865.

92   Flyers for all these lectures are held at the Historical Society of Pennsylvania, Box 11G, f 1 (6), n.d. 85 (before 1866).

93   The Reverend J. Stella Martin was a former slave who had become a popular pastor of a church in Boston. Mrs. Frances Ellen Watkins Harper, a poet and novelist, was a strong supporter of abolition, prohibition, and women's suffrage. John Mercer Langston, an attorney, educator, and activist became the first black person from Virginia elected to the U.S. Congress. William D. Kelley, a Republican politician who had fought in the civil war, was a member of the U.S. House of Representatives from Pennsylvania's 4th District from

1861 to 1890.

94 *The Liberator*, August 11, 1865. See also William D. Kelley, *The Safeguards of Personal Liberty: An Address* (Philadelphia: Social, Civil and Statistical Association of Colored People of Pennsylvania, 1865).

95 *Christian Recorder*, July 22, 1865.

96 *The Press*, July 25, 1865; *Daily Evening Bulletin*, July 25, 1865.

97 *Christian Recorder*, August 5, 1865.

98 Undated cutting from the *Philadelphia Times* held at the Harvard Theatre Collection. It is not known whether Morgan Smith received any training from Roberts. Another possible teacher could have been an individual who had placed an advertisement in Philadelphia's *Public Ledger* on June 7, 1865, stating "DRAMATIC INSTRUCTION IN THE REQUISITE accomplishments for the Stage, by SIGNOR VALLO, 532 North Tenth Street." Another announcement headed OPERA, DRAMA AND ORCHESTRA appeared in the *Public Ledger* on August 30, 1865: "SIGNOR VALLO, 532 North Tenth street, is now organizing a complete Amateur Company, which he intends training for private or public performances. Young Ladies and Gentlemen wanted for every department. Terms moderate." It is doubtful that Morgan Smith would have been welcome to join such a Company.

99 According to the *New York Clipper*, July 18, 1868, the inaugural performance at the new venue at Fifth and Gaskill streets occurred on April 17, 1868, by which time Morgan Smith had already been performing in England for nearly two years. Henry S. Morais, in *The Jews of Philadelphia* (Philadelphia: Levytype Co., 1894), 219, reports that Wheatley Dramatic Hall, "called after William Wheatley, a celebrated actor,…has been the place where more than a few followers of his art have made their first public appearance."

100 Morgan Smith may have appeared on stage in Philadelphia even a bit earlier. A report in the *Public Ledger*, December 24, 1864, mentions a "Mr. Smith" performing with a troupe at Stewart's New Apollo Concert Hall, but it is not known whether this was Morgan Smith.

101 *Public Ledger*, September 9, 1865.

102 Brown, *History of the American Stage*, 314.

103 Andrew Davis, *America's Longest Run: A History of the Walnut Street Theatre* (University Park, PA: Pennsylvania State University Press, 2010), 137.

104 John Bouvé Clapp and Edwin Francis Edgett, *Players of the Present, Part III* (New York: Dunlop Society, 1899), 307.

105 Davis, *America's Longest Run*, 116, 137.

106 *The Press*, November 1, 1865; *Public Ledger*, November 1, 1865. See also note 86.

107 *The Press*, November 1, 1865. The reference to having been in the barbering

business for seventeen years suggests that Morgan Smith had started as an apprentice barber in 1848, when he was sixteen years old.

108 Ancestry.com, citing an online database of *Massachusetts, Town and Vital Records* available at Provo, Utah, identifies the boy's birth place as Boston, but the record shows he was born in Philadelphia and that his birth was only registered in Boston shortly before his family departed for England.

109 Conway, "The Negro as Artist," 39. It is not known who the "actor of New York" was. According to Robert C. Hayden, *African-Americans in Boston: More Than 350 Years* (Boston: Trustees of the Public Library of the City of Boston, 1991), 19, "The Boston Black population numbered 2,348 in 1865." Hayden, p. 62, also records that "The Histrionic Club, the first Black drama group in Boston, was founded in the late 1840s," so it is possible that Morgan Smith may have met other aspiring Black actors while there. There is evidence that the Histrionic Club was still active and giving public exhibitions in 1858. See *The Liberator*, April 2, 1858, and April 23, 1858.

110 There are entries on William Henry Sedley Smith in a number of encyclopedias: Dumas Malone, ed., *Dictionary of American Biography* (New York: Charles Scribner's Sons, 1935), 9:363-64; Phyllis Hartnoll, ed., *The Oxford Companion to the Theatre*. 4th ed. (Oxford: Oxford University Press, 1983), 749; Martin Banham, ed., *The Cambridge Guide to World Theatre* (Cambridge, UK: Cambridge University Press, 1988), 197.

111 *Ballou's Pictorial Drawing-Room Companion*, January 1857, 44.

112 Though Conway had reported in "The Negro as Artist," 39, that Morgan Smith had not been permitted to "visit the stage and the various arrangements behind it" in Boston, in another article published in the same month he asserted that the Philadelphia negro's "whole training has been obtained in the negro-galleries of theaters in his native city and in Boston." See M. D. C. [Moncure D. Conway], "Correspondence," *The Round Table: A Saturday Review of Politics, Finance, Literature, Society, and Art*, 4 (September 29, 1866): 56. Nothing was said in this piece about the training that Morgan Smith had received from Sedley Smith, though this had been mentioned in "The Negro as Artist."

113 "House...No. 356 Commonwealth of Massachusetts," in *William Cooper Nell: Nineteenth-Century African American Abolitionist, Historian, Integrationist: Selected Writings 1832-1874*, ed. Dorothy Porter Wesley and Constance Porter Uzelac (Baltimore: Black Classic Press, 2002), 663-64. A similar report on "several influential and wealthy colored citizens [who had been] refused admission to the Boston Theatre after having purchased tickets" had appeared in *The Commonwealth*, March 31, 1866 and had provoked further comment in that paper on April 21, 1866.

114 *The Liberator*, June 10, 1853.

2
Gravesend

I t took twelve days for the ship Asia to cross the Atlantic, stopping first at Queenstown (now Cobh), a seaport in southern Ireland where a few passengers alighted on May 6th, before arriving in Liverpool the following day.[1] Within a week Morgan Smith had arranged to take over management of the Theatre Royal at Gravesend, hire a stage manager and director, and recruit a company of experienced actors to support him in a variety of standard roles. Gravesend, twenty-five miles outside London, was described in the *Kent Directory* of 1866 as "a municipal borough, seaport, railway station, union, and market-town, and a polling place for the Western division of the county."[2] The population at that time stood at approximately 20,000.[3] The Theatre Royal stood at the corner of Garrick Street and New Road, not far from the River Thames.[4]

On May 19th the *Gravesend and Dartford Reporter* carried a surprising announcement:

THEATRE ROYAL, GRAVESEND.

The Nobility, Gentry and the Public, are respectfully

informed that the THEATRE

47

WILL OPEN

THIS EVENING, SATURDAY, MAY 19,

Under the Management of

Mr. S. MORGAN SMITH

(Coloured Tragedian from the United States,)

With a powerful and HIGHLY EFFICIENT COMPANY.

N.B.—Public attention is specially directed to the
intention of the manager to court the patronage of the
upper classes and all who love the drama, by an effort
to raise the character of the Theatre to the highest
position of respectability.

Stage Manager and Director, Mr. H.D. Thompson.

Prices.—Boxes, 2s.; Private Boxes, 2s, 6d.; Pit, 1s; Gallery,
6p.

The following week a favorable review of the first performances
appeared in the same paper:

> THE THEATRE.—This place of public amusement opened on
> Saturday evening last under the management of Mr. S. Morgan
> Smith, an American coloured tragedian, whose gentlemanly
> manners and ability, combined with an excellent company,
> cannot fail to secure him a fair amount of patronage. The
> performances commenced on Monday and Wednesday evenings
> with "Othello," the part of the *Moor* being ably sustained by Mr.
> Smith. The tragedy was well put upon the stage, and the several
> actors acquitted themselves admirably, and to the evident
> satisfaction of the audiences.[5]

*The Gravesend Journal, Dartford Observer, and County
Intelligencer* praised the production in much the same terms but
also went further in commending the efforts of the major supporting
players:

> The tragedy of "Othello" was well put upon the stage, and the
> acting far above mediocrity. The *Moor* was played my Mr.
> S. Morgan Smith, who, upon the whole, ably sustained the
> character. The respective roles of *Cassio, Iago,* and *Roderigo*

found efficient representatives in Messrs. C.A. Clarke, Mr. Harry D. Thompson, and Mr. Charles Seymour. The part of the *Gentle Desdemona* was exceedingly well played by Miss Lizzy Grey, and Mr. [*sic*] C. A. Clarke's conception and acting of the part of *Emilia* elicited frequent tokens of approbation from the audience present. We trust the Gravesend Theatre will meet with all the success which it deserves...We apprehend that the length of the present season will be determined by the amount of patronage bestowed."[6]

Even *The Era*, the leading theatre journal in England, briefly mentioned that Morgan Smith "had made his first appearance on Monday, as Othello, assisted by a capital company. He deserves success, as he is doing everything in his power to increase the respectability of the Theatre."[7]

This news was picked up a month later by *The Commonwealth*, an African American paper in Boston that had read the review in the *Gravesend Journal* and relayed the information to its subscribers. Nashville's *Christian Recorder* then disseminated it more widely on June 23, after adding a few of their own editorial remarks on the surprising story:

A SUCCESSFUL PHILADELPHIAN

The Commonwealth says: "It may be remembered by some of our readers that Mr. S. *Morgan Smith* of Philadelphia, left Boston about the 25th of April last for Liverpool. He had resided with us for some months previously while prosecuting his histrionic studies. While here, he was refused admittance both at the Boston and Continental Theatres on account of his color,—a prejudice likely to be overcome by an amended law recently passed by the legislature forbidding exclusion from places of amusement unless 'for cause,' which no court will hold to be color. We learn, by letter, that Mr. Smith is the lessee of the Theatre at Gravesend, a watering place near London, and we observe by a recent English paper that he played the 'Moor' in *Othello* 'far above mediocrity.' A fine company of white ladies and gentleman rendered him efficient support."

We do not countenance theaters and theater going, but we cannot forbear to notice the success of the gentleman alluded to above, who has succeeded despite discouragement, in having his genius and manhood acknowledged.

It will be remembered that this gentleman gave some readings in Philadelphia not long since at Concert Hall, and scarcely any colored person attended. He was inspired, however, with a *grand idea,*—to develop his talent,—and though many called him "foolish" because he was determined *to try,* all feel proud of his success.[8]

Clearly Morgan Smith was off to a good start in Britain, not only as an actor but also as a theatre manager. His third performance, on May 25, won him further applause on both counts:

GRAVESEND THEATRE—We consider it a pleasing duty to call attention to the performances now taking place at the above theatre, under the able and judicious management of Mr. S. Morgan Smith. All the leading *artistes* comprising the *corps dramatique* have been carefully selected from the highest amount of talent procurable at various London and provincial theatres. Many years have elapsed since such a company as the present one have graced the boards of this theatre. Mr. S. Morton Smith has added fresh laurels to his histrionic fame by his impersonation of *Claude Melnotte*, in the "Lady of Lyons," his performance of which character was highly artistic and effective. Upon future occasions we will take opportunities of particularizing the relative merits of the various members of Mr. Smith's company. We highly commend an early visit to the Gravesend Theatre to all true lovers of the dramatic art. From want of capital, and its consequent want of the necessary resources to conduct a theatre successfully; from mismanagement, added to gross neglect; and from the still greater want of a good and effective company, and a proper selection of the pieces produced on its boards, the Gravesend Theatre had sunk into desuetude and disrepute; but, under the present liberal management, a single visit will convince the most skeptical in such matters that a place for dramatic entertainments of the highest order is now open to the public, in every respect well worthy of its most liberal patronage and support.[9]

Edward Bulwer-Lytton's *The Lady of Lyons; or, Love and Pride,* called by one authority "the most popular play of the nineteenth century" in England,[10] was a strategic choice for Morgan Smith's first attempt at playing a conflicted hero in what started as a romantic comedy and ended as a melodrama. It had been performed in

Philadelphia theatres several times every year from 1850 to 1865, so he would have had opportunities to see many different actors performing the role, perhaps most notably his mentor James E. Murdoch who appeared in it at the Walnut Street Theatre in May 1861.

In the play Claude Melnotte, a gardener's son, has fallen in love with Pauline Deschapelles, the beautiful daughter of a rich merchant, but she, encouraged by her status-seeking mother, refuses him and all other suitors who lack noble titles. Beauséant, a proud, wealthy man who has been rejected by her, seeks revenge by persuading Melnotte to pose as a foreign prince in order to win her love and marry her. Melnotte is successful in this quest, but, conscience-stricken, wants to break his contract with Beauséant and avoid the marriage. However, he is forced to comply and has to confess the ruse to Pauline on the night of their wedding. He feels great remorse for having thus disgraced her and himself, so he leaves immediately to join a military regiment in France. When he returns two and a half years later, he finds that Pauline, though still in love with him, has reluctantly agreed to marry the villain Beauséant, who has offered to rescue her father from ruinous debt. Melnotte, now a rich man himself, intercedes, pays the debt, and is reunited with the woman he has always ardently loved. In performing this role Morgan Smith would have had to display the full gamut of emotions and fluctuating qualities that Bulwer-Lytton felt defined such a character: "Claude's high-placed love; his ardent feelings, his unsettled principles (the struggle between which makes the passion of the drama), his ambition, and his career, [which] were phenomena that characterized the age, and in which the spirit of the nation went along with the extravagance of the individual."[11] Morgan Smith evidently succeeded in meeting this challenge in his initial appearance as Melnotte.

On Tuesday, May 29th, Morgan Smith reappeared as Othello, winning further commendation from *The Era* which said he had "displayed ability, and had evidently well studied the part."[12] On the following night his company performed a dramatic version of Sir Walter Scott's *Rob Roy*, but he evidently did not participate in this production.[13] A day or two later he came on as Hamlet for the first time, a play in which his "delineation of the 'melancholy Dane' was characterised by polished execution, added to a careful and effective style of acting."[14] The following Monday, June 4th, he debuted as Macbeth, prompting one of the local papers to declare, "It is only due to the gentleman to remark that upon each of his successive performances he achieves a greater triumph in histrionic fame."[15]

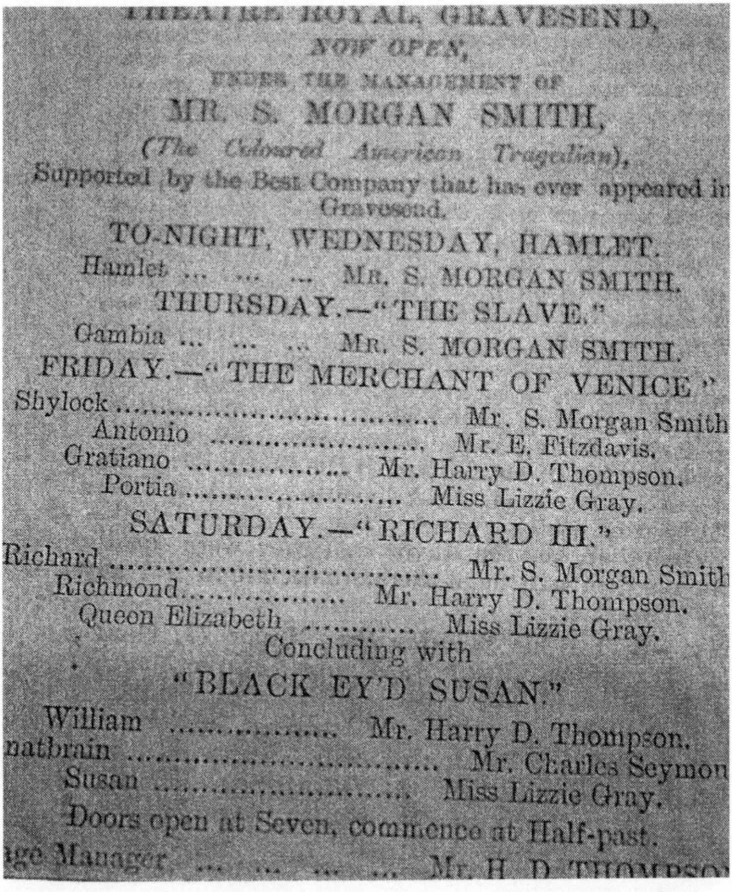

THEATRE ROYAL, GRAVESEND,
NOW OPEN,
UNDER THE MANAGEMENT OF
MR. S. MORGAN SMITH,
(The Coloured American Tragedian),
Supported by the Best Company that has ever appeared in Gravesend.
TO-NIGHT, WEDNESDAY, HAMLET.
Hamlet ... ... Mr. S. MORGAN SMITH.
THURSDAY.—"THE SLAVE."
Gambia ... ... Mr. S. MORGAN SMITH.
FRIDAY.—"THE MERCHANT OF VENICE."
Shylock .... Mr. S. Morgan Smith
Antonio .... Mr. E. Fitzdavis.
Gratiano .... Mr. Harry D. Thompson.
Portia .... Miss Lizzie Gray.
SATURDAY.—"RICHARD III."
Richard .... Mr. S. Morgan Smith
Richmond..................... Mr. Harry D. Thompson.
Queen Elizabeth .... Miss Lizzie Gray.
Concluding with
"BLACK EY'D SUSAN."
William .... Mr. Harry D. Thompson.
natbrain .... Mr. Charles Seymon
Susan .... Miss Lizzie Gray.
Doors open at Seven, commence at Half-past.
ge Manager ... ... Mr. H. D. THOMPSON

Figure 10. Advertisement in the *Gravesend Journal, Dartford Observer, and County Intelligencer* for the Theatre Royal, Gravesend, June 6-9, 1866. ©British Library Board, 072.2315. Reproduced with permission from the British Library.

During the rest of his third week Morgan Smith was extremely busy, reappearing as Hamlet on Wednesday, June 6th, and appearing for the first time as Gambia in Thomas Morton's *The Slave* on Thursday, then as Shylock in *Merchant of Venice* on Friday, and as Richard, Duke of Gloucester, in *Richard III* on Saturday. This was an extraordinary schedule for an actor who had never before played any of these last three roles in a proper theatre. He must have had a remarkable capacity to learn, retain, and speak a great number of lines when performing major roles in so many classic plays back to back, having perhaps only rehearsed them alone up to this point in his career. Is there any other actor in Britain or America who had attempted such a feat in his first few weeks of setting foot on stage before a live audience? How long would it have taken him to prepare for such a trial by fire? Morgan Smith's command of such an ambitious repertoire right from the start remains truly astonishing.

Gambia, which had been one of Ira Aldridge's staple roles, was a noble, honorable African slave who remains loyal to his owner even when this requires self-sacrifice, great courage, and extreme altruism. This was an anti-slavery drama depicting an African as an admirable, intelligent being who is better than most of those Englishmen who oppress him. There were no reviews published in the local press of Morgan Smith in this role. Nothing was said of his performance of Richard III either.

However, his portrayal of Shylock was instantly regarded as his greatest accomplishment:

> Mr. S. Morgan Smith eminently surpassed all his former performances in his excellent and finished delineation of the *Shylock*, "the Jew which Shakspeare drew." True to nature, subdued and placid at the commencement of the part, gradually rising in artistic development of the passions of hatred, thirst for revenge, and wrath; the acme, the crowning climax of the actor's art was attained, and found full scope, in *Shylock's* reply to *Bassanio's* question, "Why dost thou whet thy knife so earnestly?" Mr. Smith's burst of concentrated malice in the reply—"To cut the forfeiture from that bankrupt there," both in look and gesture, was something scathing and terrific.[16]

Even one of the major London papers, the *Sunday Times*, took notice, summarizing what had already been said in the Gravesend review:

His delineation of the part was highly impressive, and wrought wonderfully upon the feelings of his audience. It was by far the highest impersonation with which this actor has yet presented us. It was very true to nature, quiet and artistic at the commencement, arriving by gradual stages to a point at which the ascendancy of strange and terrible passions, of baffled hate and powerless longing for revenge, became exceedingly impressive. The delivery of the line "To cut the forfeit from that bankrupt there" electrified the audience. The entire performance of *The Merchant of Venice* was very complete and meritorious, and gave great delight to an overflowing audience.[17]

The last statement made here about the size of the audience appears to be at odds with what had been said locally about the reception of Morgan Smith's efforts as a theatre manager:

Mr. S. Morgan Smith has spared neither expense or exertion to redeem [the Gravesend Theatre's] character and status, by producing a succession of well-selected standard plays, by first class authors. It would be a credit to the town itself to retain such a company in it, but sorry are we to see that a class of trivial and very questionable entertainments (at least so called) are patronised elsewhere, almost to the exclusion and neglect of true worth, real talent, and undoubted respectability.[18]

There had been reports in the press of several competing attractions. On May 31st there had been an entertainment at the Gravesend and Milton Club featuring three humorous plays: J. Toole's comedietta "Intrigue; or, the Bath Road"; Charles Mathews's comedy "Used Up"; and T. J. Williams's farce "Turn Him Out." In addition, "Mr. Savery presided at the pianoforte and harmonium, and in the course of the evening favoured the audience with a song, which was well received. The attendance was not so large as on some previous occasions, the room being about three parts full."[19] All this may have been offered on the same evening that Morgan Smith was making his debut as Hamlet.

Then, starting on June 4th and possibly continuing through the week, Herr Schalkenbach, a member of the French Academy, was entertaining crowds at the Rosherville Gardens with four performances daily on an electric Military Orchestral Piano and on newly-invented brass musical instruments. The piano was said to be a machine combining "the power of a full military band, with drums, cymbals, triangles, &c., representing in the whole not less than twenty-four performers."[20] As if such a musical spectacle was not distraction enough, on the same June 4th Mr. W. W. Alcock was giving his annual concert in the National Schoolroom on Perry Street, consisting of a series of dramatic readings by amateurs, a performance by members of St. Mark's choir, several solos and duets by other singers, and demonstrations of virtuosity by instrumentalists playing pieces on the flute, violin, violoncello, and piano.[21] This was also the date that Morgan Smith was starring as Macbeth for the first time. These shows, intended for mass audiences, may have been the "trivial and very questionable entertainments" that serious theatergoers were worried about. Against such competition, Shakespeare's days on stage in Gravesend appear to have been numbered.

The end came the following week, with the theatre opening on Monday, June 11th, with a repetition of *The Lady of Lyons* in which Morgan Smith again won praise in *The Era* for his interpretation of the role of Claude Melnotte: "This gentleman is an actor of colour, and bids fair, in tragic parts, to rival the renowned Ira Aldridge. His performance of the part was excellent, and much applauded by the few persons who visited the Theatre on the occasion."[22] On Wednesday he reprised Shylock before what may have been an even smaller audience, for on that evening the Gravesend Philharmonic Union was giving their last concert of the season in the Assembly Rooms where, as usual, "although money is never taken at the doors, the room has been completely crowded by most fashionable audiences, comprising the *elite* of the town and neighbourhood."[23] Two days later, the Gravesend Theatre was nearly on its last legs:

> This place of amusement was (virtually) closed on Friday night, the 15th inst., on which occasion the manager, Mr. S. Morton [*sic*] Smith, took his benefit, appearing in the character of *Richard the Third*. At the conclusion of the tragedy Mr. Smith was called before the curtain. He thanked those who had favoured him with their support. He said that he deeply regretted that, after all the outlay, time, and attention which had been bestowed in an endeavour to place pieces on the boards of the Gravesend Theatre which deserved patronage, all his efforts,

in a monetary point of view, had been failures, but that, not even now discouraged, at a no very distant period, and in a more frequented and fashionable locality, he might again attempt to win that patronage and approbation which, unfortunately for him, had been hitherto withheld at the Gravesend Theatre.[24]

The Era wished him "better success in the next speculation."[25]

The following night his company ended their run by performing Thomas Haines's *My Poll and My Partner Joe*, a nautical melodrama, and John Maddison Morton's farce *Poor Pillicoddy*, while Morgan Smith contributed reenactments of the third act of *Othello* and the last act of *Richard III*. "With this night this unfortunate season ended, the attendance on the two evenings being *'qualis ab incepto'* [such as from the beginning]—very bad. The only circumstance on which Mr. Smith can be congratulated is the termination of the season."[26]

Again there had been no mention of how well Morgan Smith had performed as Richard III, but a friend of his later contributed an anecdote that provided some telling details:

> A gentleman of my acquaintance in London, of high culture, and a very critical writer, learning that an American named Morgan Smith had taken the Gravesend theatre, and was acting in Shaksperian characters with some success, determined to go down to Gravesend, which is near the mouth of the Thames, and a considerable distance from London. He soon found himself seated in the pit of the little theatre, and somewhat disgusted at the dreary performances of a very poor stock company. But from the moment when Morgan Smith come out—the play was Richard III—he found himself borne along on great waves of feeling and emotion, as he had rarely been in his life. This gentleman wrote to me declaring that Smith had the true fire, and would surely succeed; that he had made his acquaintance, also, and found him an extremely interesting man.[27]

Although Morgan Smith's month-long experiment at Gravesend proved to be disappointing financially, the good reviews he received there may have won him rewarding attention elsewhere, especially in London, where favorable notices had appeared not only in *The Era* but in other papers as well. The *Morning Star*, for instance, a day after the Gravesend Theatre closed, reported that

> Mr. S. Morgan Smith, a young coloured gentleman, a native

of Philadelphia, has recently appeared in this country as a tragedian. With the exception of Ira Aldridge, who is now attracting so much attention in Russia, Mr. Morgan Smith is the first of his race to seek the honours of the dramatic profession. He was trained for the stage by the most eminent teachers in America, but he had never publicly played till he came to England. He has just completed a month's engagement at Gravesend, and is arranging for a tour of the provinces. He has appeared as Othello, Hamlet, Macbeth, Lear, Richard III, and in other leading parts, his greatest success thus far having been as Shylock.[28]

The same notice subsequently was reprinted in newspapers throughout the British Isles, notably in Glasgow, Edinburgh, Dundee, Cork, Dublin, Liverpool, Leicester, Nottingham, Leamington Spa, and North and South Shields.[29] This kind of publicity no doubt helped him to secure engagements on tours of the provinces in the months and years ahead.

Endnotes

1   *Liverpool Weekly Mercury*, May 12, 1866.

2   *Post Office Directory of Kent 1866*. (London: Kelly and Co., 1866), 962.

3   According to volumes of the *Census of England and Wales, 1861* and *1871* (both published in London by G.E. Eyre and William Spottiswood for Her Majesty's Stationery Office in 1862 and 1872 respectively), the population of Gravesend in 1861 was 18,782 and in 1871 had grown to 21,265. All future references to population figures in the U. K. will be drawn from these sources.

4   John Kennedy Melling, *Discovering Lost Theatres* (Tring: Shire Publications, 1969), 46.

5   *Gravesend and Dartford Reporter*, May 26, 1866. Morgan Smith had not appeared on the opening night, May 19, when *Leah*, a drama by an unknown playwright, was performed by his company, for he preferred to wait until May 21 and 23 to make his debut as Othello.

6   *The Gravesend Journal, Dartford Observer, and County Intelligencer*, May 23, 1866.

7   *The Era*, May 27, 1866, and reprinted there on July 29, 1866.

8   *Christian Recorder*, June 23, 1866. The report, entitled "Another Colored American Tragedian Abroad," had appeared in *The Commonwealth* on June 16, 1866. The correspondent for *The Commonwealth* who broke this story

may have been Moncure D. Conway who, between May 1863 and September 1867, submitted a weekly letter from England, signing it as M. D. C. See Mary Elizabeth Burtis, *Moncure Conway, 1832-1907* (New Brunswick, NJ: Rutgers University Press, 1952), 244-45.

9   *The Gravesend Journal, Dartford Observer, and County Intelligencer*, May 30, 1866.

10 Dewey Ganzel, "Bulwer and his *Lady*," *Modern Philology*, 58, no. 1 (1960): 41.

11 Edward Bulwer-Lytton, "Preface," *The Lady of Lyons; or, Love and Pride* (New York and London: Samuel French, n.d.), 3.

12 *The Era*, June 3, 1866.

13 *The Gravesend Journal, Dartford Observer, and County Intelligencer*, June 6, 1866.

14 Ibid.

15 Ibid.

16 *The Gravesend Journal, Dartford Observer, and County Intelligencer*, June 13, 1866.

17 *Sunday Times*, July 1, 1866.

18 *The Gravesend Journal, Dartford Observer, and County Intelligencer*, June 13, 1866.

19 *The Gravesend and Dartford Reporter*, June 2, 1866.

20 *The Gravesend and Dartford Reporter*, June 9, 1866.

21 Ibid.

22 *The Era*, June 17, 1866.

23 *The Gravesend and Dartford Reporter*, June 16, 1866.

24 *The Gravesend Journal, Dartford Observer, and County Intelligencer*, June 20, 1866.

25 *The Era*, June 17, 1866.

26 *The Era*, June 24, 1866.

27 Conway, "The Negro as Artist," 39.

28 *Morning Star*, June 17, 1866. This was reprinted in London's *Court Journal*, June 30, 1866. It has not been possible to verify that Morgan Smith performed as King Lear at the Gravesend Theatre.

29 See the *Glasgow Herald*, June 22, 1966; *Edinburgh Evening Courant*, June 22, 1966; *Dundee Courier*, June 23, 1866; *Irish Examiner*, June 25, 1866; *Dublin Evening Mail*, June 26, 1866; *Liverpool Mercury*, June 25, 1866; *Leicester Chronicle*, June 23, 1866; *Nottingham Guardian*, June 29, 1866; *Leamington Spa Courier*, June 30, 1866; and *Shields Daily Gazette*, June 23, 1866.

3

Birmingham and London

For the next five weeks Morgan Smith was idle, though he may
have been busy seeking engagements in London, but without
success. During this time one more account of his activities in
Gravesend appeared in London *English Leader*, but it didn't result
in any offers of employment:

> Considerable interest is just now felt in the appearance on the
> English stage of Mr. S. Morgan Smith, a coloured actor from
> America, who is said to have very great gifts for the dramatic
> profession. He appears not only in parts with which he is allied
> by complexion, such as Othello, Oroonoko, Gambia, &c., but
> also in Macbeth, Shylock, and Hamlet. He has a noble voice,
> great facial expression, and renders with singular delicacy,
> naturalness, and power, a very wide range of sentiment and
> passion. Not the least of his merits is his high artistic ambition,
> and his desire to prove that the race to which he belongs is
> capable of successful exertion in the arduous walks of the
> Theatrical Profession.[1]

Eventually Morgan Smith decided his best course of action would
be to publicize his availability for a provincial tour by placing a
lengthy advertisement in *The Era* for four consecutive weeks,

starting on July 15th. The ad told of a dozen parts he was prepared to play, including six he had not performed in Gravesend:

MR. S. MORGAN SMITH

COLOURED AMERICAN TRAGEDIAN

will be happy to negotiate Short Engagements with Provincial Managers.

Mr. Smith's *Repertoire* consists of the following Characters:—

OTHELLO,	HAMLET,
ZANGA,	SHYLOCK,
OROONOKO,	RICHARD THE THIRD,
GAMBIA,	CLAUDE MELNOTTE,
MACBETH,	VIRGINIUS,
RICHELIEU	DAMON

Mr. S. refers to the following criticisms from the Press during his brief sojourn in England.

All communications to be addressed to H. J. TURNER, 21, Bow-street.[2]

Following were seven glowing reviews of his performances at Gravesend that had appeared in *The Era*, *Gravesend and Dartford Reporter*, *Morning Star*, *Sunday Times*, and *English Leader*, testifying to his ability to play a range of roles, white as well as black.

The publicity campaign worked, leading Mrs. Macready, the lessee and manager of the Prince of Wales Theatre in Birmingham, to offer Morgan Smith a contract for six nights during which he was to act five different characters. He opened on August 6, 1866 as Othello, and the critical response to his acting was decidedly negative. The *Birmingham Daily Post* declared

> To say that Mr. Smith's the worst *Othello* we ever saw, would be perhaps going too far, but that it is *one* of them is quite within the mark. His conception of the fiery high-souled Moor is weak and spiritless to a degree, and the manner in which he delivers his words fully worthy of the conception. Never once rising to

mediocrity, the performance very frequently sinks to depths far below it.[3]

Avis's Birmingham Gazette attributed his failure to his youth and inexperience:

> Mr. Smith is said to have been studying under eminent tuition in America, but is yet very young in his dramatic career. He has made the too common mistake to attempting to fly before his wings are strong enough for lofty flights, and has much to learn before he can hope for success in delineating great parts to an audience which knows the difference between finish and rawness.[4]

London's *Illustrated Sporting and Theatrical News* offered an equally blunt assessment but also managed to find something positive to say about this over-ambitious actor:

> He was by no means happy [as Othello]. His acting was bad, and his elocution worse; but although not equal to his pretensions he is evidently intelligent and painstaking.[5]

The *Birmingham Journal* found it pointless to criticize the performance, but thought Morgan Smith might perhaps have a chance to improve as a thespian:

> It would be inflicting needless pain both on him and our readers to enter now upon any review of his qualifications. Of Mr. Smith we would say in the words of Cowper—
>
> > "Peace to all such 'twere pity to offend
> >
> > By useless censure, whom we cannot mend,"
>
> but we doubt our warranty for the latter assertion. Mr. Smith has many good points, and as he is still young, it is not unreasonable to hope that with time and experience, a closer study of human nature and a fuller acquaintance with the canons of his art, he may ultimately develop into a competent exponent of even such lofty and subtle characters as Shakespeare's *Othello*.[6]

Nearly all the Birmingham critics chose to ignore Morgan Smith's appearances as Shylock on Tuesday, Gambia on Wednesday, Claude Melnotte on Thursday, Cardinal Richelieu on Friday, or Gambia again on Saturday. The *Illustrated Sporting and Theatrical Times* said he had appeared as Shylock "without producing any great effect,"[7] and the *Birmingham Journal* predicted that his reappearance as Gambia in *The Slave* would be "a part and a drama, we may scarcely say, for which Mr. Smith is in every respect better suited than those in which he challenged criticism on Monday night."[8]

Mrs. Macready may have been greatly disappointed with the response to her visiting star, but it is clear that the critics did not hold her to blame for Morgan Smith's performances. One called his Othello "a pity, for, on the production of good plays in a creditable manner depends the future of this house, which we should heartily like to see prosperous."[9] Another said:

> We wish the manager of this theatre greater success than has yet fallen to her lot. When the season commenced she had one of the best stock companies ever seen in Birmingham. They needed no "stars" then; all they wanted was a fair degree of popular support. That was lacking, for the fortunes of the place had fallen very low, and it takes long to retrieve character once lost. Mrs. Macready has done much to deserve success, but has not been sufficiently backed up; consequently, the company has deteriorated in quality. Nevertheless, the performances we have lately witnessed at the Prince of Wales Theatre were pleasing and well-conducted, and showed that the void requiring to be filled was in front rather than behind the curtain.[10]

It is regrettable that nothing was said about Morgan Smith's debut in Bulwer-Lytton's *Richelieu*, for it would have been interesting to know how he interpreted the Cardinal. He may have seen great actors perform this character in Philadelphia. Edwin Forrest was considered "powerful and impressive" in the role, and Edwin Booth's Richelieu "was one of the most carefully studied and elaborately finished of all his impersonation[s]."[11] One wonders if Morgan Smith would have attempted to imitate such strong models.

Richelieu; or, The Conspiracy, like *Lady of Lyons*, was one of Bulwer-Lytton's most popular and long-lasting plays on the nineteenth-century stage. According to his son,

> It was an historical drama on the grand scale, the central figure being Cardinal Richelieu....The plot is woven out of the intrigues of the Duke of Orleans and others to destroy Richelieu, and the Cardinal's measures to circumvent his enemies and save France. Everything turns on the possession of a certain

document which contains written evidence of the conspiracy and this does not get into Richelieu's hands till the last moment. At first his enemies look like succeeding; the King is deceived, the cardinal deposed; but finally the possession of the precious document turns tables and Richelieu triumphs.[12]

The Cardinal dominates the play. Relying on French sources,[13] Bulwer-Lytton created a crafty leader who could command, manipulate, and outmaneuver others by the sheer force of his personality. He told William Charles Macready, for whom he had written the part, of Richelieu's "raillery—his address—his terrible good humour. His vindictiveness—his daring—his wisdom—his

Figure 11. Playbill of *Othello* starring Morgan Smith at the Olympic Theatre, London, on August 25, 27 and 28, 1866. Reproduced with permission from Leon Robinson, Positive Steps, London.

Figure 12. Image of Morgan Smith as Othello. Reproduced with permission from the Michael A. Morrison collection.

genius in the broad events of his history."[14] The role, according to a later commentator, became "a popular one with leading men and with stars. The attractive combination of comedy and melodrama, with opportunities for declamatory climaxes, is of the sort to excite audiences; and for that reason, if for no other, would appeal to actors."[15] It is not surprising that Morgan Smith was drawn to it.

Two weeks after leaving Gravesend, he secured an engagement at London's Olympic Theatre, where he opened on Saturday, August 25, as Othello. The reaction was swift and mixed; some critics praised him, others condemned him, and a few merely mentioned him as a curiosity or experiment. The most positive assessment appeared in the *English Leader*:

> A new tragedian has appeared in London—Mr. Morgan Smith, a coloured gentleman, who in America was never suffered, by reason of his race, to go behind the scenes in any theatre, and consequently could not master stage business. In this country he can command these facilities, and on Saturday evening he appeared at the Olympic, in the difficult character of Othello, in which his success was unquestionable. That he has a natural genius for acting was manifest in the confidence and mastery of his part which he displayed. Challenging the judgment and meeting the critical eye of a new race for the first time, on whose verdict the hopes, ambition, and struggles of a life depended, was an hour for trepidation. The actor showed none. He had that self-possession which genius alone imparts, if we may credit George Sand—and we may credit her here. Though short as Garrick, Mr. Morgan Smith had so much the natural dignity of the chief, that he always looked the commanding Moor, and you forgot, or did not notice, that he was below the regulation standard for Othello. He has a splendid and well cultivated voice, with a slight American accent. There was no straining after effects, not an atom of rant, but a perfectly natural action in all he did. Gentle and brave and candid, with a noble reservation of pride and high feeling in the earlier portions of the play, he passed to the terrible agitation of consuming jealousy, with a transition so life-like and spontaneous as to take the feelings of the auditor captive unawares. When he seized Iago in his first great doubt of the tempter, the sudden southern fire of his speech took the house by storm, and left an impression of his power which was never effaced. He met Desdemona a changed being. He did not step, he stole over the stage like a panther. There was a wild animal in his tone—you expected him to

spring upon his wife. Yet he was merely savage, not brutal, or coarse. He always preserved the delicacy and refinement of a high yet terrible nature. Mr. Morgan Smith's Othello is as great a performance as Mr. Fechter's Hamlet.[16]

Lloyd's Weekly Newspaper also spoke favorably of what Morgan Smith had managed to achieve before an enthusiastic audience but pointed to some deficiencies as well and ended by questioning the implicit premise of such a performance:

> A naturally dingy Othello on the stage is no novelty since the many years of Mr. Ira Aldridge's success; and just the extreme—the deepest of the dark—is therefore taken off Mr. Morgan Smith, who made a first and successful appearance at the Olympic theatre, as Othello, on Saturday last. Mr. Smith's appearance is certainly favourable, though he might, with propriety, look more dominant, as becomes the character. And besides, to a certain extent, public feeling must be consulted, and public feeling has always ran in favour of any coloured race being strong and savage. The same want of intensity likewise marks the passions; but at times Mr. Morgan Smith seemed roused to the occasion, and revels in the lines of the poet. In the last scene, before Desdemona awakes, he created a great effect on the audience as well as in his indignant remonstrance with Cassio, and calm gravity with Brabantio. The favourite passages in the play are his best, and he seems to have studied not altogether too wisely nor too well; for whilst he seems thoroughly to understand what he is talking about, he sometimes halts, and cuts the lines about in a manner of "pointing" which might drive a fastidious printer into an immediate lunatic asylum. We may have other opportunities of seeing Mr. Morgan Smith, even during the present limited engagement; for he has already been successful in many Shaksperian characters in various parts of England which are not London. A Morocco Hamlet will be a novelty; and Richard growing white with fear will be an effect indeed....
>
> Surely, a black or a dark Othello is running realism mad. It reaches the point when acting ceases to be....The end and aim of an actor is to appear to be somebody he is not....And so we think natural duskiness no kind of advantage to a theatrical Othello; and if, moreover, he should happen to be a great general in a foreign service there would be all the less acting in the case. The stage is built for assumptions—not for realities.[17]

The *Penny Illustrated Weekly News* found Morgan Smith's appearance and acting skills satisfactory but not outstanding:

> Mr. Smith is a native of Philadelphia, of middle height, and of a deep brown complexion, with black piercing eyes, and a countenance expressive of dignity, animation, and power.... He is a good actor, his attitudes being graceful, and his movements free and natural. His delineation of the Moor must be pronounced clever, and in some parts very effective. He displayed considerable skill and energy in the exhibition of the rising of jealousy in his bosom when Iago first endeavoured to kindle that passion within him. His elocution has many good qualities, but it is not of the highest order of oratory. His acting throughout the final act, though evincing the possession of great histrionic skill, and indicative of careful study, did not, in our estimation rise to the highest standard of impersonation of the impassioned Moor. Mr. Morgan Smith was frequently and warmly applauded, and he received this mark of encouragement with great modesty, after the manner of an artist who seems to be painstaking and serious in his labours.[18]

The *Illustrated Sporting and Theatrical News* agreed that he showed great promise but was not yet a polished performer, though he did manage to please his audience:

> He has the dignity of a free man in his every aspect, and affords as favourable a proof of "the man and brother" theory of as the most ardent promulgator of that theory could wish for.... That which is most apparent in Mr. Smith's acting, judging from his performance on Saturday night, is innate capability. Unless first impressions deceive us Mr. Smith is made of that rare stuff out of which fine actors are made. He has an exceedingly fine voice, a dignified though modest demeanour, a varied fund of natural expression—of look, tone and gesture, and, best and most promising of all, *no stage vices*. All these things, however, though pointing to the capability of which we speak, do [not] make a great actor. The being capable of being and the being are two different things. For the adequate filling of the high position which we think his abilities point to, the new actor will need much artistic training, and study alike of his author and his art. As a rule he shone most in the quieter passages, many of which in his hands were more significant than usual. In the grand ebullitions of passion the fairly powerful conception

was marred in the execution by, first, the actor's short-comings as an elocutionist, and, second a certain amount of diffidence. The audience, although evidently not at all pre-disposed to enthusiasm, were at several points—not, however, always at *the* points—trapped into applauding, and at the close the applause culminating in a call before the curtain was very general and encouraging. All things considered, Mr. Morgan Smith must be congratulated.[19]

The *Morning Herald* and *London Evening Standard* jointly called the evening a "tolerable success," noting that "Mr. Smith is a powerful actor, although, perhaps, a little too stiff in his action; but the effect which is given to the part he portrays by his natural appearance in a measure counterbalances that defect, and to judge from the reception he met with last night, he appears already to have become a favourite with the Olympic audience."[20]

Meanwhile the *London Review* remarked that Morgan Smith had "succeeded in showing that Mr. Ira Aldridge is not the only actor who can represent that character in a respectable fashion without the aid of lampblack."[21] And the *News of the World* found that "His performance of the part is characterised by considerable care and discretion, but we must wait until he undertakes another character before we form any decided opinion of his ability to represent the heroes of SHAKESPERIAN drama."[22] Such commendations, even when qualified with a few complaints, were a significant improvement over what had been said about his interpretation of Othello at the Gravesend Theatre.

However, there were critics who were not at all pleased with this Othello. The *Sunday Times* was one of the first to pounce, saying,

Mr. Smith has...few qualifications for the part he undertook. He is physically small and spare; his voice lacks power; he is deficient in fire and animation, and his delivery is abrupt and inelegant. He has no correct conception of the character of Othello, and is physically unable to express such conception as he has. In his delivery of the vigorous lines which occur in the play, he was lamentably ineffective. He gave the famous exclamation, "I'll tear him all to pieces," very much in the sort of tone and manner in which Mr. Calhaem, as Jackey [*sic*], in a certain notorious drama, used to say, "I'll punch your head." In less forcible passages his delivery was equally unsatisfactory. It was abrupt and artificial. His voice dropped at the end of every paragraph—dropped not only in loudness of tone, but in inflection, and a very curious effect was thus produced. The attempt, indeed, was in all respects unsatisfactory; and Mr. Smith, if he is to attain any success on an English stage, must be contented with a less ambitious effort than that of shining in the very highest walk of tragedy.[23]

The *Sporting Times* was even more emphatic in denouncing what it had witnessed on stage:

I am of the opinion that what is intrinsically and inevitably bad is most effectually "wiped out," to use a Yankee phrase, either by contemptuous silence or by a few lines of absolute and unqualified condemnation; and as there exists in my mind a deeply-rooted conviction that Mr. Morgan Smith's Othello reached the supreme degree of defectiveness, I think my best course will be to resort to the last of the two above-named expedients. The term "puerile" is the adjective that most adequately conveys an impression of this gentleman's pitiable endeavour to portray the different phases in the character of the jealous Moor. It was in truth a boyish attempt. If magnificent costumes and an inexhaustible amount of confidence could of themselves ensure success, then Mr. Smith would have achieved a triumph. But unhappily for abortive aspirations, the impersonator of tragedy must be possessed of voice, gait, figure, intelligence, education, &c., but in Mr. Smith most of these essentials are conspicuous by their absence. I should not be speaking frankly did I fail to give expression to my belief that this gentleman is totally unfit for the profession he has chosen.[24]

The *Morning Post*, after summing up Morgan Smith's professional qualities as a "black skin, fine flashing eyes, and teeth of snowy whiteness," went on to describe at some length his many inadequacies as an actor, noting in particular that he was "frequently monotonous," lacked "creative power and poetic imagination," and was "textual, not histrionic."[25] Five other papers joined in the chorus of condemnation:

Not withstanding that he has the advantage of being more than one-third *white*, the distinction has not bestowed on him any histrionic merit. His *Othello*...was without exception one of the worst that we have seen for many years. It was not only deficient in an intelligent conception of the *Moor*, but wanted his dignity and feeling as much as the traits of a finished treatment....At the same time, it is necessary to say that he has considerable natural advantages. He has an expressive, handsome face, but very far from the negro type—and a manly voice and person.[26]

The gentleman possesses two possible qualifications for the part—he "knows his lines" well, and is by nature as black as any Othello need be...and though the sun's livery on the face and hands of a gentleman of colour may enable his Othello to dispense with lampblack, the inside of the head cannot well dispense with those cerebral advantages without which an actor becomes a mere energetic "spouter;" leaving his weary, parboiled critic to wish Othello had contrived to kill himself before the last act came to end his misery and our self-imposed penance.[27]

So far as regards complexion, he is unquestionably the genuine article for personating the copper-coloured Moor; but beyond this natal advantage, there is assuredly nothing else to warrant his assuming so difficult a part. He seems to be a conscientious actor with some power, but no genius, not grace, dignity, *verve*, and impulse. If there be nothing offensive in his performance of *Othello*, there is no indication whatever of present or even possible excellence. Most of our "eminent tragedians" are very sorry sticks, but even these may all claim precedence of Mr. Morgan Smith.[28]

Mr. Morgan Smith [is] a gentleman who is described in the bills as a coloured American tragedian, but who, neither in physiognomy, figure, nor voice, exhibits in any marked degree the specialities of the negro race. Whatever peculiarities Mr. Morgan Smith possesses are rather such as will be recognised as American, and these are displayed so unmistakeably as must greatly interfere with his success with an audience accustomed to a pure English pronunciation. Neither has Mr. Smith the power of expressing intense passion or the more level quality of refined elocution. The points he made, and the passages in which he called forth marks of approval from an audience undoubtedly friendly, were those in which the poet has done everything for the actor, and in which common sense and ordinary intelligence only are necessary to ensure effect.[29]

Mr. Morgan Smith...does not realise [the] ideal of the unhappy Moor, in spite of his natural advantages. He is conscientious and sensible—nothing more; and he has an unpleasant way of wrapping up his words in small parcels of three or four, and firing off a speech in the shape of isolated cartridges, instead of making it a general volley. In the third (and most important act) Mr. Morgan Smith was disappointing.[30]

Though most of these reactions were hostile rather than friendly assessments of Morgan Smith's credentials as a tragedian, the audience who saw him perform evidently approved of what he was able to do on stage and applauded him for his efforts. Even some of the critics had to admit that he possessed certain qualities that worked to his advantage—notably his voice, face, person, his self-confident and conscientious manner, and enough common sense and ordinary intelligence to be effective. They also seemed to be surprised that he did not look or behave like a negro. Perhaps they had not expected an African American to offer such a tame performance of Othello. Or maybe they remembered the vigor with which Ira Aldridge, allegedly a native African, had played the role. In any case, they appear to have been disappointed as much by Morgan Smith's color as by his conception of the jealous Moor.

His first appearance on stage in London also was covered by Moncure D. Conway, a correspondent for an American periodical, *The Round Table*, who provided a number of interesting new details on how and by whom it was received:

I witnessed a novel and very impressive scene the other evening at the Olympic—or as it is called now, Tom Taylor's—theatre. It was announced that the play of *Othello* would be presented there, with the character of Othello rendered by a negro from Philadelphia—Mr. Morgan Smith. Mr. Smith had never found in America a theatre willing to admit him to its stage. He has only of late arrived in England, and this was but his twentieth appearance in any theatre. That he should appear on any London stage was a formidable ordeal under such circumstances. The theatre was well filled, and it was strange to see the most fashionable row of seats in it occupied by a well-dressed and, by general agreement, decidedly good-looking array of colored people. Amongst these was Ellen Craft, the celebrated fugitive slave who escaped some fifteen years ago from Macon, Ga., in the disguise of a Southern gentleman, attended by her husband, William Craft, who acted the part, in that very real drama, of her (his) body-servant. There were with her two handsome mulatto women. Then there was the Rev. Sella Martin, his wife, and her cousin, who would both be called anywhere very handsome brunettes. There were two or three others. These ladies in their rich opera-cloaks were a parterre of African beauties such as one scarcely sees, and on this occasion attracted the opera-glasses of the fashionable audience almost as much as the actors on the stage. Mr. Smith's appearance in the make-up of the Moor was most admirable, and he received a round of applause. Never was there a man on the stage who more perfectly looked the character he was about to represent. And when in addition to this he showed that he was a complete master of the grand Shakespearian conception; when from first to last he gave the most chaste and finished readings, never ranting, never at a loss; when with new electric movements and tones he kindled and thrilled those present in a way which, in the present decadence of the Shakespearian drama on the London stage, none had dared expect, his triumph was complete. From first to last he moved the entire assembly with him; again and again the house echoed the plaudits and bravos; and when the curtain fell he was called before it by the most deafening and long-continued applause. So great was the success that the manager announced amid cheers that he had then and there made an agreement with Morgan Smith to continue his representations. It is even said that the Olympic and Sadler's Wells are to have a lawsuit for his services. I risk nothing in saying that the most distinguished theatrical success in London at the present moment is that of the Philadelphia negro, whose whole training has been obtained in the negro-galleries of theatres in his native city and in Boston. A friend who has seen Ira Aldridge, the negro who has been making such a stir in St. Petersburg and other cities of the continent, assures me that Morgan Smith has far more dramatic genius, and will be a greater man in the end. It has always been my conviction—formed from a long acquaintance with negroes in the Southern States—that the negro race has very important artistic gifts, and particularly that they have great dramatic qualities. There is at this time another American negro in London training for the stage for whom great things are predicted.[31]

Ellen and William Craft had lived in Philadelphia and Boston for two years after their escape from Georgia but had decided to emigrate to England in December 1850 following the passage of a Fugitive Slave Law that allowed slave owners to pursue their runaways anywhere in the United States and return them to slavery. William and Ellen spent some time giving antislavery lectures throughout the British Isles and attending an agricultural trade school in Ockham, Surrey, where they learned to read and write. In 1857 they moved with their small children to London, settling in Hammersmith.[32] In 1860 William's book *Running a Thousand Miles for Freedom, or, The Escape of William and Ellen Craft from Slavery* was published, lending "further authenticity and support to the effort to isolate proslavery America."[33] When William in 1863 went off to Dahomey for three and a half years to start a school and business, Ellen remained at home seeing to their children's education and continuing her involvement in the abolition movement.[34] "Life in Hammersmith was quiet, interrupted only by visits from friends and American abolitionists touring London."[35] Reverend John Sella Martin, a family friend, had escaped from slavery in Alabama and had become a Baptist preacher in Boston and a prominent abolitionist. He too traveled to England to lecture against slavery and was working there to raise funds to build schools for blacks in the American South after the civil war. He happened to be in London when Morgan Smith was debuting at the Olympic Theatre, so he and members of his family joined Ellen Craft and other friends for the performance there.[36] Moncure D. Conway, the author of the piece in *The Round Table*, was a white preacher and abolitionist who had come to England as an unofficial ambassador from the American antislavery movement. He had visited Ellen Craft at her home in 1864.[37]

Morgan Smith continued performing Othello at the Olympic Theatre for the next four nights. The Olympic management resorted to puffery in an attempt to lure audiences, placing an advertisement in *The Times* that called his appearance there "the greatest legitimate triumph for years,"[38] but no further reviews turned up in the press. The following week he reappeared in the role only on Tuesday and Thursday,[39] having been displaced on other nights by Miss Marriott, an actress from Sadler's Wells who had been brought in to star as Hamlet; one paper called it "an admirable and exceedingly clever impersonation. Probably it is as near perfection as it is possible for a woman to approach."[40]

During his third week at the Olympic he was back in a starring role as Shylock for five nights, but only a single review appeared, *The Era* finding his interpretation of the moneylender disappointing:

In giving our impressions of our clever coloured friend's achievement in the character of the Jew we cannot avoid saying that, while we felt there was much to admire in his delineation of the crafty, vindictive usurer, it was not all that could be desired. There are not two opinions as to the prodigious power displayed by the poet in this picture, but the same cannot be affirmed of Mr. Smith's copy of it. There was the correct outline, the same details, and the same colours, but the reproduction lacked the bold relief and the strong warm tints of the great original. A learned Shakespearian commentator has compared the fierce hate and insatiate greed of the old extortioner to "the convulsions of an earthquake, or the outbreak of a volcano," but certainly that is not the simile which would be suggested by Mr. Smith's rendering even of the most impassioned passages of the part. This gentleman's great deficiency is the lack of a deep-seated and sustained feeling and power, yet he is not emotionless by any means, nor is he wanting in energy and activity. In a word, for ourselves we think that he is a skilful, careful workman, but that he has not the high genius of the consummate artist. His delivery of the text was almost unexceptionally good; he spoke with distinctness, correctness, fluency, and thoughtful discrimination, and in his acting displayed much tact in the manner in which he gave expression to various feelings.[41]

Finally, there was an announcement that on Wednesday, September 19, "Mr. Morgan Smith will appear as HAMLET! Being that Gentleman's Benefit, and Last Appearance previous to his Provincial Engagements."[42] The critics remained completely silent about this performance.

Moncure D. Conway, who saw Morgan Smith perform in a more intimate setting than a theatre, offered this account of him:

I found the actor a remarkably handsome man of about thirty years of age, of a deep brown color, singularly strong lines of face, and an expression full of dignity, animation and power. He consented to read for us, and a little company was collected, amongst whom were several literary personages, and one who had been connected with the stage. To this group, seated in an English drawing-room, the Philadelphian negro read the speech of Othello to the Senate, and several portions of Hamlet. There was no one present but was thrilled by these readings. His voice was clear, rich, and resonant, perfectly modulated, and capable of uttering the widest range of emotion, from tenderness and pathos, to terror and rage. And there was, too, a chasteness, an absence of all noisiness and affectation, which is ever the sign of a true artist. I think I have never seen such an eye since I saw Rachel's—a magazine of the weapons of passion. There is but one opinion amongst those who have seen and heard Morgan Smith, on or off the stage, and that is that the provincial tour upon which he is now about to enter as a star-actor, will end with a position on the London stage as eminent as that of Ira Aldridge on the continental stage; and that America may ere long have more food for reflecting how well she is leading the van of Humanity, whilst some of her finest spirits can find a free arena for their development and movement only under the monarchies and aristocracies of the old world.[43]

Figure 13: Image of Samuel Morgan Smith as Othello published on the letterhead of a message sent by him to Moncure Daniel Conway on December 13, 1866 and held among the Moncure Daniel Papers, Box 20, at the Rare Book & Manuscript Library, Columbia University in the City of New York. Reproduced with permission.

Endnotes

1   *English Leader*, July 7, 1966, quoted in *The Era*, July 22, 1866. It has not been possible to verify that Morgan Smith performed as Oroonoko at the Gravesend Theatre.

2   *The Era*, July 15, 1866.

3   *Birmingham Daily Post*, August 7, 1866.

4   *Avis's Birmingham Gazette*, August 11, 1866.

5   *Illustrated Sporting and Theatrical News*, August 11, 1866.

6   *Birmingham Journal*, August 11, 1866.

7   *Illustrated Sporting and Theatrical News*, August 11, 1866.

8   *Birmingham Journal*, August 11, 1866.

9   *Birmingham Daily Post*, August 7, 1866.

10 *Aris's Birmingham Gazette*, August 11, 1866. This Mrs. Macready, described in T. Edgar Pemberton's *The Birmingham Theatres: A Local Retrospect* (Birmingham: Cornish Brothers; London: Simpkin, Marshall [1889]), 45, as "a strange being, who was fond of acting Shylock," was not related in any way to the famous tragedian William Charles Macready nor to the former manager of the Bristol Theatre Royal, Sarah M'Cready.

11 Both remarks are quoted in Charles N. Mann's unpublished "History of the Arch Street Theatre," 5 (1861): 193-94, held in the M. Kendall Collection at the Harry Ransom Center, University of Texas at Austin. Forrest had performed Richelieu at the American Academic of Music on December 9 and 20, 1861, and at the Chestnut Street Theatre on February 2, 5, 6, and 20, March 20, November 23, December 17 and 28, 1863, and December 15 and 16, 1864. Booth had performed the same role at the Arch Street Theatre on August 27, 1859, May 11 and November 2, 1860, April 13, 1861, as well as at the American Academy of Music on August 22, 1863.

12 [Edward Robert Bulwer Lytton] Earl of Lytton, *Bulwer-Lytton* (Denver: Alan Swallow, 1948), 72.

13 Charles B. Qualia, "French Dramatic Sources of Bulwer-Lytton's *Richelieu*," *PMLA*, 42, no. 1 (March 1927): 177-84.

14 A letter quoted in Charles H. Shattuck, ed., *Bulwer and Macready: A Chronicle of the Early Victorian Theatre* (Urbana: University of Illinois Press, 1958), 94. In the same letter Bulwer-Lytton provides Macready with a "list of Books [in French] relative to Richelieu."

15 M.A., "Introduction," in Sir Edward Bulwer Lytton, *Richelieu; or, The Conspiracy* (Boston: Walter H. Baker & Co., 1896), 4. For a discussion of occasional "splendidly melodramatic" aspects of this play, see Richard Bevis, "'Mightier than the Sword': The Anatomy of Power in Bulwer Lytton's

Richelieu," *Essays in Theatre*, 8, no. 2 (May 1990): 95-106.

16 *English Leader*, September 1, 1866. According to George Henry Lewes, *On Actors and the Art of Acting* (London: Smith, Elder & Co., 1875): 130-31, Charles Albert Fechter, an Anglo-French actor, surprised theatergoers in England when he gave a "new and charming representation" of Hamlet, playing him in a natural style that was "more conversational and less stilted than usual." Lewes said "His Hamlet was one of the very best" he had ever seen. For the response to Fechter's interpretation of Hamlet in America, see Charles H. Shattuck, *Shakespeare on the American Stage: From Booth and Barrett to Sothern and Marlowe* (Washington, DC: Folger Shakespeare Library, 1987), 143-48.

17 *Lloyd's Weekly Newspaper*, September 2, 1866.

18 *Penny Illustrated Weekly News*, September 1, 1866. Errol Hill, in "S. Morgan Smith: Successor to Ira Aldridge," *Black American Literature Forum*, 16 (1982): 133, quotes a similar assessment in *The Era*, September 2, 1866.

19 *Illustrated Sporting and Theatrical News*, September 1, 1866.

20 *Morning Herald*, August 29, 1866; *London Evening Standard*, August 29, 1866.

21 *London Review*, September 1, 1866.

22 *News of the World*, September 2, 1866.

23 *Sunday Times*, September 2, 1866. Stanislaus Calhaem was a popular actor who had played the role of Jacky, an Australian, to great acclaim in C. H. Hazelwood's stage adaptation of Charles Reade's novel "It's Never too Late to Mend" at Leeds in January 1865. A review of the play can be found in *The Era*, March 12, 1865.

24 *Sporting Times*, September 1, 1866.

25 *Morning Post*, August 27, 1866.

26 *Weekly Dispatch*, September 2, 1866.

27 *Sportsman*, August 28, 1866.

28 *Reynolds's Newspaper*, September 2, 1866.

29 *Observer*, August 26, 1866.

30 *Illustrated Times*, September 1, 1866.

31 [Conway], *The Round Table*, 56. The other American negro mentioned may have been either Gustavus Allenborough, a "Coloured Tragedian" who had performed as Othello in Northampton and Woolwich in June 1866 and was to reappear in the same role in Red-Hill in August 1867 (for details see the *Northampton Mercury*, June 30, 1866, *The Era*, July 1, 1866, and *The Era*, August 4, 1867) or G. P. Dunbar, the "American Coloured Tragedian, who was to appear as Antoine in *Antoine, the Savage of the Rocks* at Latimer's

Mammoth Theatre, Pool Meadow, Coventry, in June 1867 (for details see the *Coventry Herald*, June 21, 1867). A third possibility might be G. A. Gross, "the South American Coloured Actor," who later performed as Othello and Richard III at Liverpool's Royal Adelphi Theatre in September 1868 (for details see the *Liverpool Daily Post*, September 4 and 11, 1868).

32   Jerome Farrell, "Craft, William (*c.* 1825-1900)," *Oxford Dictionary of National Biography* (Oxford: Oxford University Press, 2004).

33   R. J. M. Blackett, *Building an Antislavery Wall: Black Americans in the Atlantic Abolitionist Movement, 1830-1860* (Baton Rouge and London: Louisiana State University Press, 1983), 198.

34   R. J. M. Blackett, *Beating Against the Barriers: Biographical Essays in Nineteenth-Century Afro-American History* (Baton Rouge and London: Louisiana State University Press, 1986), 119-21.

35   Ibid., 121.

36   For further details on the career of Reverend Martin, see Blackett's chapter on him in *Beating Against the Barriers*, 184-285.

37   Dorothy Sterling, *Black Mothers: Three Lives*. 2nd ed. (New York: Feminist Press at The City University of New York, 1998), 45. Conway was also a prolific journalist who regularly contributed pieces to prominent British and American journals. The *National Anti-Slavery Standard*, August 11, 1866, said, "His services in England to the negro's cause and the nation's honor are surpassed by those of no other American in Europe; while his contributions to the American press are the most racy, brilliant, well-chosen, well-timed and instructive of all our foreign correspondence."

38   *The Times*, August 27, 1866.

39   On Thursday, September 6, he performed only the last three acts of the tragedy, the main offering that evening being a production of a comedy, *All That Glitters is Not Gold* in which he did not take part.

40   *Illustrated Sporting and Theatrical News*, September 8, 1866.

41   *The Era*, September 16, 1866.

42   Olympic Theatre playbill dated September 15-19, 1866, held at the Harvard Theatre Collection.

43   Conway, "The Negro as Artist," 39.

4
Off to the Provinces

The week before Morgan Smith started his run at the Olympic Theatre on August 25 a notice appeared in *The Era* publicizing his appearance there and stating that he "has accepted Engagements for Preston, Paisley, Leicester, Cheltenham, &c."[1] Apparently his earlier advertisement running for a month in *The Era* from July to August, as well as the first reviews of his performances at Gravesend—and perhaps also the efforts of his agent H. J. Turner to secure contracts for him at provincial theatres—had paid off. Ira Aldridge had appeared earlier at all four of the towns mentioned, two of them, Cheltenham and Leicester, as recently as 1859 and 1860: at least one current manager, George Owen at Leicester, had acted with Aldridge when serving as theatre manager at St. Helier, Jersey in September 1856 and had acted with him again at Leicester in 1857. So there was no reluctance on the part of such managers to hire another black actor who could play some of the same roles in which his famous predecessor had excelled.

Aldridge happened to be back in London resting from the end of August to mid-November 1866. A nine-month tour that had taken him to Odessa, Constantinople, and possibly parts of Crimea and

Southern Russia had ended disastrously in Kiev on July 12th when a thief entered his hotel room, broke into a chest of drawers containing his valuables, and made off with nearly 10,000 silver roubles, two gold watches, nine rings, a brooch set with 52 diamonds, and important papers. Aldridge moved on to parts of Poland where he performed for a few weeks in August before heading back to England.[2]

He certainly would have been curious to see Morgan Smith's performances at the Olympic, and it is entirely possible that he may have accompanied Ellen Craft and her friends there when the Philadelphia actor opened as Othello on September 4th. Her husband William was still in Whydah, Dahomey at that time, so the man sitting beside her had been misidentified in the report that Moncure D. Conway had submitted to *The Round Table*. Perhaps it was Aldridge.

The Crafts had come to know Aldridge earlier in London, and evidence of their continuing friendship can be found in notes that he and his young Swedish wife Amanda gave Ellen when she visited them in their home at Hamlet Road in Upper Norwood on October 19, 1866. Aldridge had presented her with handwritten lines from the *Merchant of Venice*:

Extract

"Mislike me not for my Complexion

The Shadow'd livery of the burnish'd Sun"

The Prince of Morocco in Shakespeare's

Merchant of Venice

Copied for Mrs Ellen Craft

By Ira Aldridge K.S.

Upper Norwood

19th Oct. 1866

Amanda had quoted lines from the second stanza of a Swedish poem, "I rosen doft" (In the fragrance of the rose), written by Herman Sätherberg and set to music by Sweden's Prince Gustaf in the nineteenth century:

O fråga ej: vad är att lycklig vara,

O fråga ej: vad är att vara nöjd.

Blott hör naturens egen röst,

Och göm dess ord uti ditt bröst,

Oh sök att dem förklara.

Amanda von Aldridge

To my [illegible] Ellen Craft

London

Oct. 19th 1866

An English translation of which is

Oh, do not ask what it is to be happy,

Oh, do not ask what it is to be content.

Only listen to the voice of Nature,

and hide its word in your breast,

and try to explain it.[3]

It would be interesting to know if Morgan Smith had accompanied Ellen on this visit to Aldridge's home. He was due to open at Leicester's Theatre Royal three days later, however, so he may have already left London.

A week earlier Morgan Smith had sent a letter to Moncure D. Conway thanking him for sending a copy of something he had written:

12 Cambridge Rd

Hammersmith

Oct 13 1866

My dear Mr. Conway

I have just received per post an article from the "Anti Slavery Standard" of the states signed with yr name & doubtless to you I owe the reception of the same.

I am prompted my dear Sir to seek this means of the acknowledgement of the article not from any vanity of the friendly & kindly manner (& indeed complimentary) to which you have been pleased to allude to my humble efforts—though being very far from indiferent [*sic*] & feeling a certain degree of pride for the same[.] But seek this medium to express to you on behalf of my *Race* to whom you have so wisely & justly referred, my sincere gratitude & appreciation for such noble hearted humanity, & kindliness, & must give expression to the wish that yr life may be prolonged to witness the result you predict, and which must surely arrive, their recognition & elevation to the loftiest rounds of artistic development of the age in which we live. [R]eceive from me personally my sincere gratitude & appreciation for this & the many of evidences of good feeling manifested, & express to yr kind Lady my sincere regards & respect & believe me ever

Truly yrs

S. Morgan Smith

PS. I might here remark for yr information that I open in "Lecister" [*sic*] next Monday week & soon after play an engagement of one month in several provincial towns.[4]

One surprise is that this letter was written from the address where Ellen Craft lived.[5] Perhaps Morgan Smith and his family were living with her, or perhaps he was merely using this address as a place where he could occasionally pick up his mail while traveling outside London.

He opened at Leicester's Theatre Royal on October 22nd. The theatre had started its fall season on September 5th under a new lessee and manager, George Owen, a man with considerable experience as both an actor and manager, and hopes were high that the company he recruited "may lay claim to an amount of excellence which shall defy its opponents at rival houses....We take it that the Theatre should be always the leading and prominent resort for amusement-seekers, and we trust Mr. Owen will offer something which will be worthy of our excellent and commodious house."[6]

There were only two reviews of Morgan Smith's performances, the first saying "The part of Othello was sustained by Mr. Morgan Smith, who has been engaged for six nights. There was a good house, and Mr. Smith met with a hearty reception....On Tuesday 'The Merchant of Venice' was played. Mr. Smith played Shylock in a manner which showed that he had evidently made it his especial study."[7] The second review reported that "Morgan Smith laboured under severe disadvantages last week through the company not knowing their parts, either in *The Merchant of Venice, Hamlet*, or *The Slave*. When the latter piece was produced on Wednesday, the audience got impatient and *hissed*. With all these drawbacks, the dark stranger, who continually *assisted the company* to their parts, had a good attendance at his benefit, and on his last appearance the Theatre was crowded to the doors."[8]

This brought a response from the prompter who had been working there:

> Mr. EDITOR.—Sir,—Pardon the liberty I take in addressing this to you, but in justice to myself, and the rest of the Leicester company, I feel it my duty to do so. In your impression of November 4th, a very unfavourable criticism of the Leicester company appeared, accusing them of being very imperfect, so much so that they were hissed by the audience. If your reporter would adhere to the truth (which in this case he certainly has not), there would be no occasion for any remarks by me. As prompter, I ought to be the best judge, whether the company were perfect or not. I can safely say that they were perfect, almost without exception...
>
> Apologising for troubling you with this subject, I am, Sir, yours respectfully, H. MAYHEW, Prompter, Theatre Royal, Halifax, November 11th.[9]

Another letter followed in the same issue of *The Era*, confirming what the first commentator had said:

> Mr. EDITOR.—Sir,—Seeing a few remarks made by your Leicester correspondent upon the company engaged at the Theatre in that town, I beg to say what he stated was quite correct, for I never witnessed pieces worse performed, and it was a great injustice to the star (Mr. Morgan Smith), whom they had to support. Scarely [sic] one of them knew their parts, and what few people were there hissed, as the prompter's voice was distinctly heard. I cannot imagine where the Manager could be, certainly from home, or such a farce at acting would not have been tolerated. Hoping the Manager will look into it, and have this state of things altered, yours truly, ONE WHO DOES NOT LIKE TO SEE SHAKESPEARE'S PLAYS MURDERED.[10]

At this point the Editor of the paper intervened:

[Upon receipt of the above letters we wrote to our "Leicester Correspondent," asking him further particulars, and from his answer (which he has not the least idea of seeing in print) we extract the following sentences—Ed. of THE ERA]

"I assure you what I said about Morgan Smith's supporters was all perfectly true. I spoke generally, *not* individually, and I do not mean to say but that *one* or *two* parts *might* be properly delivered, but the majority were out of their parts. I was present all through *Merchant of Venice*, to my sorrow, and saw as much of *The Slave* and *Hamlet* as I could bear. Indignation was expressed in the Theatre on the latter evenings at the weak support given by the company. I can give the names of several persons present on various evenings referred to, who all fully testify to the truth of my assertion. I do not, therefore, wish you to rest on my bare word alone * * * * * * I need not enter into the faults which the company endeavour to lay upon Smith in the affair; but when I have heard him repeatedly put into their mouths various passages, so shamefully audible, and their restless motions toward the prompter's box, &c., I should say sufficient aggravation was caused to the audience to bring down the hisses complained of.

Your LEICESTER CORRESPONDENT."[11]

This drew a rebuttal from the Stage Manager, who felt the charges made were unjust, particularly to other members of the company who were not at fault:

Mr. EDITOR.—Sir,—In reply to the gentleman who does not like to see Shakespeare's plays murdered, I feel it my duty, as Stage-Manager, to state that in the performance of *Hamlet* there was but one person imperfect, and it is unfair to throw disgrace upon the entire company for the fault of one. In the performance of *The Merchant of Venice* the same thing might be observed, the majority of the company being perfect; and I feel certain if this should meet the eye of Mr. Morgan Smith he will bear me out in what I say, as he himself returned thanks to the members of the company [for] the able manner in which he was supported during his visit here. If a person sitting in the front expects to hear Shakespeare's plays word for word as set down in the text he will be labouring under a delusion, as there are many judicious and desirable alterations made so as to adapt them for stage representation.—Yours respectfully, J. HUDSPETH (Stage-Manager), Theatre Royal, Leicester.[12]

This controversy may reveal how difficult and frustrating it must have been for visiting stars to tour the provinces and work at theatres where the standard of acting by a local or itinerant company was not uniformly high and might on occasion be abominably low. As these negative reactions show, it might take only one or two inept performers to ruin a play. And the excuse that Shakespeare was seldom heard verbatim in such theatres would have been regarded in London as a sign of professional degradation. Charles Kean, a distinguished veteran of the stage who had spent many years on tour in the British Isles, complained in a letter he wrote to a friend on March 25, 1860 that

> the Provincial Performers in tragedy are as a rule vile beyond measure—I find them with scarcely an exception totally uneducated and perfectly ignorant—their only qualities being conceit and impudence—Not a single instance of rising talent has come under my observation since I commenced my tour in October last.
>
> This is a sad falling off—I am assured that as far as the English drama is concerned, the Dress Box people never come out except *to me*. Consequently the managers & actors indulge in pieces and in style suited to the lower classes, and all knowledge of high art has disappeared.[13]

Attempting to revive an appreciation of classic English drama in provincial theatres appears to have been the challenge that Morgan Smith was willing to undertake while on tour, for the roles he enacted most frequently, at least initially, were those in major Shakespearean tragedies. Here is a record of the number of his known performances from mid-May to the end of December 1866:

Othello	19
Shylock	12
Hamlet	8
Gambia	7

Richard III	6
Fabian	5
Melnotte	3
Richelieu	2
Macbeth	1

After finishing his week at Leicester, Morgan Smith may have taken a week off before returning to Kent to perform for six nights at Rochester, only nine miles from where he had started out at Gravesend. Some of the performers he met there were the same who had supported him during his first month-long engagement. To give a few examples: Miss Lizzie Gray who had played Desdemona earlier was now starring as Pauline in *Lady of Lyons*, while Miss Hambleton, who had been cast as Nerissa before, was the new Desdemona. Also, Mrs. C. A. Clarke, who had originally been given the role of Emilia in *Othello*, was now playing Julie in *Richelieu*, and her husband Mr. C. A. Clarke, formerly appearing on alternate nights in Gravesend as Iago or Cassio, was currently fully occupied as the manager of Rochester's Lyceum Theatre.

While waiting to go on at Rochester, Morgan Smith evidently worked up an entirely new role that had not been among the dozen he had offered to play when he arrived in England. This was Fabian, the mixed race hero in the French melodrama *The Black Doctor; or, the Fated Lovers of Bourbon*, which he acted for the first time on November 11th. After the play had become available in an English translation in 1846, Ira Aldridge had appeared as Fabian many times on tours of the British Isles, and he is credited in the Dicks' Standard Plays edition with actually having adapted this romantic drama for the English stage.[14]

The plot has been neatly summarized by Keith Byerman:

> Fabian, once a slave on the Isle of Bourbon, gained his freedom by saving the lives of the master's family, through both his courage and his medical skills. One of those he saved was the Marquis de la Reynerie's daughter Pauline; when her mother, now a widow, apparently perishes at sea, Fabian once again comes to her aid. He falls in love with her, but knowing the rules of his society, he isolates himself rather than admit his feelings

to anyone. When Pauline comes to his cabin to thank him and to seek his help for another of her servants, he arranges to meet her at an isolated cove. In the meantime he also manages to save the Chevalier de St. Luce, who turns out to be the man her mother had designated as her betrothed. At the cove, with the sea rising, he confesses his love and says that they will die together. Believing this to be true, she admits her love for him. They are, in fact, saved and married by a local priest, offstage.

The scene then moves to Paris, where the mother, who in fact did not die, is arranging the marriage to the chevalier. Pauline refuses and finally reveals the truth about her relationship to Fabian; recognizing the mother's racism, Fabian renounces the marriage in order to save his beloved. The marchioness then betrays them by sending Pauline to a nunnery and Fabian to a dungeon in the Bastille. The villain dies, the Bastille is stormed, but Fabian has lost his sanity in the meantime. Released, he goes to Brittany with the man who freed him and is reunited with Pauline momentarily. She is threatened by the mob as an aristocrat, but can be saved by her marriage certificate, which Fabian initially fails to produce, thinking that he is saving her by keeping it a secret. When one of the mob fires a shot at her, Fabian takes the bullet and, in a dying gesture, produces the paper and declares his love.[15]

Byerman goes on to say that Aldridge gave "particular emphasis to race and class issues in creating a Romantic hero" who challenges the conventions of French society and exhibits a high level of integrity and courage.[16] Aldridge's revisions included changing Fabian from a black man to a "handsome Mulatto, yellow and brown," an alteration that enables him to "present the melodramatic aspects of emotional intensity and madness without reverting to racial caricatures of the irrational black or the unstable mulatto."[17] This is an important point, for it forces us to recognize Fabian as the kind of Romantic hero who suffers and dies for love but asserts his value as a person in the end. Though a man of color, he is a traditional melodramatic protagonist, not a racial stereotype.[18]

Hazel Waters has also observed that "Fabian is a serious character, with an emotional range—albeit expressed within the conventions of melodrama—that the black character of this period is not often endowed with."[19] To play this role, an actor had to portray a gamut of emotions ranging from love, sorrow, and misery to anger, jealousy, and mental derangement. Morgan Smith immediately decided to add Fabian to his permanent repertoire and played him at every town he visited during the rest of the year.

After Rochester, he was engaged for seven consecutive weeks, first at Northampton, then in Scotland at Kilmarnock for twelve nights, followed by six nights each at Paisley, Coatbridge, and finally Carlisle near the Scottish border. In each place his last performance was on a Saturday, so he had only a day to move to his next assignment and begin rehearsals for his opening night on Monday as either Othello or Hamlet. Fortunately, the Scottish sites were close together, so the longest distance he had to travel during this period were the 359 miles from Northampton to Kilmarnock, but a well-established transportation network of trains would have enabled him to reach his destination without too much difficulty or delay.

There were hardly any reviews of Morgan Smith's performances published in the provincial press during the last two months of the year, so we have to rely almost entirely on reports that appeared in *The Era*, but the few remarks that made it into print were quite positive, though usually quite brief. As Othello in Rochester "Mr. Smith's physical peculiarity, added to his fine elocution and evident talents as a first-rate tragedian, gave his representation of Othello an air of reality not to be surpassed,"[20] and as a consequence, "he elicited much applause from a well filled house."[21] As Richelieu later in the same town, he was also said to have "appeared to great advantage, and the audience seemed thoroughly satisfied, if we may judge by the continued rounds of applause. At the conclusion of the play Mr. Smith was honoured by a call."[22] In Northampton his Richard III was "well impersonated,"[23] and in Paisley he appeared as Othello, Fabian, Richard III, Shylock, and Gambia "with considerable success to good houses."[24] As Othello, Hamlet, and Fabian at Coatbridge, he "certainly showed that he does possess great dramatic powers, a good voice, clear and distinct in utterance, and his delineation of each was impressive and betokened great care and study....We may mention that Mr. Morgan Smith has had nightly calls before the curtain."[25] A Glasgow paper also stated that his performances of

Hamlet and Othello in Coatbridge were "characterized by polished elocution and altogether showing careful study and an effective style of acting,"[26] to which *The Era* added that such acting "called forth the hearty applause of the audience"[27] In Carlisle Morgan Smith played Othello "most effectively,"[28] but as Hamlet, though "his performance throughout was most satisfactory," yet "we cannot but think, however, that Mr. Smith's representation of the philosophic Dane would have been improved had he taken a little more time."[29]

This was the only slightly negative remark made about him on his first prolonged provincial tour, and it sharply contrasts with what was said about him in parts of London and in Birmingham. Perhaps he was actually improving as he gained more experience on the road, where he had to play a different role every night. He may have quickly acquired much greater professionalism. Or maybe he was just far better than the mediocre performers he played with in these small towns. Whatever the reason, he clearly was becoming more consistently successful as an actor.

Morgan Smith rested during the Christmas week, but he was ready and eager to resume touring in the new year, so on December 30th he inserted another ad in *The Era* announcing his availability:

> MR. MORGAN SMITH, the Coloured American tragedian, is now at Liberty to arrange dates with Provincial Managers for 1867. Acknowledged as one of the most attractive Stars in the United Kingdom. Lithographs, Posters, Opinions of the Press, &c.

> Address: MORGAN SMITH, Cambridge-road, Hammersmith, London, W.; or Theatrical Agents, Bow-street.[30]

The following day Morgan Smith's wife Mary Eliza gave birth to their second surviving son, Edgar Jessup Smith, at 4 Cambridge Road, not far from the home of Ellen and William Craft at 12 Cambridge Road.[31]

Endnotes

1   *The Era*, August 19, 1866.

2   For further details on these events, see Bernth Lindfors, *Ira Aldridge: The Last Years, 1855-1867* (Rochester, NY: University of Rochester Press, 2015), 227-39. Aldridge left Warsaw for London on August 27th.

3   Both notes are held at the Avery Research Center for African American History and Culture at the College of Charleston, South Carolina. I am grateful to Jeffrey Green for calling these notes to my attention and to Raoul Granqvist for translating the Swedish poem. Amanda was Aldridge's second wife, whom he married a year after his first wife died in 1864.

4   Letter dated October 13, 1866 and held among the Moncure Daniel Conway Papers, Box 20, at the Rare Book & Manuscript Library, Columbia University in the City of New York. It was published in William Norris, "Additional Light on S. Morgan Smith," *Black American Literature Forum*, 20, no. 1-2 (1986): 76. My transcription of it differs slightly from his. The article in the *National Anti-Slavery Standard*, September 29, 1866, was a reprint of Conway's article on "The Negro as Artist: Morgan Smith," published in *The Radical*, 2 (September 1866): 39.

5   Jeffrey Green mentions this in "S. Morgan Smith, the black actor 1832-1882," an article available at his website: http://www.jeffreygreen.co.uk/072.

6   *The Era*, September 2, 1866.

7   *Illustrated Sporting and Theatrical News*, October 27, 1866.

8   *The Era*, November 4, 1866.

9   *The Era*, November 18, 1866.

10   Ibid.

11   Ibid.

12   *The Era*, November 25, 1866.

13   This letter is held at the Claremont College Library in California. It was addressed to a Mr. Donne and sent from Newcastle upon Tyne.

14   [Ira Aldridge], *The Black Doctor. A Romantic Drama in Four Acts. Adapted to the English Stage by Ira Aldridge.* Dicks' Standard Plays, 460 (London: John Dicks, n.d.).

15   Keith Byerman, "Creating the Black Hero: Ira Aldridge's *The Black Doctor*, in *Ira Aldridge: The African Roscius*, ed. Bernth Lindfors (Rochester, NY: University of Rochester Press, 2007), 204-6.

16   Ibid., 204.

17   Ibid., 206.

18   Ibid., 214.

19   Hazel Waters, *Racism on the Victorian Stage: Representation of Slavery and the Black Character* (Cambridge, UK: Cambridge University Press, 2007), 79.

20   *Illustrated Sporting and Theatrical News*, November 17, 1866.

21   *The Era*, November 11, 1866.

22   *The Era*, November 18, 1866.

23 *The Era*, November 25, 1866.

24 *The Era*, December 23, 1866.

25 *The Era*, December 16, 1866.

26 *Glasgow Herald*, December 14, 1866.

27 *The Era*, December 23, 1866.

28 *Illustrated Sporting and Theatrical News*, December 22, 1866.

29 Ibid.

30 *The Era*, December 30, 1866.

31 Dinte Nightingale Overell Masters McFarlane file, Ancestry.com.

5

1867

On January 6th *The Era* again carried Morgan Smith's advertisement. His theatrical agents were presumably still H. J. Turner and E. Danvers, but he appears to have been prepared to make his own arrangements with theatre managers wishing to employ him, so he also gave an address where he could be reached in Hammersmith.

The publicity brought an immediate response, for by mid-January he was able to set off on a three-month tour of provincial theatres in England, Scotland and Wales, playing in each venue for a week or two with hardly any breaks between consecutive engagements. The tendency was for him to play a different role every night for a week and repeat a few roles only when he remained at a theatre for a second week. The blend of roles was split more evenly between Shakespearean tragedies and popular melodramas, so audiences were able to see him portray a variety of characters.

This must have been an exhausting routine. In his first six weeks he had to travel nearly 1500 miles, moving from Worcester to Hartlepool, to Dundee, to Bradford, and on to Aberdeen, each venue separated by more than two hundred or three hundred miles, and he usually had only a Sunday to reach his next destination.

The reviews of Morgan Smith's performances on this strenuous tour were generally quite positive, noting in particular his good figure, prepossessing appearance, and considerable natural talent, which, despite a few flaws in execution, gave promise of future excellence.[1] The fullest assessment of the range of his abilities came when he reached Hanley in Staffordshire at the end of February, where he was described as

> a specimen of the highest type of mulatto, possessing an intelligent and expressive countenance, very considerable histrionic abilities and stage requirements, and a rich, musical voice, tinged, however, with an American accent. His acting is characterised by natural dignity and force, an accurate reading, and a clear enunciation, which renders his tragic personations highly effective. The qualities which Mr. Smith possesses are those which fit him best for tragedy; his comedy is stiff and strained, though there is a good deal of merit in the evident efforts he makes to acquire an ease which, however, he does not seem able to command. His *Hamlet*, *Shylock*, and *Richard III*, were very creditable performances, and possessed more individuality than one might have expected from one labouring under the disadvantages of race. There was at times a slight excess of nervous energy, which marred the otherwise carefully wrought picture, but, taken as a whole, the personations were far above average. Mr. Smith with many good qualities, is conspicuous for the absence of a very bad quality—he is often energetic, but he never rants, or "tears passion to tatters." In "The Slave," as *Gambia*, who devotes himself with almost unparalleled courage and generosity to rescuing a beautiful white female slave...from the lust of his master, Mr. Smith was at home, and acted with considerable success.[2]

Briefer remarks on his appearances in Dundee claimed he had been more successful as Othello than as Hamlet,[3] and that "his Othello was a remarkably able portraiture—his reading of some of the passages, indeed, truly grand....By the way, we may mention that Mr. Smith introduces a novelty into the dressing of Othello, which is worthy of attention. In the scene where the Moor puts an end to the brawl between Cassio and Roderigo it is usual for the actor to appear with the same dress he wore previous to retiring, but Mr. Smith comes on with what to us appeared to be a magnificent morning or dressing gown, as if he had been aroused from bed, which is obviously correct."[4] As Shylock, he also had "acquitted himself with great credit, his impersonation of this difficult character being at least equal to that of any one we have seen undertake it in Dundee,"[5] and his "impersonation of the deformed and dissembling Richard was splendid, and is, to our thinking, the best of his many excellent assumptions. The entire performance was so uniformly excellent that we are unable to point out any particular scene in which he most excelled."[6] The only performance that was panned during these months on tour was his interpretation of Macbeth in Bradford:

> His readings are often strained and forced, and his gesticulations greatly over-done. On the other hand, his makes-up [*sic*] are excellent, and his desire to excel so evident, that we hope time may mend his faults, among the most prominent of which is the introduction of convulsive sobs in almost all the more passionate parts of his speeches.[7]

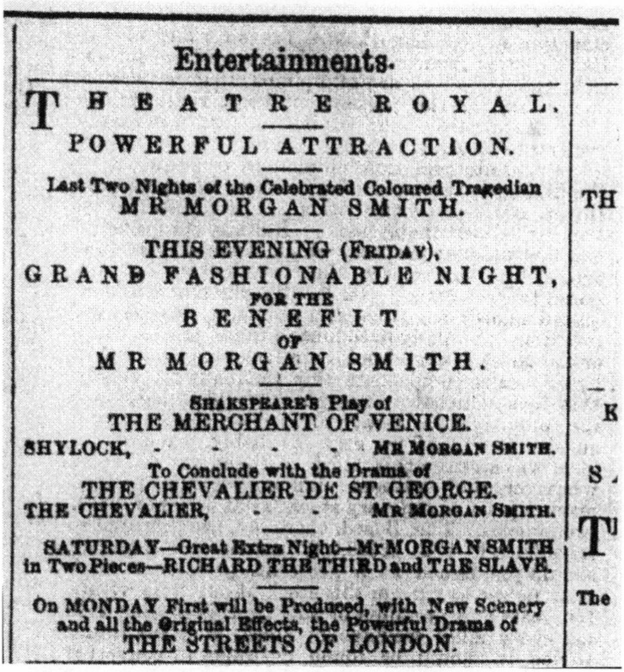

Entertainments.

THEATRE ROYAL.

POWERFUL ATTRACTION.

Last Two Nights of the Celebrated Coloured Tragedian
MR MORGAN SMITH.

THIS EVENING (FRIDAY),
GRAND FASHIONABLE NIGHT,
FOR THE
BENEFIT
OF
MR MORGAN SMITH.

SHAKSPEARE'S Play of
THE MERCHANT OF VENICE.
SHYLOCK, - - - - - MR MORGAN SMITH.
To Conclude with the Drama of
THE CHEVALIER DE ST GEORGE.
THE CHEVALIER, - - - MR MORGAN SMITH.

SATURDAY—Great Extra Night—Mr MORGAN SMITH in Two Pieces—RICHARD THE THIRD and THE SLAVE.

On MONDAY First will be Produced, with New Scenery and all the Original Effects, the Powerful Drama of
THE STREETS OF LONDON.

Figure 14. Advertisement in the *Northern Warder and General Advertiser for the Counties of Fife, Perth and Forfar* for the Theatre Royal, Dundee, February 8, 1867. ©British Library Board, 072.9127. Reproduced with permission from the British Library.

While in Dundee, Morgan Smith experimented by playing for the first time the dashing hero of *The Chevalier de St. George*,[8] an adaptation by Thomas William Robertson[9] about Joseph Bologne, a famous eighteenth-century mulatto who had excelled as a fencer, dancer, rider, violinist, composer, and military officer. A handsome man, he was also known to be a favorite among highborn ladies.[10] The play focuses on his love for a wealthy countess who is being courted by a nobleman on behalf of his son, a wastrel who has amassed debts. But the Chevalier, who in his youth had been her playmate and slave until disgraced and sent away by her family, has always been the one she truly loved. The Chevalier, more honorable than the spoiled son, pretends to be from Peru, not from the Countess's plantation in St. Domingo, but they eventually come to recognize one another as former companions. The son, jealous and aware of the Chevalier's background as a disgraced slave, challenges him to a duel, and the noble Chevalier feels obligated to fight it, until the son's father reveals that he is father of the Chevalier too, so the duel will be fought between two brothers. The Chevalier then declines to fight the duel, accepting the shame of having done so, but the Countess pledges to marry him and defend his honor.

The play affords opportunities for the Chevalier to display his superior skills as a swordsman, horseman, thinker, and lover. He always outperforms and outsmarts his antagonists, even when the odds are against him. He is a typical romantic hero, a Victorian stereotype, albeit of a French flavor.

In a study of Robertson's stagecraft, Maynard Savin has commented on some of the merits of this comedy despite its obvious crudeness and flaws:

> Melodramatic, cloyingly sentimental, totally deficient in characterization, the play nevertheless marches. Scenes effectively theatrical succeed each other too rapidly to permit the audience to engage in fatal analysis. The plot combines the standard motif of the last-minute discovery of a blood relationship and...the motif of mésalliance....The expository speeches, like a side of beef, had to be plunked down on the counter in a solid chunk of interchange, but the speeches themselves are short and humanly rhythmic. Moreover, they cap one another, and in view of the considerable past history

of the principal characters which must be presented to the audience, they achieve a seemingly casual coherence. While the pace of the dialogue throughout the play is generally natural, in scenes of emotional intensity, the playwright shuts his ear to human speech and indulges in literary language. Such scenes are replete with attitudinizing....Seemingly they are mandatory show pieces in which the stage self-consciously assumes the office of the pulpit. Declamatory speeches in no uncertain terms reassure audiences that the theater is a moral force.[11]

Morgan Smith's initial attempt at performing this role followed his appearance as Shylock on his benefit night, February 8, 1867, and the only paper to notice it said, "His representation of the Chevalier de St. George was also one of great excellence."[12] However, when he revived it a few weeks later in Aberdeen, he was reported to have been "exceedingly lame" as the Chevalier.[13] Morgan Smith, perhaps as a consequence, chose not to star in the role again until he reached Hartlepool in mid-April and could advertise the play under a new title, *Child of the Sun!*[14] This performance elicited no response in the local press.

During the spring there had been reports filtering back to the British press of Ira Aldridge's triumphant tour of France, which had been launched with an appearance at the Grand Théâtre de Versailles the previous November. *The Era* said he "has achieved a great success....He has visited sixty-eight towns, and received an ovation in most of them."[15] At the end of March, after Morgan Smith's visits to Tredegar and Cardiff, London's *Athenaeum* carried the news that "Ira Aldridge, the black tragedian, has been greatly admired in the French provinces.—An actor of colour, Mr. Morgan Smith, has been playing, successfully it is said, in the Welsh towns."[16]

This prompted comments in the British provincial press concerning the intellectual ability of black people, Aldridge and Morgan Smith being cited as interesting exceptions to the widely accepted notion that blacks were inferior to whites mentally:

> I see by the French papers that Mr. Ida [*sic*] Aldridge, the black tragedian, has been playing to crowded audiences in several of the provincial towns of France; and I notice that a Mr. Morgan Smith, also a black actor, has been very well received in Wales. These two facts put together will do something to counteract

what may be called the very bad intellectual reputation that the black race has throughout the world; and I have sometimes thought that that party whom others call negrophilists would do well to "bring out" a few negroes, if it can be done, to show that they are not intellectually inferior to white folks. At present, the number of men (and there have never, I believe, been one woman) among the black races who have displayed remarkable intellectual power is wofully [*sic*] small; and it is very desirable that if that power does exist it should be proved. Toussaint l'Ouverture is the one great exception in the intellectual history of the black races, but can anyone cite a dozen, or even half a dozen names of black men who have made themselves a famous name in history from an *intellectual* point of view?[17]

Nonetheless, Morgan Smith continued to receive commendation and applause as he made his rounds through a series of small towns during the summer months playing his familiar roles. In Bolton he was praised when representing Hamlet for having "displayed talent rarely to be found among our own countrymen,"[18] and in Great Grimsby, too, his Hamlet was said to be "a first-rate performance, casting aside a little defect in his elocution, here and there, peculiar to his race."[19] Morgan Smith was continuing to tour without the help of an agent by asking theatre managers to contact him at his address at 4 Cambridge Road in Hammersmith,[20] but this did not result in a reduction in the number of his engagements until August, when many theatres were closed.

In September Morgan Smith appeared for the first time in Ireland, where he performed almost exclusively in a variety of Shakespearean roles for a week in Belfast followed by a week in Dublin. Here, unlike his experiences in small provincial towns in England and Scotland, he received ample press coverage, so it is possible to discern how he was regarded by theatergoers who had been accustomed to seeing such roles interpreted by some of the best actors of the day. Morgan Smith was introduced to the Belfast public as "the Celebrated American Coloured Tragedian" and "the only successor to the late Ira Aldridge,"[21] who had died on tour in Poland a month earlier. Aldridge had spent many years performing in parts of Ireland, especially in Belfast and Dublin, so comparisons were inevitable.

Morgan Smith made his debut as Othello, and responses to his performance varied. The kindest and most tolerant assessment appeared in the *Banner of Ulster* which provided a sympathetic account of the difficulties he had faced as an aspiring actor in America:

> In the present day, when there is such a dearth of actors who are really capable of embodying the great characters of Shakspeare, it is gratifying to welcome a new candidate for fame in the highest field of dramatic art. The pleasure is not the less sincere, because in the case of Mr. Morgan Smith, a coloured tragedian, who made his appearance for the first time at the Theatre Royal last night, we have a gentleman belonging to another country and a different race, who seems destined to take a creditable position among the most gifted of our tragedians. Mr. Smith, we believe, is a native of Philadelphia, and though long anxious to become a member of the theatrical profession, he was precluded from doing so, owing to the laws of his country, which were enacted, at least before Abraham Lincoln's glorious proclamation, with special reference to the continued bondage of the African exiles in America. In England, however, no such impediments obstructed the path of the young actor, and besides a successful tour of the provinces, he made a brilliant *debut* in the metropolis itself. Mr. Smith is of medium stature, and as may readily be supposed of deep brown complexion. His countenance beams with intelligence and animation, while his large, dark, penetrating eyes are full of expression—whether in the calmness of repose, or the lava-like torrent of passion. The house last night was densely crowded, and the audience, with that desire to encourage merit, for which Belfast is deservedly famed, gave Mr. Smith a most enthusiastic welcome. His impersonation of *Othello* evinces design and intelligence, and has many traits of independence and originality. Whilst we say so it is only fair to Mr. Smith that we should keep in view the fact that he has had many difficulties to contend with, not only as regards his limited opportunities for study, but also with respect to the American school of acting, which, according to our ideas of the stage, is but ill adapted to foster a pure and refined taste in theatricals. Mr. Smith's voice, which is rather deficient in range, was not as clear last night as it is wont to be, owing to his recent passage across the Channel. The intellectual

and emotional features of the portraiture we must regard as truthful, but without any unnecessary parade of honesty or independence, we are bound to state that in his delineation of this difficult character, his physical powers seemed scarcely adequate to the task of giving full voice to the development of his conceptions. Mr. Smith's acting elicited hearty applause with several calls before the curtain.[22]

The *Belfast News-Letter* also treated him with some respect but did not refrain from commenting on the lack of subtlety in his portrayal nor on the peculiarities of his American accent:

Mr. Morgan Smith, a colored gentleman—the only negro tragedian with whom the public have an opportunity of becoming acquainted, now that Ira Aldridge has flitted off this mortal stage—has commenced an engagement here for six nights. The announcement that he would appear as *Othello* brought together a house crowded to remarkable excess in the pit, upper boxes, and gallery. The coincidence of color had, no doubt, a great deal to do with this, as well as the laudatory announcements which heralded the advent of Mr. Smith. Mr. Smith, on presenting himself, was received with a genuine Irish welcome. He is rather beneath than above the middle stature, so that he is without the physical advantage of a commanding presence. We cannot say that he is opulently endowed by nature with those other and higher qualifications essential to a good tragedian, though we have no hesitation in saying that he is quite fitted to become an accomplished average actor. We have heard that one of the motives which have led him to adopt the stage is to endeavor to show that his race are not incapable of acquiring distinction in those liberal arts which are made to minister to the amusement of civilised and refined communities. It would be ungenerous to discourage Mr. Smith in his patriotic design. His race have given statesmen to the world; and is there not at this moment in America a liberated negro who discusses State problems like a politician and a man of culture? But success on a political platform may be more easy of achievement than a legitimate triumph on the mimic stage. At any rate, Mr. Smith comes before us from America without the necessary pre-liminary training—a privilege which, it is said, was denied him in that land of "equality." Besides, last night he appeared to serious disadvantage, for the character of the noble Moor has been made familiar to Belfast play-goers by an actor who was endowed beyond ordinary men with native dignity and grace. If it is a great pleasure to witness a highly-gifted actor, it is a pleasure that brings with it some alloy, for with the recollection of the excellence which we have admired vividly before us we fail to enjoy a less artistic portraiture. Hence we may judge Mr. Smith somewhat unfairly. If he seemed at times oblivious of the delicacy of a character whose delicacy is obvious to even the most casual reader, and negligent of the finesse of the stage, he at least produced a strongly-marked and forcible picture. But, as the actor was incessantly at his utmost pitch of rage, we missed *Othello's* off-recurring recollections of the lovely past that seem to revisit him in his tumultuous passion, like gleams of sunshine on a storm-tossed ocean. The sorrow, and the trouble, and the pain were obvious enough in the convulsive motion of the body and agonised expression of the countenance of the actor, but there was no mellow light to relieve the prevailing gloom. The character, as we have been accustomed to regard it, is marked by a rapid succession of alternating passions—by the subtle conflict in a noble mind between love and jealousy, and the perplexities of which they are the fruitful parents. It may be a comparatively easy task to tear a passion to tatters, but it requires a keen insight and patient study to portray the varying phases under which, with inimitable skill, the character of *Othello* has been drawn by Shakspeare. In this the actor was conspicuously remiss. Unfortunately, Mr. Smith has imported some of the Transatlantic peculiarities of accent, and as on English soil these are generally relegated to the comic drama, the effect was sometimes provocative of mirth. It is not without reluctance that we have thus referred to a man undoubtedly possessed of natural ability, and who may be destined to reach an important position on the stage of these countries; but the demerits of last night's performance are not such as we can wholly overlook. Had the artist not shown that he possessed some grounds upon which to justify his ambition, we should have dismissed his performance with a line. In the present destitution of provincial tragedians of respectable ability, we are bound to regard him as an accession to the stage such as we would not willingly dispense with. It should be mentioned that Mr. Smith was several times recalled by a section of the audience—a fact accounted for on the *de gustibus* theory. We gladly pass from the language of censure to the more grateful duty of awarding a well-deserved compliment.[23]

The *Belfast Morning News* offered a much briefer critique, singling out some obvious defects in Morgan Smith's performance:

> The *role* selected for his *debut* was that of "Othello," a rather unfortunate selection, for the play going public here have often seen the part performed in first-class style, and are extremely fastidious about it. It may not be fair to criticise an actor on first appearance, but it is to be hoped that Mr. Smith is better able to personate other characters than that of the Moor. The piece had not proceeded far when it was apparent that Mr. Smith was not gifted with a very strong voice, and as the acts advanced this defect became more painfully evident. His rendering of the soliloquies was certainly very impressive, but several of the most striking passages were slurred over in such a way as to hide their beauty.[24]

But the most devastating review was published in the *Illustrated Sporting and Theatrical* News, a London paper:

> On Monday night last Mr. Morgan Smith, the coloured tragedian, made his first appearance in Belfast in the character Othello, and certainly a worse representation of the part we have not witnessed. With the exception of the dress circle the theatre was crowded to excess, the greater portion of the audience being, doubtless, impelled by the motives of curiosity. We will "nothing extenuate, nor set down aught in malice," but Mr. Smith does not possess the qualifications requisite for a correct representation of this great part. His reading was stilted and in bad taste, his gestures broken and awkward, his pronunciation anything but correct, and in the passionate scenes there was an entire absence of that fire and force which always must be considered necessary to a correct delineation of the noble, but unfortunate Moor. He dresses with taste, and introduces some original business. His last act was his best, but the performance on the whole smacks strongly of the amateur. At the conclusion of the piece he was called before the curtain.[25]

After this, all *The Era* could add were a few random remarks:

Mr. Smith's performance of the Moor presents many points to recommend it, though a great way from the perfection the character shall yet attain to in his hands. The business throughout, while entirely distinct and free from any of the old beaten track of many of his predecessors, is at the same time true and consistent with the implication of the text.[26]

Morgan Smith's performance of the only non-Shakespearean role he performed during the engagement, Gambia in *The Slave*, on Tuesday night, was considered superior to his Othello, partly because it had

a poorly-constructed plot, and abounds in fustian and bombast. The *role* of the slave was better adapted to Mr. Smith's capacity than that of "Othello," and in some passages last evening he was really very effective. His gesticulation is rather abrupt, and he would do well to tone it down a little; but he possessed more command over his voice than on Monday, and was audible to the entire audience, who frequently applauded him. At the close of the play he was recalled.[27]

Another critic said,

He is earnest and painstaking. He also has some knowledge of melo-dramatic effect, as was shown last evening in the combat between *Gambia* and his unscrupulous master, and by the manner in which he cut the bridge in order to save *Zelinda* and her child. The applause which he received, however, was as much due to the strength of the situations as to his acting; and a virtuous slave declaiming in favour of freedom while suffering from a tyrannical master, and disinterestedly sacrificing himself for those he loves, appeals powerfully to the sympathies of the gallery....

Mr. Smith has not a good stage appearance, and his voice is neither musical nor of much compass. He is sadly deficient in the knowledge of elocution, having formed himself on some American models which ought rather to be avoided than imitated. He is restless and self-conscious, without dignity and without repose. As *Gambia*, the slave, he was tolerable. For a part like *Othello*, he must be considered unqualified in everything but the coloured face; and it is but charity to tell him the truth.[28]

When he appeared as Macbeth on his third night, he was again contrasted with Aldridge:

> Mr. Smith has been described as the legitimate successor to Mr. Ira Aldridge, but we must confess that, in our opinion, he falls far short of the African Roscius, both in professional acquirements and in natural ability. Waiving the anomaly of a coloured Scotch thane, nature has denied him other physical qualifications for the first rank of his profession. His stage appearance is bad, and his voice is rather husky, and limited in power. His act last evening reminded us more of a clever amateur than of an *habitue* of the stage. The dagger scene was particularly open to this objection, and in the subsequent interview with Lady Macbeth, his impersonation of the aspiring chieftain was much too lachrymose. The crying, craven coward presented to the audience was certainly not the *Macbeth* that Shakespeare drew.[29]

On Thursday night Morgan Smith reappeared in *Othello*, but this time as Iago, a new role for him, rather than as the Moor, but what must have been a surprise for his audience did not further disturb his critics, who remained almost entirely silent on the change. More remarkable was their response on Friday night to his interpretation of Hamlet, which they found better than all the rest of his performances for the week:

> Since our last notice Mr. Smith has appeared in several Shakspearean characters to well-filled houses. His Macbeth on Wednesday and his Iago on Thursday were not performances calculated to make us alter the opinion we had formed after witnessing his Othello, but on Friday night on the occasion of his benefit he played Hamlet to the satisfaction of everybody, and to the surprise of not a few. His performance of this part was immeasurably superior to anything he had hitherto attempted here, and the audience, with their usual discrimination, were not slow to display their appreciation of the excellent impersonation. In the last scene he handled his foil with a grace and dexterity which we have not seen equaled. On being called at the end of the piece he made a short but feeling speech, in which he thanked the people of Belfast for the very kind manner in which they had received him, and modestly expressed the hope that on his next visit he might be able to give more satisfaction to the press than on the present occasion.[30]

The Era called his Hamlet "the grandest and most successful effort of his engagement,"[31] and the *Banner of Ulster* confirmed that

> He was frequently applauded, and several times called before the curtain. In response to the wish of the house, enthusiastically expressed, Mr. Smith appeared before the footlights, and in the course of a short address, he thanked his patrons most sincerely for the warm reception they had accorded to him since he appeared before them, notwithstanding the strictures—and in one case, he must say, rather harsh strictures—of the press.... [He] assured them that whatever might be his future career in the profession of his choice, he would entertain a lively and pleasing recollection of his visit to Belfast.[32]

Morgan Smith's final performance of Richard III was ignored by the local press but was condemned in rather gruff terms by the correspondent for a London paper who was apparently unaware of the extraordinary success he had achieved the previous night when playing Hamlet before an enthusiastic Belfast crowd:

> In the Theatre Royal, Belfast, Mr. Morgan Smith (the coloured tragedian) concluded a short engagement on last Saturday night. Those who had formed favourable opinions of Mr. Smith's histrionic abilities had them totally dispelled by that gentleman's acting. The novelty of a real Ethiopian drew large houses, but the delineations were in every case coldly received by the audience.[33]

Morgan Smith's reception in Dublin was better than what he had experienced in Belfast. As usual, he opened in *Othello*, but the response to him as the Moor was more favorable now:

> Mr. Smith has considerable personal advantages: his figure is light and graceful: his features handsome and intelligent: and his walk without any apparent strut or staginess. His rendering of the Shakesperian text betokens considerable study, and the possession of a highly educated mind—every salient point being grasped, and each speech given in a manner most natural. The address to the assembled council, in the first act, and the working of love, trust, and jealousy in the third, drew down the warmest applause, and resulted in a unanimous call before the house. His dresses are exceedingly rich and appropriate, so that nothing is wanting to render Mr. Smith's 'Othello' an exceptional performance.[34]

The *Evening Freeman* concurred in this evaluation:

> Report, which had heralded his praises, was not exaggerative, as he is an actor of fine presence and undoubted talent. As a reader he is intelligent, and gives expression to the conception of the author with due dignity and effect. The character which he selected for his *debut* was *Othello*, and the noble deceived Moor was represented in all the phases of the character, whether as the valiant soldier, the tender lover, or the husband maddened by the jealousy instilled into his soul by the deceptive Iago, in such a way as to prove that genius does not belong exclusively to the Caucassian [*sic*] race, but finds its expression in men of all colours. The applause which Mr. Smith received repeatedly during the performance of the play was hearty, sincere and spontaneous.[35]

Saunders's Newsletter was also complimentary but spoke vaguely about some defects in his performance that needed to be corrected:

> The mere blackening of the face cannot make a negro, and we therefore hail with satisfaction a successor to poor Ira Aldridge. Mr. Smith possesses some good qualities, but is not free from defects. The language of *Othello* is generally violent, and before attempting the performance of this character the actor must have learned to be passionate and vehement without degenerating into that ranting style so common to bad actors and so disagreeable to a discriminating judgment. Mr. Smith generally avoids this fault, and further study and practice will, we are sure, raise him to a respectable position in the dramatic world.[36]

The *Irish Times* was more specific in identifying defects but also praised some of Morgan Smith's qualities:

> His representation of a character which has severely tested the abilities of our most celebrated tragedians was witnessed by a large and discriminating audience. The performance went well, but was not successful in every particular. The actor's reading and elocution were in some instances defective. However, generally speaking, Mr. Smith rendered Othello naturally, and was vigorous and powerful when occasion served. The character, and similar ones, will gain him favour in Dublin as a coloured tragedian.[37]

Morgan Smith's appearance in *The Merchant of Venice* the following night also won approval:

> His acting possessed all the concentrated earnestness, and malignant utterances so peculiar to this great part, and above all, he never lost sight of the spirit of deliberate revenge struggling with the love of gain, which distinguishes the Jew. His rendering of the lines—"I am not bound to please thee with my answer"— and "To cut the forfeit from that bankrupt there," called forth loud expressions of applause.[38]

For the next two nights he reappeared as Othello, winning further commendation from the *Dublin Evening Post*:

> This gentleman bids fair to follow in the footsteps of the late famous Ira Aldridge, whose artistic personation of those parts which formed his particular line will be long remembered by lovers of the drama. Mr. Smith has evidently made the character of the Moor a special study, and has succeeded admirably in pourtraying it free from what might be considered rant or artificial outbursts of feeling. His reading of the part is also careful and well modulated throughout, besides which he possesses the physical advantages of a clear, manly voice and good appearance—two indispensible requisites in the walk of tragedy. During the progress of the play he received from the audience frequent acknowledgments of their appreciation.[39]

His rendering of Hamlet on Friday evening also was admired:

> Mr. Smith is the second actor of colour who has become favourably known to European audiences for his clever and effective representation of Shaksperian characters. He is a fitting successor to the mantle of Ira Aldridge. To a good *personnel* he adds considerable natural dramatic power and careful cultivation of those powers. His impersonation of Hamlet was forcible and dignified, and his elocution was clear and expressive. Frequent bursts of applause testified to his success with the audience.[40]

However, a report from a London correspondent asserted that "In 'Hamlet' he was far from realising our ideas of the character."[41]

On his last night in Dublin the *Irish Times* congratulated Mr. George Owen for his discrimination in bringing such a performer to the local stage:

The engagement of Mr. Morgan Smith, the only actor of colour on the stage, was a happy hit, and one worthy of Mr. Owen's discernment. The bill of fare on Saturday evening was unusually heavy, and selected more to give Mr. Smith an opportunity of showing the result of an indefatigable perseverance in the study of the Shakespearian characters than to produce an exponent in the field of tragedy to be compared with Kemble, Kean, or Brooke. The programme comprised…the third acts of Hamlet and Othello, and the fifth act of Richard the Third, in which Mr. Smith certainly "worked like a black," and again and again called down the plaudits of the house.[42]

Dublin's *Daily Express* concluded that

Although very young, he possesses many of the first-rate qualities of a good actor, and after a little more experience and careful study there is no doubt he will enjoy a high position on the stage. On Saturday evening he…sustained the leading character in each [play] with much ability. Throughout the evening he was frequently applauded.[43]

This survey of the responses of Irish audiences and critics to Morgan Smith in September 1867 reveals that during his sixteen months on the stage he had managed to acquire a range of skills that had earned him a measure of respect as a professional actor, someone whose natural talent and evident dedication to his craft showed promise of further development in the future. There were still areas in which he could improve, but he was learning from his mistakes and trying to correct what others saw as his defects and deficiencies. The fact that he now was being perceived in some quarters as a competent successor to Ira Aldridge suggests that he had made a lot of progress in relatively short span of time. The question remained whether he would fulfill his potential in the years to come.

Upon leaving Dublin, Morgan Smith moved to Scotland, where he played Othello, Shylock, Hamlet, and Richard III to great acclaim in Arbroath[44] before heading south to Rochdale, near Manchester. However, on October 6th, a day before opening there, his engagement had to be cancelled when he received word that his wife, Mary Eliza, at age 27, had died of epilepsy and apoplexy at Angelo House, Shaftsbury Road, Hammersmith, a new address to which she and their two sons had recently moved.[45] Ellen Craft, who lived nearby, was present when she died.[46]

The shock of her loss kept Morgan Smith grounded for two weeks until he received an invitation to appear at the Theatre Royal, Barnstaple, for six nights starting on October 21st, followed by two weeks at Rochdale, and a string of new engagements for six or seven weeks that in the interim had been organized for him in parts of England and Scotland by his new agent, Samuel May, 35 Bow Street, Covent Garden, London.[47] May, who ran a Masquerade and Theatrical Repository, had designed splendid costumes in 1866 for Ira Aldridge's tour of France.[48] He was an effective agent, for he had useful contacts with theatre managers throughout the British Isles.

When Morgan Smith returned to Rochdale at the end of October, he found that the town for the past month had been conducting a vigorous debate in the press on the question of whether theatres were good or evil. Shareholders in a local theatre company were in the process of building a new theatre, and some member of the religious community objected to this on moral grounds. The controversy began when Reverend John Ashworth wrote a lengthy letter to the editor of the *Rochdale Observer* expressing his belief that

> [H]undreds of Sunday school teachers, and all who are anxious for the welfare of the young, will deeply deplore this fearfully counteracting influence; for evil can only produce evil, and the theatre, as all experience proves, is the hotbed of every iniquity....No one need be informed of the truth of this statement, for the theatre is the meeting place of the abandoned, whether man or woman, the theatre, the brothel, the gin palace, and the prison, all, and always were, inseparably connected....I believe that the money spent on the place truly called PIT, a pit leading to another *pit*, will be a double curse, a curse to those that formed it, and a fearful curse to the poor young inexperienced victims that will perish by it.[49]

This was answered a week later by the chairman of the shareholders, James Buxton, who argued that

> With respect to the drama, I have invariably found the parties that are its most bitter opponents are those that are practically the least acquainted with it. For one great intellect opposed to the drama, I can find ten in support of it. Christ himself quotes from the Greek comedians....In fact, our greatest men, ministers of the gospel, statesmen, and philosophers, have all given their support to the theatre.[50]

109

Another respondent, signing himself as "a member of the Good Will Society," said, "I am sorry to find your correspondent 'Ashworth' has not improved his faults, which are rashness, bigotry, and excitement....He has heaped calumnies on...others in language that is unbecoming a professed Christian."[51]

These letters prompted further discussion by others on whether stage plays had a good or bad influence on the morals of those who attended them. The debate raged on for a month and included ad hominem attacks voiced by participants on both sides.[52]

This kind of deep-rooted antagonism between the church and the theatre was typical of moral debates on religious issues that flourished in nineteenth-century Britain. There were preachers who were famous not only for regularly delivering sermons denouncing theatergoing as a terrible form of sin but also for publishing them as pamphlets for wider circulation. And there were theatre managers and theatergoers who fought back by responding to such attacks in the press or with their own publications, accusing the preachers of narrowmindedness, intolerance, and an unChristian bias against harmless public amusements.

While this characteristic dispute was going on in Rochdale, hardly any attention was being paid to what was actually being staged at the Rochdale theatre. Only two appearances by Morgan Smith were discussed in the local press. The first concerned his debut as Othello:

> On Monday evening [Morgan Smith], who was announced to appear in Rochdale about three weeks ago, but was prevented by some domestic affliction, made his appearance at the theatre in Newgate, in the character of *Othello*. Being dark, and possessed of a good figure, his appearance as the *Moor* was extremely good, and judging by the frequent and hearty plaudits of a crowded house, his reading of this part, although both original and novel, appeared to give satisfaction, but we would suggest that his intonation was not over pleasant or natural; a want of elocution was perceptible, and with a little study of this art (if the natural power of his voice is not deficient in itself,) he would be more effective. But, of course, we must remember that we are not speaking of a native, and the theatre being full, some portion of the audience was rather unruly, which would have a

very material influence on the general effect of the play; and he would indeed be a clever actor who could successfully pourtray the extremes of love and jealousy, revenge and remorse, with a perfect interpretation of the immortal author's conceptions.[53]

The second review dealt with his reappearance in *Othello* on November 7th, but this time in the role of Iago, which he played opposite a popular young local actor, William Mallalieu, as Othello. Most of the commentary inevitably focused on the native son, but as the *Rochdale Pilot* pointed out,

Mr. Smith, being a gentleman of colour, we had the singular novelty of a naturally black Iago and an artificially copper-coloured Moor. The novelty ends, however, in the rarity of the occurrence, for it seems well that the villain should have the blackest exterior of the two, and, though we said last week that Mr. Smith appears as Othello himself, it is perhaps better that he should sustain the deeper dyed character of Iago. However such a point may be decided, both gentlemen acquitted themselves with very considerable ability.[54]

The *Rochdale Spectator* was of the opinion that

Mr. Morgan Smith makes a better *Iago* than *Othello*, though as our notice last week would show, we are not unmindful of the merits of his impersonation of the gentle Moor. But while his style of delivery goes against him in *Othello*, it is rather in his favour in *Iago*. His byplay and general action are also very good, and his rendering of some portions of the text is so apt that it gives to the listener perceptions of its excellency and applicability which he did not have before.[55]

The *Rochdale Observer* agreed with this view of Morgan Smith's Iago, saying, "No doubt the fact of Mr. Morgan Smith, the coloured tragedian, supporting [Mr. Mallalieu] as *Iago* would tend materially to make Mr. Mallalieu less effective, by comparison. The *Iago* of Mr. Smith was a considerable improvement on his *Othello* of the previous week."[56]

This was not the only surprised reaction to the effectiveness of Morgan Smith's interpretation of a white role. A week later in Birkinhead a paper reported that

When the novel impression created by a *black Hamlet* wore off, we were struck with the genuine ability which Mr. Smith displayed. We do not pretend to rank him with the best tragedians of the present day. He bids fair, however, to eclipse the fame of his compatriot Ira Aldridge, who, despite the prejudices excited by his race and colour, at a time when such prejudices were more stern than they are now, won his way to an honourable position amongst the tragedians of the world. We have no hesitation in recommending Birkenhead playgoers to witness Mr. Morgan Smith's acting.[57]

But the major surprise in Birkenhead was Morgan Smith's appearance in another new white role: that of Sir Edward Mortimer in George Colman the Younger's *The Iron Chest*, a popular role for many nineteenth-century tragedians, which he played for two consecutive nights. The character chosen was a gloomy, melancholy nobleman who had committed a murder but had been acquitted of the crime, so his conscience bothered him greatly. In a lengthy preface to the play, Colman the Younger had said he required for the role a man

"Of a tall stature, and of sable hue,"

"Much like the son of Kish, that lofty Jew."

A man of whom it might be said,

"There's something in his soul"

"O'er which his melancholy sits, and broods."

I have endeavoured, more-over, to pourtray *Sir Edward Mortimer* as a man stately in his deportment, reserved in his temper, mysterious, cold, and impenetrable, in his manner... .I demanded a performer who could enter into the spirit of a character proceeding upon romantick, half-witted principles, abstracted in his opinions, sophisticated in his reasonings, and who is thrown into situations where his mind and conduct stand, tiptoe, on the extremest verge of probability.[58]

Philip Cox has expanded upon this by pointing out that Sir Edward Mortimer

is throughout a potentially tragic figure: he is seemingly

aristocratic, honourable and noble-spirited but, in addition, he possesses an intrinsic flaw relating to his misguided and excessive sense of reputation and fame. He has an acute sense of justice and yet is tragically led to violate both the spirit and the letter of the laws he is trusted to enforce.[59]

This would have been a challenging melodramatic role for Morgan Smith to play, for it required handling a subtler range of fluctuating emotions, some bordering on insanity, than he was experienced in expressing. Unfortunately, there were no descriptions in the press of the way he performed this character. However, *The Era* reported that his impersonation of Iago in Birkenhead was "exceedingly well sustained."[60]

His Hamlet was likewise appreciated as a "highly intelligent and satisfactory exposition" when he was reengaged in Dundee for the first of twelve different roles he was to play there over the next eleven nights. He received rave reviews almost every evening. His Shylock was "on the whole very excellent."[61] His Othello was "as nearly perfect as we have ever seen it," and in certain scenes "we have never seen Mr. Smith's acting surpassed."[62] When he appeared as Iago, he "gave a very able portrayal of the part. His acting throughout was very quiet, and remarkably free from exaggeration, and he received a hearty call at the end of the tragedy."[63] "A character better suited for the display of Mr. Smith's abilities than that of Fabian [in *The Black Doctor*] could scarcely be found. His impersonation of it is most excellent and deserving of the highest praise."[64] "The audience testified their appreciation of his impersonation of [Gambia in *The Slave*] by repeated bursts of applause."[65] Theatergoers were also looking forward to his benefit night when he was scheduled to appear as the Chevalier de St. George, as well as Mephistopheles in a "magical drama," *Faust and Marguerite*, translated from the French of Michel Carré by Thomas William Robertson.[66] He was also to recite Tennyson's "The Charge of Six Hundred."[67] Dundee newspapers remained uncharacteristically silent about these final performances.

Morgan Smith closed out the year by performing in Dunfermline for a week beginning December 16th:

[He] commenced a six nights' engagement with a task of no

ordinary magnitude—the play selected being Hamlet. Like a skilful painter and man of genius, Mr. Smith brought out all the lights and shadows of the royal Dane, showing a profound knowledge not only of his author, but of the human heart. Hamlet beyond any of the plays of our immortal Shakspeare, presents the finest scope for exhibiting to advantage the taste of a scholar. The accomplished tragedian ably acquitted himself, and was applauded to the echo....On Tuesday, the "Merchant of Venice" was produced, Mr. Smith taking the part of "Shylock." His skilful rendering of this very difficult part is evidently the result of deep study. So natural and finished is this gentleman's acting—without straining after effect—that we look, as it were, not on the actor, but on the individual he represents. On Wednesday, the "Slave." On Thursday, the "Lady of Lyons." On Friday, "Othello"; and to-night, Mr. Smith will appear for the last time of his present engagement in "Richard III." To those who can appreciate the play as written, or can enjoy that quiet, calm calculation which is the real character of the opening soliloquy in the original—

"Now is the winter of our discontent

Made glorious summer by this sun of York"—

I would say, go and see Mr. Morgan Smith, the sable tragedian.[68]

He returned to London on December 24th and placed an ad in the next issue of *The Era*, saying he "will be happy to hear from Provincial Managers for SPRING TOUR. Engagements will also be made with Literary Organizations, &c, for Readings."[69] He evidently was seeking to maximize his opportunities for employment by offering to draw upon his experiences in Philadelphia as a solo elocutionist.

1867 had been a very good year for Morgan Smith. He is known to have appeared at least 132 times in thirty cities and towns in England, Scotland, Ireland, and Wales, playing at least thirteen different roles, four of which were entirely new ventures he had added to his repertoire while touring. Two-thirds of his performances were in Shakespearean plays, but he was now beginning to appear in more melodramas and romances. He never appeared in two of the roles he had originally advertised in London as being available: Virginius in *Virginius: or, The Liberation of Rome,* a tragedy by James Sheridan Knowles, and Damon in *Damon and Pythias*, a tragedy set in ancient Greece by John Banim and R. L. Shiel. Perhaps tragedies set in classical antiquity were not popular in the provinces. Or perhaps theatre managers there preferred to have him play Shakespearean parts or characters in more contemporary plays. In any case, he now had a sufficiently large and diverse repertoire to offer to any theatre willing to employ him for up to two weeks. He was ready to resume touring in 1868.

Endnotes

1   See, e.g., the reviews in the *Worcester Journal*, January 19, 1867; *Illustrated Sporting and Theatrical News*, January 26, 1867; *South Durham and Cleveland Mercury*, January 26, 1867; *Dundee Courier and Argus*, January 29, 1867; *Northern Warder*, January 29, 1867; and *The Era*, February 3, 1867.

2   *Staffordshire Sentinel and Commercial & General Advertiser*, March 2, 1867.

3   *The Era*, February 3, 1867.

4   *Illustrated Sporting and Theatrical News*, February 9, 1867.

5   *Dundee Courier and Argus*, February 9, 1867.

6   *Illustrated Sporting and Theatrical News*, February 16, 1867.

7   *Bradford Observer*, February 14, 1867.

8   *The Chevalier de St. George: A Drama in Three Acts, Adapted from the French of MM. Melesville & Roger de Beauvoir* (London: Thomas Hailes Lacy, n.d.).

9   Allardyce Nicoll, *A History of English Drama, 1660-1900* (Cambridge, U.K.: Cambridge University Press, 1959), 76, states that, "Although this play is ascribed to T. H. Reynoldson, T. W. Robertson seems to have been the author."

10 See, e.g., Gabriel Banat, *The Chevalier de Saint-Georges: Virtuoso of the Sword and the Bow*. Lives in Music Series, 7. (Hillsdale, NY: Pendragon Press, 2006) and Emil F. Smidak, *Joseph Boulogne called Chevalier de Saint-Georges* (Lucerne: Avenira Foundation, 1996).

11 Maynard Savin, *Thomas William Robertson: His Plays and Stagecraft* (Providence, RI: Brown University, 1950), 46.

12 *Dundee Courier and Argus*, February 9, 1867.

13 *Northern Telegraphic News*, February 23, 1867.

14 Playbill 963/5/8 C11568 held in the Robert Wood Collection, Theatre and Entertainments Section, the Tyne and Wear Archives.

15   *The Era*, February 24, 1867.

16   *The Athenaeum*, March 30, 1867. The same announcement appeared in the *Illustrated Sporting and Theatrical News*, April 6, 1867, as well as in a number of provincial papers.

17   On April 6, 1867 this article was published in the Surrey Comet, Middlesex Chronicle, Walsall Free Press and General Advertiser, Whitby Gazette, Watford Observer, and Louth and North Lincolnshire Advertiser. Obviously the author of this piece had never read Abbé Henri Baptiste Grégoire's *De la littérature des nègres, ou recherches sur leur facultés intellectuelles, leur qualités morales, et leur littérature* (Paris: Maradon, 1808), translated by D. B. Warden as *An Enquiry Concerning the Intellectual and Moral Faculties of Negroes, Followed with an Account of the Life and Works of Fifteen Negroes and Mulattoes, Distinguished in Science, Literature and the Arts* (Brooklyn: Thomas Kirk, 1810) or W. Armistead's *A Tribute for the Negro: Being a Vindication of the Moral, Intellectual, and Religious Capabilities of the Coloured Portion of Mankind; with Particular Reference to the African Race* (Manchester: W. Irwin; New York: W. Harned, 1848), but this may be expecting too much of newspaper journalists in England in the nineteenth century.

18   *The Era*, June 23, 1867.

19   *Gramsby Free Press*, August 2, 1867.

20   *The Era*, June 2, 1867. On June 23, this contact address in *The Era* was changed to 9, Grove Terrace, opposite station, Hammersmith. Three months later, on September 29, Morgan Smith announced in *The Era* that "In consequence of the Richmond Railway Company's purchase of the premises, 9, Grove Terrace, Managers will address for the future to Angelo House, Shaftesbury-road, Hammersmith, London, W."

21   *Belfast Morning News*, September 2, 1867; *Belfast News-Letter*, September 5, 1867; *Banner of Ulster*, September 5, 1867.

22   *Banner of Ulster*, September 10, 1867.

23   *Belfast News-Letter*, September 10, 1867.

24   *Belfast Morning News*, September 11, 1867.

25   *Illustrated Sporting and Theatrical News*, September 14, 1867.

26   *The Era*, September 15, 1867.

27   *Belfast Morning News*, September 11, 1867.

28   *Northern Whig*, September 11, 1867.

29   *Ulster Observer*, September 14, 1867.

30   *Illustrated Sporting and Theatrical News*, September 21, 1867.

31   *The Era*, September 22, 1867.

32 *Banner of Ulster*, September 14, 1867.

33 *The Orchestra*, September 21, 1867.

34 *Dublin Advertising Gazette*, September 21, 1867; *Commercial Journal and Family Herald*, September 21, 1867.

35 *Evening Freeman*, September 17, 1867; *Freeman's Journal*, September 17, 1867.

36 *Saunders's Newsletter*, September 17, 1867.

37 *Irish Times and Daily Advertiser*, September 17, 1867.

38 *Dublin Advertising Gazette*, September 21, 1867; *Commercial Journal and Family Herald*, September 21, 1867.

39 *Dublin Evening Post*, September 20, 1867.

40 *Evening Freedman*, September 21, 1867; *Freeman's Journal*, September 21, 1867.

41 *Illustrated Sporting and Theatrical News*, September 28, 1867.

42 *Irish Times and Daily Advertiser*, September 24, 1867.

43 *Daily Express*, September 23, 1867.

44 For details, see the *Arbroath Guide*, September 25 and October 5, 1867.

45 See note 20. Mary Eliza and their sons apparently did not travel with Morgan Smith on his provincial tour. Instead, she handled some of his correspondence with theatre managers while he was away.

46 *England and Wales, Free DNB Death Index 1837-1915* [database online].

47 *The Era*, October 27, 1867. We do not know what happened to Morgan Smith's sons, one two-and-a-half years old, the other ten months old, during this period, though it is possible that Ellen Craft may have taken care of them. At this time she would have been bringing up two children of her own, eight-year-old Ellen and six-year-old Alfred. See Jeffrey Green, "Black American Children in England in the 1850s," online at jeffreygreen.co.uk/059

48 Bernth Lindfors, *Ira Aldridge: The Last Years* (Rochester, NY: University of Rochester Press, 2015), 154. See also Aldridge's letter thanking May for having made for his performance of Othello a costume that was "the surprise and admiration of all," 247.

49 John Ashworth, "The New Theatre," *Rochdale Observer*, September 28, 1867. In the same paper on October 5, a religious leader from Bamford, James P. Kay-Shuttlesworth, described Ashworth as "the missionary of Rochdale. He has published tracts of which some hundred thousand copies have been sold. He has done more than any other man to keep alive and spread the faith of Christ among the manual labour class in the valley of the Roche, and his missionary labours extend to many distant places....My conviction is that he is a noble-hearted man, with a natural genius for his work as an evangelist."

50 "Replies to Mr. John Ashworth's Letter on the New Theatre," *Rochdale Observer*, October 5, 1867.

51 Ibid.

52 See, e.g., A Looker On, "Mr. Buxton in a Muddle about the Drama," *Rochdale Observer*, October 12, 1867; James Buxton, "Mr. Buxton and 'Looker On,'" *Rochdale Observer*, October 19, 1867; J. E. S., "A Defence of the Theatre,"*Rochdale Observer*, October 19, 1867; Anon., "The Theatre: A Peep Behind the Scenes," *Rochdale Observer*, October 25, 1867; D. L. N., "The Theatre: The School of Vice and Immorality," *Rochdale Observer*, October 25, 1867; J. E. S., "The Poor Persecuted Theatre Again," *Rochdale Observer*, November 2, 1867; Wm. Cooper, "Theatres and 'Strange Tales,'" *Rochdale Observer*, November 2, 1867, and reprinted in the *Rochdale Pilot*, November 2, 1867.

53 *Rochdale Observer*, November 2, 1867. I have not been able to access reviews of this performance from the *Rochdale Pilot* and *Rochdale Spectator*, though both are known to have commented on it.

54 *Rochdale Pilot*, November 9, 1867.

55 *Rochdale Spectator*, November 9, 1867.

56 *Rochdale Observer*, November 9, 1867.

57 *Liverpool Daily Post*, November 13, 1867.

58 George Colman, the Younger, *The Iron Chest: A Play; in Three Acts* (London: Printed by W. Woodfall. For Messrs. Cadell and Davies [etc], 1796), v, and reprinted online by Chadwyk-Healey (Cambridge, UK, 1966).

59 Philip Cox, *Reading Adaptations: Novels and Verse Narratives on the Stage, 1790-1840* (Manchester and New York: Manchester University Press, 2000), 31.

60 *The Era*, November 24, 1867.

61 *Dundee Advertiser*, December 4, 1867.

62 *Northern Warder*, December 6, 1867.

63 *Illustrated Sporting and Theatrical News*, December 14, 1867.

64 *Dundee Advertiser*, December 11, 1867.

65 *Northern Warder*, December 13, 1867.

66 This play will be discussed in the next chapter.

67 *Dundee Courier*, December 13, 1867.

68 *Dunfermline Saturday Press*, December 21, 1867.

69 *The Era*, December 29, 1867.

6

1868

Morgan Smith continued to receive offers of employment at a fairly steady pace in the early months of the new year, but it is impossible to determine with any certainty exactly how often he performed or even where he played his roles because he sometimes appeared in small towns that had no local or regional papers that covered what was happening in provincial theatres. *The Era* was the only London paper that made a concerted effort at reporting such news, but it, too, had its limitations and blind spots. Yet it sometimes provided hints or intriguing clues about possible forthcoming engagements that were newsworthy.

For instance, the first mention of Morgan Smith in the new year appeared in an advertisement in *The Era* placed by Charles Gill, proprietor of the Victoria Music Hall in Rotherham, a small town (population 25,087 in 1871) northwest of Sheffield, who had a vacancy for "a First-class LEADING GENTLEMAN....Stars can be received at any time for Six or Twelve Nights. Glad to hear from Mr. MORGAN SMITH."[1] It is likely that Morgan Smith would have been eager to accept this invitation, but we do not know whether he did because there was nothing further said in *The Era* about

Rotherham's Victoria Music Hall in the months that followed.

Morgan Smith's first known performances in 1868 took place at Kidderminster, another small town (population 20,814 in 1871) southwest of Birmingham, where he acted for six nights in *Merchant of Venice, Othello, Richard III*, and other plays, giving "the greatest satisfaction, and each evening [receiving] repeated calls before the curtain."[2] Three weeks later he was at Cheltenham further south, playing more Shakesperean roles as well as Claude Melnotte in *The Lady of Lyons*.[3] The *Cheltenham Chronicle* some years later recorded a memorable incident that occurred during that week:

> One of our well-known tragedians, whilst starring the provinces, played an engagement at Cheltenham. He opened in "Othello," and after the play, being in a hurry to join some old friends, he raised a loud outcry because there was no hot water to take the colour off. When the man whose duty it was to look after such matters arrived he was met with a torrent of such reproach as fairly startled him. Some time after another star arriving also played *Othello*, and when he had finished his performance, he sought his room gasping and out of breath. Scarcely had he done so when the old attendant burst into the room, and planting a huge can of boiling water on the floor, exclaimed, "There! All right this time: you can take your confounded black off as soon as you like!" But again he was startled with a burst of indignation, for the *Othello* on that occasion was poor Morgan Smith, the coloured tragedian!"[4]

At the end of February Morgan Smith secured an engagement for a week at the Royal Amphitheatre at Leeds, and one of the local papers commented at some length on his opening night there:

> Mr. Morgan Smith, a gentleman with a deeply copper-coloured complexion, began an engagement here last evening. In the first appearance of a celebrated tragedian there is always simple curiosity almost out-weighing the ordinary anticipations which intelligent playgoers cannot suppress on such occasions. The fame of an intending visitor never reaches us for the first time without extorting from the fancy some idea of the manner of man he is who is shortly expected. In the case of Mr. Morgan Smith, however, the curiosity felt is quite out of the common kind, for a black man on the English stage is something we have not been accustomed to dream of since in our schooldays *rara*

avis in terra nigroque similima cygno [a rare bird upon the earth and very like a black swan] became a familiar apparition. But where should there not be at least one black tragedian, when we have a black bishop, black senators, and black governors already taking part in the affairs of civilized institutions? There is indeed every reason why a coloured tragedian should be welcome, and that Mr. Morgan Smith felt that he was made welcome at the Amphitheatre last night we verily believe. Most appropriately, his *debut* took place in the part of *Othello*, and his gifts, both natural and acquired, made the performance unusually interesting. In more than one respect he gave a native hue to the character of the fiery Moor, and succeeded in obtaining frequent applause.[5]

A London paper remarked "from the little we saw of Mr, Smith we are bound to say he well deserves all the laurels he has gained. His rendering of the Moor showed a perfect knowledge of the character, and tragic powers of rare magnitude."[6]

Morgan Smith performed as Gambia, Chevalier de St. George, Shylock, and Fabian in *The Black Doctor* during the rest of the week, and won commendation for having "drawn appreciative audiences by his impersonation of several Shaksperian and other characters. His acting is careful and precise, indicating a full realisation of the lights and shadows of the characters presented."[7]

His next stop was at nearby Dewsbury, where he was reported as "the African [*sic*] tragedian, who has played Othello and Hamlet. He has drawn good houses, and appears to be a favourite."[8] He then returned to Kidderminster, having been re-engaged there for another week.

Much, therefore, was expected from him, and it is only just to say that he quite equaled or excelled the expectations of those who heard him. As Richard III, he performed the part of the crafty and cruel hunchback admirably. His hypocritically declining the crown when offered to him, the scene with the Lady Anne, where she first reproaches him with the murder of her affianced husband Edward, his dream, and finally the battle scene with Richmond, were all powerfully taken and proved him to be an actor of very great merit. His Shylock on Tuesday was in its way equally good, especially in the last act, where the greedy and revengeful Jew demands his pound of flesh, and is circumvented by the disguised Portia. On Wednesday he took Macbeth, and on Thursday, Sir Edward Mortimer in *The Iron Chest*, in both of which he increased the good opinion already formed of him. The playing of the rest of the company was excellent, and Mr. Smith stated that for a small company he had seldom met with one that worked so well together.[9]

From there he journeyed 220 miles northward to Tyne and Wear to play at little Jarrow-on-Tyne (population 18,179 in 1871) as well as at sizable Sutherland (population 112,643 in 1871) where "the reception he received was most flattering."[10] His next engagement was a hundred miles south at Wakefield, near Leeds, after which he reversed direction and went back up to Newcastle-upon-Tyne, where his performance of Gambia in *The Slave* excited an extraordinary amount of attention in one of the local papers:

The piece teems with "situations" of unusually thrilling melo-dramatic interest—situations which ill-natured critics would say seem purposely contrived for the numerous reappearances of Gambia at most opportune crises. Did anybody want a drink, Gambia would have been ready with a pot of water; was Captain Clinton to be released from prison, Gambia was ready with self sacrifice; was a retreat to be cut off, Gambia with the simple assistance of a short sword, in a couple of seconds hewed down a rustic bridge and tumbled it into the howling torrent beneath; was a child to be rescued, Gambia could do it; was the villain of the play to be knocked on the head, Gambia alone could perform the ceremony in the most artistic manner. Did Zelinda call, in times of trouble, for the faithful black, wasn't Gambia at her side in the twinkling of an eye? Indeed he appeared with such promptitude as almost warranted the belief that he was in waiting at one of the wings until Zelinda should shout for him. Talk of general utility men! Gambia is unapproachable. Eclipse is first, and the rest nowhere: from pitch and toss to manslaughter nothing came amiss to this wonderful fellow. He was perhaps one of the most remarkable men in the country. We fancy he never told his love for Zelinda—except to the audience. He spouted about freedom like Curran, and almost in the very words; he explained that a negro had feelings just as one Shylock in a play written some three hundred years ago by a certain Mr Wm. Shakespeare informed his supercilious neighbours that a Jew had a number of points of resemblance in common with the high and mighty Christians. Indeed we ratherly think Mr Shakespeare must have seen Mr Morton's play of the Slave, and regardless of the laws of meum and tuum *conveyed* some sentiments into his worthless Merchant of Venice. When we say that some of the situations in the Slave are remarkably like some of the actions in Pizarro, we think we have given a fair idea of the many merits of this singular production. Whatever demerits there may be in the piece the burden of them does not rest on Mr Morgan Smith's shoulders. In it there are many happy expressions and noble utterances. The solemn business is very happily relieved by the fun of the Sharpsets and of the venerable Miss Von Trump. Mr Smith spoke with vigour, and at times with touching pathos. He is, however, too fond of attitudinizing, and his poses though picturesque and telling are not unattended with awkwardness. Mr Smith was frequently applauded and his many declamations elicited noisy and general approval.[11]

The few negative remarks recorded here about Morgan Smith's acting were the first to have been uttered by any reviewer up to this point in 1868, but there were good things said too, and it is made abundantly clear that he had pleased his audience.

Morgan Smith moved on to Wishaw next, a hamlet northeast of Birmingham so tiny (population 6,112 in 1871) that there were no press reports telling what he did there.[12] But at Blackburn the following week there was discussion of some of the roles he played:

On Monday evening, there was a good house to witness his representation of "Othello," the novelty of the thing proving an attraction which many could not withstand. From the manner in which his rendering was received—a recall being made before the close of the piece—we should say that the audience was well pleased; and indeed the delivery of the less passionate speeches was graceful and highly effective. In his delineation of the sublime passion attained in "Macbeth" and "Othello," Mr. Smith seemed to fall short—particularly in the latter; and this, we should suppose, arose rather from physical incapacity than from want of perception as to the meaning of the author. So far "Richelieu" has been his best effort, the apparent bodily decrepitude of the old minister contrasting in a striking manner with his portrayal of the indomitable will which governed his actions.[13]

The criticism here is again muted, with commendations balancing what was said about his shortcomings. On Thursday, April 23, Morgan Smith had performed Macbeth in commemoration of the 304th birthday of Shakespeare.[14]

One measure of Morgan Smith's growing fame as a peripatetic performer was the fact that he was now known well enough by some audiences to be imitated by comic actors who attempted to simulate features of his distinctive style. Though he had performed at Belfast's Royal Theatre for only a week in September the previous year, on May 1st and again in mid-October, a young satirist there, Thomas Verney, "who on different occasions has achieved success of an unmistakable character, displayed his genuine talent at a comedian to great advantage" by cleverly imitating in Charles Selby's operatic farce *The Widow's Victim*, not only such stars as J. L. Toole, Barney Williams, T. C. King, Charles Kean, John Clarke, and Henry Webb, but also Morgan Smith in a performance that "could hardly have been excelled."[15]

For the next four months, stretching from May throughout the summer, Morgan Smith was frequently unemployed. He had adopted the practice of advertising his availability in *The Era* weekly, noting in particular where and when he was scheduled to perform in coming weeks so theatre managers could contact him directly to arrange future engagements or could deal with his agent, Samuel May, in London. But during this fallow period there was little to report aside from ten more nights in Wishaw in mid-May, a single night at the Marylebone Theatre in London on May 26th when he was due to perform as Gambia in a benefit performance for Miss Nellie McEwan, who was to play opposite him as Zelinda, then a week at Preston toward the end of June, followed by six more nights at London's Pavilion Theatre, and finally three nights in Margate late in August. Morgan Smith had tried to stimulate interest by publishing in *The Era* excerpts from very positive reviews of his appearances in Newcastle, Leeds, and Blackburn,[16] but most theatres in the provinces and a good number in London were closed during the summer months, so he had very few options to pursue.

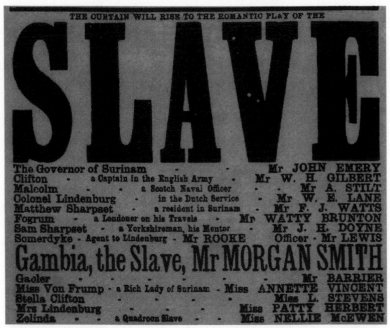

THE CURTAIN WILL RISE TO THE ROMANTIC PLAY OF THE

SLAVE

The Governor of Surinam	-	Mr JOHN EMERY
Clifton - a Captain in the English Army	-	Mr W. H. GILBERT
Malcolm - a Scotch Naval Officer	-	Mr A. STILT
Colonel Lindenburg - in the Dutch Service	-	Mr W. E. LANE
Matthew Sharpset - a resident in Surinam		Mr F. J. WATTS
Fogrum - a Londoner on his Travels	-	Mr WATTY BRUNTON
Sam Sharpset - a Yorkshireman, his Mentor	-	Mr J. H. DOYNE
Somerdyke - Agent to Lindenburg - Mr ROOKE		Officer - Mr LEWIS

Gambia, the Slave, Mr MORGAN SMITH

Gaoler	-	Mr BARRIER
Miss Von Frump - a Rich Lady of Surinam - Miss ANNETTE VINCENT		
Stella Clifton	-	Miss L. STEVENS
Mrs Lindenburg	Miss	PATTY HERBERT
Zelinda - a Quadroon Slave	-	Miss NELLIE McEWEN

Figure 15. Playbill of *The Slave* starring Morgan Smith as Gambia at the Marylebone Theatre, London, on May 26, 1868. Reproduced with permission from the Westminster Archives Centre, London.

Reviews of his infrequent performances during this interval were scarce as well. In Preston he had appeared as Hamlet, Gambia, Chevalier de St. George, and Sir Edward Mortimer in *The Iron Chest*, but all that was said about him was that he had been well received as the Chevalier, having acted that role "with considerable ability and intelligence."[17] At the Pavilion, where he appeared as Gambia every night, he

> showed himself to be an intelligent, careful, and agreeable elocutionist, and a talented and painstaking actor, who, with greater physical energy, might take a higher position in his Profession than that respectable one which he already occupies. He gave an interesting delineation of the noble qualities of the high-souled Gambia. The liberated slave's delight on gaining his liberty, and the gratitude and heroic self-abnegation which he displays in selling himself back to bondage to serve his benefactor, Captain Clifton, and his chivalrous devotion to

125

Zelinda, were all vividly and feelingly depicted. Though Mr.
Smith is not a very powerful actor, he is a thoroughly earnest
and spirited one, and in many respects a superior performer.[18]

This was a considerable improvement over much of what had been
said about him two years earlier in London, but the familiar complaint
about his lack of physical energy and power indicated that he still
fell short of expectations even though he was now recognized as
possessing qualities that won him respect as a professional thespian.
In Margate (population 13,903 in 1871), as in other small provincial
towns, nothing at all was said about him.

His fortunes changed in September and October, when, after a
week in Ipswich and at least two nights in Aberystwith, he earned
a nearly unbroken string of seven consecutive weeks of back-to-
back engagements, mainly in parts of Wales and Ireland. In Ipswich
Morgan Smith was praised as "a very good Shaksperian actor,
who has a good idea of reading as well as acting the works of the
great poet."[19] For instance, "His conception and representation of
[Shylock] were alike excellent, and he was well supported."[20]

But the big surprise came on Saturday, September 9th, when he
appeared for the first time as Rolla in a translation of August von
Kotzebue's *Pizarro*, a martial melodrama that Richard Brinsley
Sheridan had brought out with great success at Drury Lane more
than half a century earlier. The play, which focused on a Spanish
military intervention in Peru, created a great sensation because it was
"partially responsible for bringing the 'oppressors of unfortunate
persons in India' to the attention of the British public,"[21] a topic
of special interest because it alluded quite directly to a political
controversy in England at that time. In fact, Rolla's famous speech
rallying his Peruvian troops against the invaders was based on an
oration Sheridan himself had delivered in the House of Commons
in 1787 during the impeachment trial of Warren Hastings, who
was accused of high crimes and misdemeanors conducted during
his tenure as Governor General of Bengal.[22] It was a critique of
corrupt British imperial practices against a vulnerable opponent,
and it continued to reverberate in reverse in subsequent decades in
England as a nationalistic rallying cry against threats from powerful
European neighbors.

Julie A. Carlson observes that Rolla's speech "highlights the patriotic service of the orator by considering public speaking as the most effective means for preserving a people's liberty."[23] So here was a role that would enable Morgan Smith to utilize his training in dramatic elocution. Back in Philadelphia he would have been able to witness James E. Murdoch, E. L. Davenport, and Edwin Forrest playing this role,[24] and, now aware of its continuing popularity in England, he must have decided that it would be worth his while to learn to play Rolla during the summer, when he had plenty of free time. It turned out to be a role he performed fairly frequently thereafter, especially during long runs when he needed something new to offer.

Wrexham was the next town to welcome him, noting that he "created great applause" when he appeared as Claude Melnotte on Monday, that "his representation of Othello "was lifelike [and] was played in a manner never excelled in Wrexham" on Tuesday, and that he "displayed his superior histrionic abilities as Hamlet" on Wednesday.[25] On Thursday and Friday the Wrexham company moved to nearby Oswestry in Shropshire, where Morgan Smith reprised his roles of Melnotte and Othello.[26]

Then, at his benefit night on Saturday, September 20th, he tried another experiment by performing for the first time as "the stranger" in Benjamin Thompson's translation of August von Kotzebue's eponymous drama of that title.[27] This was a play Morgan Smith also would have known well from his theatergoing days in Philadelphia, for he would have had opportunities to see the role played many times by visiting and local stars, among them his mentors, James E. Murdoch, James B. Roberts, and William Wheatley.[28]

For more than a century *The Stranger* remained a very popular play in British and American theatres, even though it had been widely condemned by religious leaders because it dealt with a controversial topic: marital infidelity by a woman. Mrs. Haller, the false name assumed by the heroine, had left her husband and two small children and run off with a "villain" from whom she soon separated, taking refuge for three years at the home of a wealthy Count and Countess who knew nothing of her past but admired her grace, beauty, and modesty. She regretted having betrayed and shamed her husband, whom she still loved, but feared she would disgrace him further by returning to him. Meanwhile, the husband, who also still loved her deeply, had become a moody recluse and misanthrope, known initially only as "the stranger," but later revealed to be Count Walbourg, who continued to help others in distress but preferred to live alone without revealing to anyone the cause of his unhappiness. After leaving his children with a widow in town in order to brood in solitude, he rented a small cottage for three years in the park owned by the same family who had taken his wife in. He did know that she was then living with them, nor did she know the whereabouts of her husband and their children. At the climax of the play, a mutual friend managed to bring the husband and wife together in the presence of their children.

> They press the children in their arms with speechless affection; then tear themselves away—gaze at each other—spread their arms, and rush into an embrace. The children run, and cling round their parents. The curtain falls.[29]

This highly emotional and sentimental ending caused many members of the audience, male and female, to weep profusely. Some women even had to be removed from the theatre in hysteria. Myron Matlaw, who has studied the impact of this scene over time, has noted that "The adultery and final reconciliation, which evoked the greatest amount of tears, were criticized almost invariably throughout the history of the play."[30] Matlaw may be right in suggesting that "'Immorality' of this sort has always been attractive on the stage [because of] the rigid moral code of the Victorians, with its taboo on the recognition and its consequent denial of the existence of sexual drives."[31]

Morgan Smith, in choosing a controversial play of this kind to expand his repertoire, may have been making a judicious professional decision, for it clearly was a drama that many people wished to see. Unfortunately, there were no reports on how well he performed this role in Wrexham, so we must wait for later responses to his appearances as this "stranger."

Morgan Smith spent the next two weeks at Queen's Theatre in Dublin, where he played a variety of familiar roles, most of them for two nights in succession. On his arrival, one paper said, "Judging by the success which this gentleman achieved last year, we are sure that the engagement will be most successful."[32] He opened as Othello and won immediate but qualified approval for his handling of this character:

> Mr. Smith has, of course, in this part the great advantage over ordinary actors, that he needs no recourse to the means generally employed for getting up the appearance proper to the sable-visaged Moor. But, notwithstanding this, one may be allowed to doubt whether it is altogether prudent in a young actor to attempt the interpretation of an author so subtle as Shakspeare. Ambition, however, is generally a good fault; and as Mr. Smith has acquitted himself with at least so much credit as to show that though bold he is not too presumptuous in undertaking the part of *Othello*, we are disposed to regard his appearance in the character with favour. He seems to have a wholesome dread of "rant," but is betrayed by this feeling into an opposite fault, and now and then fails to impart sufficient animation to those passages in which *Othello* gives expression to the conflicting passions by which his breast is rent. But this error is easy of correction, and we are on the whole inclined to believe that Mr. Smith will attain a good position in the profession he has chosen.[33]

The following night the play was repeated, but this time Morgan Smith chose to play Iago, a change that prompted one reviewer to remark that

> Mr. Smith is an actor of decided talent, some of his impersonations of characters in the higher walk of dramatic art being intellectual and dignified....On the first night the noble but jealous Moor was played by Mr. Smith to Mr. Clifford's Iago, and the beauties of both parts were fully brought forth by the *artistes*....On the following night, Mr. Clifford played Othello, and it became evident that, though the conceptions of each actor were in some respects different, both had realized the genius of the author, and were fully capable of giving fitting expression to it.[34]

Another reviewer went so far as to say

> We are inclined to think that both gentlemen appear to still greater advantage, when the colour and nationality are changed.

Mr Smith has evidently deeply studied the characteristics of the villainous 'Ancient,' and knows when, where, and how, to exhibit some really excellent by-play of reading. Both in dress and bearing he was superb, and although his colour would tend to neutralize any very considerable facial expression, yet it was surprising the amount of meaning he was able to convey without descending in the slightest degree to grimace or buffoonery—a prevailing fault with many white actors who have played the part.[35]

His performances for the rest of his first week attracted less attention. Nothing at all was said about his appearance for two nights as Fabian in *The Black Doctor*, and when he took the part of Chevalier de St. George on Friday, performing it under a new title, *The Child of the Sun*, the only remark made in the press was that he had been "warmly applauded for the manner in which he acquitted himself."[36] It was also disappointing that nothing of substance was reported on his next offering, which was advertised as *El Moresco, or the Moor's Revenge*.[37] This melodrama was more correctly identified in another paper as Edward Young's *The Revenge*, in which Morgan Smith was to play Zanga, a Moorish slave who succeeds in avenging himself on his Spanish master, but the paper erred in claiming this to be "one of the characters which has most made [Morgan Smith's] reputation."[38] In fact, this may well have been the first time he ever attempted this role, for there is no other prior record of it in the available published literature on his career, even though it was among the characters he stated he was prepared to play when he first advertised his availability as an actor in *The Era* more than two years earlier.[39]

Morgan Smith continued to attract large audiences during his second week in Dublin, which began with his appearance for two nights as Gambia, in which he was acknowledged to be "most successful."[40] For the next two nights he reappeared as Chevalier de St. George, on which the critics were silent, but on Friday, his benefit night, he gave the Dublin audience a sample of his other Shakespearean roles, playing

no less than four of the leading characters in the most popular of the dramas of that author, selecting an act from each play which exhibited the most striking action of the piece. The characters selected were Shylock, Hamlet, Macbeth, and Richard III. Though generally we would wish to see one of these great productions represented in its entirety and not in detail, we must say that the performance last night was a highly interesting one, as it allowed Mr. Smith to show that he has versatility sufficient to enable him adequately to personate four characters, each one of which differs so widely from the other.[41]

And on Saturday he was to play Rolla in *Pizarro*, "a character in which we have before had occasion to speak highly of him."[42] This too was not true, for this drama had not been part of his repertoire when he had performed for a week in Dublin the previous year or during the two weeks of his current run.[43]

Upon leaving Dublin, Morgan Smith returned to Wrexham for a one-night stand as Richard III, and then quickly moved on to Swansea, where he made a very good impression as Othello on his opening night:

> We have certainly never seen an actor possessed of a more admirable appearance for the part or who "dressed" it better; he did not appear to be simulating a person of whom he had no mien, but he looked the veritable Othello. Of his elocution we can scarcely speak too highly, and, indeed, his general histrionic capacity is of a very high order; whilst there is a bright intelligence and frankness in his face that lends no small force to his acting. He has a slight tinge of foreign accent, which under exciting circumstances is more plainly apparent; it is not such, however, as to be a serious detraction. We can neither imagine, nor could we wish for anything more genuine than Mr. Morgan Smith's impersonation of the confiding but betrayed Moor of Venice. We recommend those who like good acting to betake themselves to the Theatre during the week.[44]

He filled out most of the rest of the week by repeating Othello, then playing Shylock, Sir Edward Mortimer, as well as Chevalier de St. George combined with the third act of Hamlet as an afterpiece, but it was his performance in a double bill on Saturday evening that no doubt was best remembered by the audience because of a terrible mishap that occurred:

> During a desperate encounter in one of the pieces Mr. Smith had been furnished with a loaded pistol, which had, unfortunately, been rather too heavily charged. When he had to fire at the

heroine in the plot, the loud report startled the audience, and the unfortunate actress staggered back desperately wounded in real earnest. The wadding struck her on the arm, causing a severe lacerated wound, which rendered it necessary to have her removed to the infirmary, and there the poor woman will remain for some time. The lady's name is Miss Marie d'Alvera.[45]

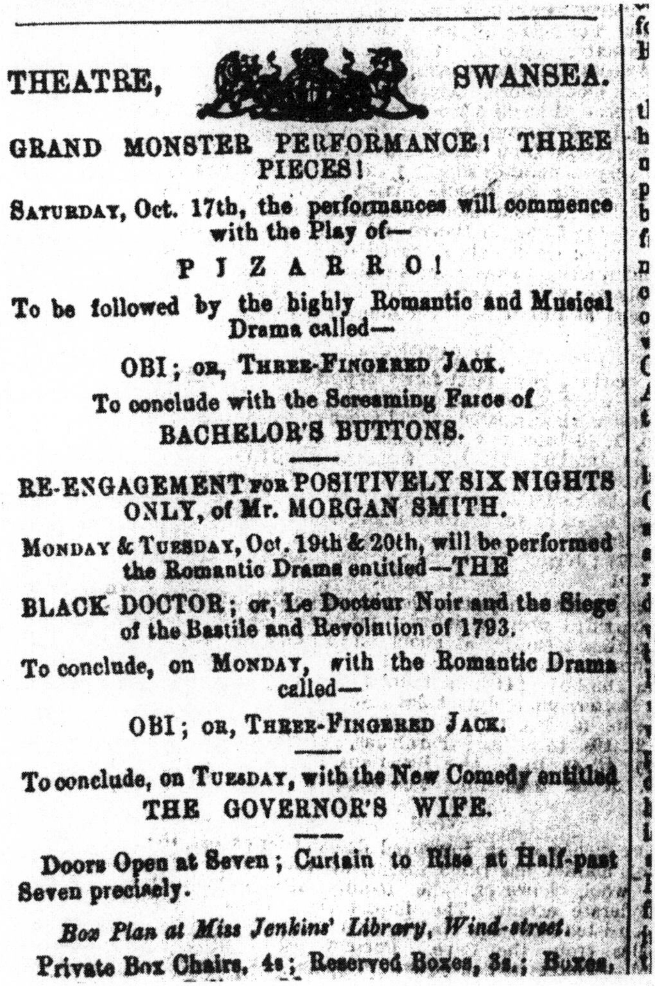

THEATRE, SWANSEA.

GRAND MONSTER PERFORMANCE! THREE PIECES!

SATURDAY, Oct. 17th, the performances will commence with the Play of—

P I Z A R R O !

To be followed by the highly Romantic and Musical Drama called—

OBI; OR, THREE-FINGERED JACK.

To conclude with the Screaming Farce of
BACHELOR'S BUTTONS.

RE-ENGAGEMENT FOR POSITIVELY SIX NIGHTS ONLY, of Mr. MORGAN SMITH.

MONDAY & TUESDAY, Oct. 19th & 20th, will be performed the Romantic Drama entitled—THE

BLACK DOCTOR; or, Le Docteur Noir and the Siege of the Bastile and Revolution of 1793.

To conclude, on MONDAY, with the Romantic Drama called—

OBI; OR, THREE-FINGERED JACK.

To conclude, on TUESDAY, with the New Comedy entitled
THE GOVERNOR'S WIFE.

Doors Open at Seven; Curtain to Rise at Half-past Seven precisely.

Box Plan at Miss Jenkins' Library, Wind-street.
Private Box Chairs, 4s; Reserved Boxes, 3s.; Boxes,

Figure 16. Advertisement in the *Swansea and Glamorgan Herald and South Wales Free Press* for the Swansea Theatre on October 17, 1868. ©British Library Board, 072.092982. Reproduced with permission from the British Library.

The two plays that were staged that night were *Pizarro* and W. H. Murrey's version of John Fawcett's musical pantomime entitled *Obi; or, Three-Fingered Jack*, a melodrama about a notorious Jamaican outlaw who uses the magic of Obeah (Obi) to strengthen his powers and intimidate his foes. There is no scene in *Pizarro* where Rolla shoots the heroine Cora. There is no such scene in *Obi; or, Three-Fingered Jack* either, but at one point in that drama, Jack "levels a pistol" at Rosa, the heroine he has captured, but does not fire it.[46] So Morgan Smith must have playing yet another role he had never attempted before when the prop in his hand suddenly discharged. This would have been his third effort since the summer to expand his repertoire by experimenting with new characters. He apparently had not wasted his time when unemployed. He must have been very eager to develop new resources.

Despite this dreadful accident, Mrs. C. Pitt, the lessee at the Swansea Theatre, must have been very pleased with Morgan Smith performances, for she immediately reengaged him for another week, starting on the following Monday with *The Black Doctor* and a repetition of *Obi; or, Three-Fingered Jack* as the afterpiece.

Morgan Smith delivered another surprise on Wednesday evening when he reappeared as Mephistopheles in Thomas William Robertson's translation of Michel Carré's *Faust and Marguerite*, a retelling of Goethe's Faust legend that he had first performed in Dublin the previous year. This had been a signature role of James B. Roberts, in which, according to one of that actor's playbills, he gave "an unrivalled impersonation which has created a veritable sensation in nearly every city in the union," as well as at London's Princess's Theatre where he played it for nearly two successful seasons in 1857-58.[47] He may also have appeared as Mephistopheles as he toured "about thirty cities and towns in England, Ireland, and Scotland" during the same period.[48] Thereafter, almost every year between 1859 and 1866, he performed the role regularly in long runs at Philadelphia's Walnut Street Theatre, where Morgan Smith would have had a chance to see him in it. A local reviewer there said, "Mr. Roberts' [Mephistopheles] is alone an artistic study worthy of the price of admission."[49]

There had been many versions of the story of Faust published or performed in English before Robertson's translation appeared in 1854. Allardyce Nicoll lists more than twenty of them,[50] and he also notes that the script of the original production of *Faust and Marguerite* staged at London's Princess's Theatre on April 19, 1854, with Charles Kean as Mephistophiles, "has been attributed variously to [Dion] Boucicault and T. W. Robertson."[51] There is in addition a source that claims that Roberts himself wrote the English version of the play in which he played Mephistopheles in Philadelphia.[52] Two editions of the play were subsequently published, one by Kean himself, who subtitled it "a magical drama" because special effects were created to simulate Mephistopheles's supernatural powers.[53] The other, slightly shorter popular edition, published by Thomas Hailes Lacy, offers this description of the costume of Mephistopheles:

> Black velvet doublet, trunks and cloak slashed with red and gold, red cap and high single red feather, red tights and shoes, thin black eyebrows and moustache, peaked beard, hooked nose, short black wiry hair, cadaverous complexion.[54]

Morgan Smith had bushy black eyebrows, a moustache, and short black wiry hair, and he would have had to rely on make-up for the peaked beard, hooked nose, and cadaverous complexion to appear sufficiently devilish.

After the positive reviews he received in Dublin and Swansea, it is surprising to read what was said about him in this role in Cardiff, especially by one critic who found more to condemn than to praise:

> To say that Mr Morgan Smith, the gentleman who is now fulfilling an engagement at the Theatre Royal Cardiff, is a great Shakespearian actor, would be unjust to himself, the public, and to histrionic art. That he has a very intelligent appreciation of Shakespeare from a purely histrionic point of view, few, we dare say, will deny; and his personation of *Othello* on Monday night was, if faulty enough in all conscience in some respects, exceedingly good in others. With a voice something like that of the late Charles Kean, Mr Morgan Smith lacks the consummate art of that great artist in the management of his voice, and at times his intonation is exceedingly harsh and disagreeable, and his pronunciation jars somewhat upon ears accustomed to the speech of the average educated Englishman. In pronouncing corner, for example, he sounded the first vowel Bristol fashion,

like "a" in car, and numerous other examples might be quoted which sounded very uncouthly. With all its drawbacks, however, the performance, upon the whole was a highly creditable one. There was a picturesqueness, dash, and animation, about it which made it "go" with the audience, and Mr Smith has one quality which all true actors possess, viz, thorough earnestness. The speech to the Senate was well spoken, and the passionate scenes in the third act were given with a force and power which left little to be desired, except perhaps a little toning down of the passion. Mr Smith has got into the bad habit of moving his head about too much, which he ought to guard against, and although the farewell to his occupation in the third act was forcefully delivered, the words were drawled out too much.[55]

Another commentator there was more favorably impressed, saying, "Mr Morgan Smith's Othello was marked by great intelligence, and he must with study take rank with the ornaments of the stage."[56] On his second night Morgan Smith represented Iago instead of Othello, and the same reviewer felt that his rendition of this role "afforded additional proof of his intellectual capacity."[57] Little was said about his appearances later that week as Shylock, Macbeth, and Hamlet except that he "performed a series of Shakespearian characters in a highly creditable manner."[58]

At the beginning of November, an odd notice appeared in a few Irish and Scottish papers, reporting

A REPUDIATION,—Poor Mr Morgan Howard! He aspires to represent Lambeth in the constitutional interest. A gentleman bearing the same name, and known as the 'Coloured Tragedian,' writes from the Theatre Royal, Bath, to say he is not the candidate, though vulgar rumour has been cruel enough to announce so. He contradicts this as likely to do him a serious professional injury.[59]

Since Morgan Smith had been busy performing under his own name during the preceding six weeks in Dublin, Swansea, and Cardiff, and had never appeared in Bath, this must have been an erroneous report. Perhaps it was intended as an amusing political hoax.

When Morgan Smith resurfaced a week later in Tunbridge Wells, the local press ignored him altogether, and a London paper merely reported that he had "appeared in a succession of his favourite characters" there.[60] At the end of November he publicized in *The Era* that he was "disengaged,"[61] and this may have earned him two weeks of employment in Hastings, but again there were only fragmentary reports of the Shakespearean roles he performed there, his Othello having been "very well placed upon the stage, and…received with much applause by a well-filled house,"[62] and "several of the 'divine Will's' most famous characters—Shylock, Richard III and Hamlet [having also been] much applauded."[63] A few of his other roles—notably Rolla, Gambia, and Macbeth—were singled out too as having given "great satisfaction."[64]

All things considered, it had been another good year for Morgan Smith. He had played before large audiences on much of his tour through two dozen cities, town, and villages in England, Ireland, and Wales, and he had been invited back to several theatres for return engagements. And while on this extensive excursion, he worked up some popular new roles to play, thereby making himself eligible for longer engagements. Audiences were impressed with his care in handling and understanding Shakespearean characters, though some reviewers at first continued to expect him to be more passionate when playing certain scenes in *Othello*. He was usually warmly applauded for his efforts, even when he could not fully satisfy those who found some faults in his acting. He was now a more professional and polished performer, and he still gravitated toward those roles that he tended to play best. Performances of five Shakespearean parts— Othello, Hamlet, Shylock, Richard III, Macbeth—still comprised half of his repertoire, but he now played Gambia more frequently and further diversified his offering by adding the new plays and by continuing to perform a number of familiar melodramas.

Endnotes

1   *The Era*, January 12, 1868.

2   *The Era*, January 19, 1868.

3   *The Era*, February 9, 1868.

4   *Cheltenham Chronicle*, November 6, 1886.

5   "Leeds Amphitheatre—Engagement of the Coloured Tragedian," *Leeds Evening Express*, February 25, 1868.

6 "Royal Amphitheatre," *Illustrated Sporting and Theatrical News*, February 29, 1868.

7 *Leeds Times*, February 29, 1868.

8 *The Era*, March 8, 1868.

9 *Kidderminster Times*, March 14, 1868.

10 *The Era*, March 29, 1868.

11 *Newcastle Guardian and Tyne Mercury*, April 11, 1868. The name Curran may be an allusion to John Philpot Curran (1750-1817), a radical Irish politician and lawyer famous for his eloquence in debates about reforms.

12 Morgan Smith was invited to return to Wishaw for a run of ten nights starting on May 6, 1868, and again there was nothing said in print about what he performed there.

13 *Blackburn Times*, April 25, 1868.

14 *The Era*, April 26, 1868.

15 *Northern Whig*, May 4, 1858; *The Orchestra*, October 24, 1868.

16 *The Era*, May 10, 1868.

17 *The Era*, July 26, 1868.

18 *The Era*, July 5, 1868.

19 *Illustrated Sporting and Theatrical News*, September 5, 1868.

20 *Ipswich Express and Essex and Suffolk Mercury*, September 1, 1868. Also, in Aberystwith, *The Era*, September 13, 1868, reported that as Hamlet, Morgan Smith "was most heartily received by the friends he made last season."

21 Julie A. Carlson, "Trying Sheridan's *Pizarro*," *Texas Studies in Literature and Language*, 38, no. 3-4 (1996): 359.

22 Ibid.

23 Ibid., 363.

24 Murdoch had appeared in this role at the Walnut Street Theatre on February 23, 1861, Davenport at Walnut Street Theatre on December 25, 1862, and Forrest both at the American Academy of Music on January 4, 1862 and at the Chestnut Street Theatre on December 29, 1863.

25 *Wrexham Advertiser*, September 19, 1868.

26 Ibid.

27 The translation had been enhanced and made more suitable for production by Richard Brinsley Sheridan, who was then running Drury Lane Theatre, where the play was first performed in 1798. For details, see Dougald MacMillan, "Sheridan's Share in *The Stranger*," *Modern Language Notes*, 45, no. 2 (February 1930): 85-86, and Cecil Price, "Sheridan at Work on *The Stranger*,"

Neuphilogishe Mitteilungen, 73, no. 1/3 (1972): 315-25.

28   The play had been performed in Philadelphia at least once every year from 1857 to 1859, thrice in 1860, four times in 1861, thrice in 1862, four times in 1863, and twice in both 1864 and 1865. These performances took place mainly at the Arch Street Theatre or the Walnut Street Theatre, but also occasionally at the Chestnut Street Theatre. Wheatley had appeared in it at the Arch Street Theatre on February 4, 1860 and January 25, 1861, Murdoch at the Walnut Street Theatre on February 17, 1860 and February 9, 1861, and Roberts at the Walnut Street Theatre on July 16, 1864. E. L. Davenport had also played the role on August 31, 1857 at the Arch Street Theatre, on November 14, 1861 and December 27, 1862 at the Walnut Street Theatre, and on May 26, 1865 at the Chestnut Street Theatre.

29   Benjamin Thompson, *The Stranger* (Cambridge, U. K.: Chadwyck-Healey, 1996), 5: 71.

30   Myron Matlaw, "Adultery Analyzed: The History of *The Stranger*," *Quarterly Journal of Speech,* January 1, 1957: 23.

31   Ibid., 28.

32   *Dublin Advertising Gazette*, September 19, 1868.

33   *Saunders's Newsletter*, September 28, 1868.

34   *Freeman's Journal*, September 26, 1868.

35   *Dublin Advertising Gazette*, September 26, 1868.

36   *Dublin Evening Post*, September 26, 1868.

37   *Dublin Advertising Gazette*, September 26, 1868.

38   *Freeman's Journal*, September 26, 1868.

39   *The Era*, July 15, 1866.

40   *Dublin Evening Post*, September 30, 1868.

41   *Freeman's Journal*, October 3, 1868.

42   Ibid.

43   Perhaps the reviewer for *Freeman's Journal* was confusing Morgan Smith with Ira Aldridge, who had performed as Zanga twice during an engagement in Dublin in December 1855, but Aldridge had not appeared as Rolla during that series of appearances.

44   *Swansea Herald and Neath Gazette*, October 14, 1868.

45   *The Era*, November 1, 1868. The news spread quickly, having been reported in the *Birmingham Daily Post, Dublin Evening Mail, Manchester Courier and Lancashire General Advertiser, Edinburgh Evening Courant, Irish Examiner*, and a number of other provincial and London papers. Swansea's *Cambrian*, October 23, 1868, provided a few additional details, saying surgeons "were

immediately in attendance, and after some delay in procuring a cab, the injured lady was removed to the infirmary, where she still remains, and is doing well up to the present time."

46   W. H. Murrey, *Obi; or, Three-Fingered Jack*, (London: Dicks' Standard Plays No. 478, n.d.), 8.

47   Playbill of "Faust and Marguerite," performed at the Boston Museum on April 14, 1862, and held at the Harry Ransom Center, University of Texas at Austin.

48   T. Allston Brown, *History of the American Stage* (New York: Dick & Fitzgerald, 1870), 314.

49   *North American and United States Gazette*, December 26, 1859.

50   Allardyce Nicoll, *A History of English Drama 1660-1900* (Cambridge, U.K.: Cambridge University Press, 1959), 6:158.

51   Ibid., 5:268.

52   John Bouvé Clapp and Edwin Francis Edgett, *Players of the Present, Part III* (New York: Dublin Society, 1899), 307.

53   Charles John Kean, *Faust and Marguerite: A Magical Drama (1854)* (London: John K. Chapman, n.d.).

54   William Robertson, *Faust and Marguerite. A Romantic Drama. In Three Acts. Translated from the French of Michel Carré* (London: Thomas Hailes Lacy, [1856]), 4.

55   *Cambria Daily Leader*, October 27, 1868.

56   *The Era*, November 1, 1868.

57   Ibid.

58   *The Era*, November 8, 1868.

59   The story, purportedly from the *Shipping Gazette,* was published in the *Dublin Evening Mail*, November 2, 1868, and then reprinted in the *Edinburgh Evening Courant*, November 4, 1868, and the Greenock *Advertiser*, November 5, 1868. The Dublin paper had added that "It would be interesting to know whether the actor wishes to have a hit at the House of Commons, the new constituencies in general, or Lambeth in particular, or whether he means the rub for an individual—say Mr Morgan Howard himself, or some former representative of whom Lambeth has no reason to be proud."

60   *Illustrated Sporting and Theatrical News*, November 21, 1868.

61   *The Era*, November 29, 1868.

62   *Illustrated Sporting and Theatrical News*, December 12, 1868.

63   *Illustrated Sporting and Theatrical News*, December 19, 1868.

64   *The Era*, December 20, 1868.

7

1869

Morgan Smith began the new year at Queen's Theatre at Londonderry, opening on successive evenings as Othello, Shylock, and Hamlet,[1] but nothing further was said in the local press about his activities there until two weeks later when he appeared for the first time as Romeo in Shakespeare's *Romeo and Juliet* and a few days later gave a reading.[2] No additional details were provided.

On January 17th he saw an advertisement in *The Era* placed by Sophie Brown, the manager of the Standard Theatre in Port Glasgow, encouraging him by name to join a full company she was recruiting. Morgan Smith accepted the invitation and spent the first week of February performing a variety of his standard roles: Hamlet, Shylock, Macbeth, Richelieu, Othello, and Richard III. Again no reviews appeared telling how well he handled this repertoire, but "this little theatre" was reported to have been "still doing well."[3]

However, when he subsequently appeared for a week at the Royal Pottery Theatre in Hanley in a round of three of his Shakespearean characters supplemented with impersonations of Gambia, Fabian, and Richelieu, the *Staffordshire Sentinel* found it could "say little laudatory, the leading star being in some instances outshone by the local [s]atellites."[4]

For the next five weeks the press remained silent about where Morgan Smith was and what he was doing, but at the end of March he managed to find employment for a week at Northampton's Theatre Royal in a characteristically wide range of roles. He opened as Macbeth. In early April, the *Illustrated Sporting and Theatrical News* reported that

> "The Slave," "Richelieu," "Hamlet," and "Othello" have been the leading attractions here. The trial scene from "The Merchant of Venice" was introduced in addition to "Othello" on the occasion of Mr. Morgan Smith's benefit on Friday evening last. The attendance, however, was not large; indeed, the house as a rule has been but scantily supported. On Saturday we had "Richard III" and "Pizarro," Mr. Morgan Smith taking the chief characters with some success. Mr. Smith has, however, one great drawback: when declaiming passionately one is at a loss to understand the meaning of the words he utters.[5]

On April 11th Morgan Smith advertised his availability for engagements in coming months, especially in two new roles he was developing:

> MR. MORGAN SMITH (Coloured Tragedian), having just concluded a very successful tour of Five Months, is prepared to arrange dates for the Summer season. Mr. Smith begs to direct the attention of London and Provincial Managers that he is prepared to produce a New and Original Drama, in three acts, written expressly for him by F. Warrington, Esq., of London, entitled "All But Lost; or, the To-tem of the Tortoise." Time, 1757. Scene—Canada and State of New York. Also a highly sensational Drama, in two acts, founded on the historical incidents and results of the late Abyssinian expedition. (The sole right to these Plays are legally secured to Mr S.) Managers can address as heretofore, care of S. May, Esq., 35, Bow-street, Covent-garden, London, W.C.; or General Post-office, Glasgow).[6]

Morgan Smith lingered in Glasgow for a few weeks. Somewhere on his travels he had met a woman named Harriet Goldspring, and they had fallen in love. On April 27th they were married in Milton, a district of Glasgow north of the River Clyde. Little is known of her background except that she had been born in Norwich thirty-five years earlier as the last of her parents' six children.[7] She was reported to have been "formerly an actress,"[8] and by the fall season she was frequently playing Desdemona opposite Morgan Smith's Othello.[9] She went on to co-star in many other roles with him and later sometimes became a headliner herself in plays in which he did not perform. In early reviews she was praised for displaying considerable ability as Desdemona[10] and for being a "correct and painstaking actress" when playing the part of Julie De Mortimer in *Richelieu*.[11] Together, they were an effective team.

Unlike his first wife, Mary Eliza, who remained in Hammersmith with their young children while her husband traveled, Harriet accompanied him on his tours, presumably bringing along sons Samuel and Edgar, who were then four years old and two and a half.

Morgan Smith's next engagement was not until a month later in Wales at Wrexham's Theatre Royal, which was "filled to overflowing" on his opening night, and where he "was greeted with great cheering on making his appearance [as Macbeth] and well did he sustain his character."[12] He reenacted this role on Tuesday "in order to give those persons an opportunity of seeing the play who were unable to gain an admission the previous evening,"[13] and he went on to play the Stranger, Shylock, Othello, and Rolla to fill out the rest of the week. This was a town in which he had been successful four times before, and a paper in neighboring Chester excused itself from commenting on his performances, claiming that "as an actor he is so well known in Wrexham and elsewhere, that it is unnecessary for us to say more than that he appeared at this theatre for several nights."[14]

Morgan Smith's search for summer employment yielded few results. He responded to an advertisement inviting applications from "a few Ladies and Gentlemen [who were] required to complete the Company" at London's Royal Alfred Theatre for a short season beginning July 10th[15] and won a week-long contract playing Fabian in a production of *The Black Doctor* that was advertised under a new title, *The Turning of the Tide; or, the Fated Lovers*. The only available review of this show, published a month later in the *New*

York Clipper, stated that Morgan Smith had "found favor with the audience, who had him before the curtain three times. His style of acting, while it is original in some cases, is wanting in finish in many points."[16]

A few weeks later, on August 4th, he appeared as "the crook-backed tyrant" Richard III at Sadler's Wells Theatre in a benefit performance for another actor, Augustus Whitby, who was also acting in London during the summer season.[17]

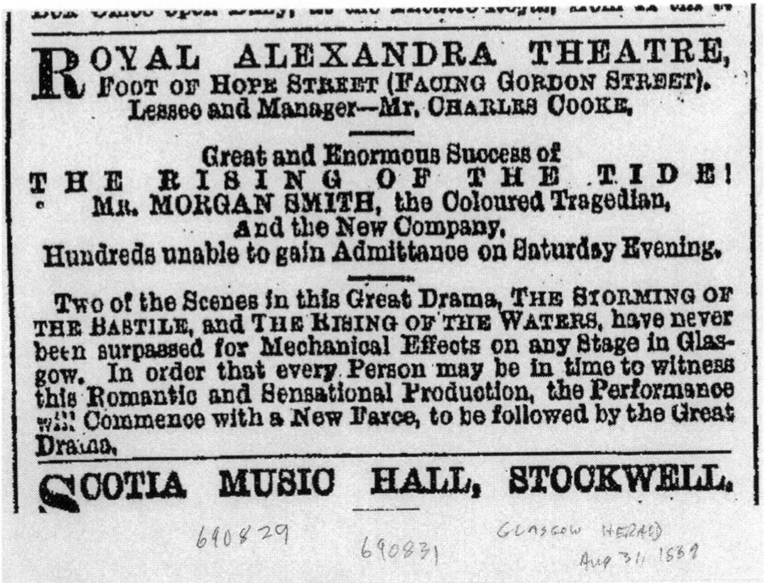

Figure 17. Advertisement in the *Glasgow Herald* for the Royal Alexandra Theatre, Glasgow, August 31, 1869. ©British Library Board, 072.9144. Reproduced with permission from the British Library.

Morgan Smith's fortunes turned at the end of August, when he secured an engagement to play Fabian in what was now called *The Rising of the Tide* for three consecutive weeks at the Royal Alexandra Theatre in Glasgow. This was the first time he had performed a single role for such a long period, but by the third week he was adding a second play to the bill to diversify his offerings. Here he was received with the same degree of enthusiasm he had experienced in Wrexham. Reviewers also had good things to say about the way *The Rising of the Tide* was put on the stage:

> Whether as regards acting or scenery nothing appeared to be left undone, as the hearty rounds of applause with which the entire representation was received testified. Several excellent *tableaux* were exhibited, the Rising of the Waters and the Storming of the Bastille being particularly effective. Altogether, the piece, which presents many striking features, was mounted and acted in a manner that reflects great credit both on the Management and *artistes* engaged, and will doubtless attract numerous audiences. Mr Morgan Smith, coloured tragedian, has been specially retained for the leading part, Fabian, the Creole. This gentleman, who is an actor of intelligence and experience, rendered all his scenes with excellent judgment and ability.[18]

The *Glasgow Herald* added that

> The piece must have satisfied all who relish incidents of a stirring and exciting kind; and Mr Morgan Smith, "the coloured tragedian," who is specially engaged to give it due effect, and who appeared as *Fabien* [sic], the Black Doctor, had no reason to be dissatisfied with his reception. He was frequently applauded, and had more than once to come to the front of the curtain.[19]

Only a London paper found something odd about such a sensational production:

> To those of a certain taste, the drama will no doubt be acceptable, but the change from Robertson's comedies to a play of this stamp is like the old step from the sublime to the ridiculous. It must be admitted, however, that Mr Smith fills the principal part excellently, his complexion filling the character *apropos*. Mr. Charles Cooke deserves encouragement for the liberal way in which the accessories of this piece, no doubt very expensive, are got up.[20]

Indeed, Cooke may have been justified in claiming that "Two of the Scenes in this Great Drama, THE STORMING OF THE BASTILE, [sic] and THE RISING OF THE WATERS, have never been surpassed for Mechanical Effects on any Stage in Glasgow,"[21] and that the Royal Alexandra was "now the most popular Theatre in Glasgow."[22]

On the first four nights of his third week there, Morgan Smith added *The Slave* to the bill, a production "which not only has been carefully mounted, but what is far better, been well acted. Mr Morgan Smith's Slave was a bit of really effective acting."[23] At his benefit night on Friday he added Othello, and he concluded his run on Saturday by combining *The Rising of the Tide* with *Dred, a Tale of the Great Dismal Swamp*, a dramatic adaptation of Harriet Beecher Stowe's novel about a black rebel in the antebellum American South. This was a role he had never played before.

The novel was excessively didactic, weighed down with heavy moral messages drawn from scripture, and inhabited by characters who were either wholesomely good or thoroughly evil. Prominent among the evildoers were most plantation owners and Southern Christian clergy who opposed the abolition of slavery. In contrast, all the blacks and mulattos were depicted as good, decent people, even those who suffered most grievously under harsh racial oppression.

Dred, the eponymous hero, is different from almost all the other blacks we see in both the novel and the play because he is not enmeshed in plantation life. He is a free spirit, a runaway slave who has chosen to live in the Great Dismal Swamp, where his expert hunting, fishing, and farming skills are sufficient to sustain him, his wife, and any other runaway slaves who come to him for assistance or shelter. He also happens to be an insightful, intuitive visionary with a deep knowledge of the Bible, which he is fond of quoting to justify actions he takes in struggles against injustice. But the characteristic that most strikingly sets him apart from all other blacks, physically and symbolically, is that he always carries a gun.

Allardyce Nicoll lists half a dozen adaptations of *Dred* performed in English before 1869,[24] and we don't know which one Morgan Smith chose for his debut in this role, but it may be significant that he kept it in his repertoire for at least eleven years. He must have found some satisfaction in playing this kind of character. Ira Aldridge, in contrast, had abandoned the play entirely after only four attempts at playing it, twice in Belfast, and twice in Cork.[25] Perhaps he had found this revolutionary hero too dreadfully melodramatic.

Upon arriving in Glasgow, Morgan Smith had been mentioned in a letter to the editor of the *Glasgow Herald* complaining about "A

MULATTO PERSONATING AN AFRICAN PRINCE":

Sɪʀ—The above heading is a mistake as applicable to the impostor Wallace. He is a little, mean, dwarfish black, full of low cunning, and has neither address nor any of the higher class accomplishments to enable him to follow out with anything like success a systematic course of swindling. My only reason for correcting the above error is that I, for good or evil, belong to the mulatto race, and I have some little objection in 30 days hence of being brought under the surveillance of the police as the real Mr Doyle Wallace, *alias* His Royal Highness, an African Prince. And now, Sir, before concluding, please allow me to call your attention to the inroads that civilisation is making in the negro race. On Sabbath day last a Glasgow pulpit was talently filled with a son of Africa; to-day our police dock was filled by another of her sons; and to-night, if all go well, another son of the South is to play his part on a Glasgow stage. If this is not proof positive that the great differences that do exist between the white and the negro races is to be found only in the colour of their skin I must give it up for a bad job, and turn my attention to something that the public and the press are capable of doing justice to.

By giving these lines a space in your columns you will oblige

A Mᴜʟᴀᴛᴛᴏ ᴡʜᴏ Tᴏɪʟs Hᴀʀᴅ ғᴏʀ ʜɪs Bʀᴇᴀᴅ

ᴀᴛ Pᴀᴛᴇʀsᴏɴ Sᴛʀᴇᴇᴛ, Kɪɴɢsᴛᴏɴ,

1ˢᵗ Sept. 1869[26]

Morgan Smith's appearance on a local stage was here being offered as evidence of racial equality.

On leaving Glasgow, he immediately moved on to Arbroath (population 17,618 in 1871), where he played for at least four nights, three of which were commented on in the local press:

On Tuesday night Mr. Smith appeared as Richard III. Although there is something *outré* in a black-faced Richard, Mr Smith gave a very powerful embodiment of the character, with perhaps a slight tendency to loudness in the stronger scenes of the drama. As Shylock in the "Merchant of Venice," on Wednesday night, Mr Smith appeared very effectively...But of any of

Mr Smith's characters that of "Othello" in which he played on Thursday, is by far the most careful and finished. This is a character for which Mr Smith is in every way well suited, and he has evidently studied it with great care. His representation on Thursday night was very fine, such as to bring out many of the more delicate points in the tragedy. His voice and manner were excellently fitted to embody the combined strong passion and childlike simplicity of the character.

This review also mentioned that "'Desdemona' was represented by Mrs Morgan Smith—very creditably."[27] This was the first time she had been noticed as performing with her husband.

For the next two weeks Morgan Smith was busy at the Princess's Theatre in Edinburgh, performing for the first six days only in *The Rising of the Tide*, and the second week appearing in a medley of roles: Gambia, Fabian, Othello, Dred, and the Chevalier de St. George, whose play was retitled *The Child of the Sun*.

The *Scotsman*'s review of *The Rising of the Tide* included an elaborate plot summary:

The action in this exciting piece opens in the island of Bourbon, where Fabian, the hero, who there figures as a "black doctor," contrives to fall in love with Pauline, the daughter of a French Marchioness. Of course, the damsel, being beautiful and an heiress, is wooed by another, and the Mulatto seems to stand but a poor chance. In the long run, however, an extraordinary interview occurs in a grotto by the sea-shore, where, in the midst of much ardent protestation, the parties are surprised by the rising tide, and Miss Pauline, believing that her last hour has come, is surprised into the confession of a mutual flame. The scene changes to a gilded saloon in Paris, and we find Fabian, who in the interim has been privately married to Pauline, occupying a decidedly anomalous position. Out of doors he does a little amateur doctoring; within doors it is not quite clear what he does, except that he goes about bewailing the circumstances which necessitate his playing the part of a lackey in presence of the woman whom he claims as his wife. Such a state of matters cannot last. The young lady gets presented at Court; and with a view to qualify her for some office there, the diplomatic Marchioness suddenly arranges that she shall marry her cousin. An *eclaircissement* ensues as to the union with

Fabian, the result being that Pauline falls into deep and lasting disfavour with her mother, while the unfortunate Mulatto gets consigned to an underground cell in the Bastille, there to repent his presumption. Next comes a peep into the interior of the prison, and in the midst of a scene in which Fabian dismally bemoans himself, the Sansculottes of Saint Antoine burst in with fire and sword, and afford swift deliverance. The *dramatis personae* are finally discovered at the sea coast, where Fabian, driven mad by his misfortunes, is living under the protection of a fisherman, to whom he did a good turn in better days. Pauline, now, through the death of her mother, Marchioness de la Reynerie, has been denounced as an aristocrat, and before she can effect her escape is surrounded by a mob of savage Republicans. In the scrimmage the Black, whom she recognises as her husband, gets shot, apparently by accident. His wits thereupon return to him; and by producing the marriage-certificate, and proving Pauline the wife of a good Sansculotte, he as his last act saves her neck from the guillotine. With nothing to recommend it in the dialogue, the piece presents several of those strong situations on which playwrights now-a-days place so much reliance. One great sensation is the grotto scene, with its rising tide, though this would be none the worse for a little more verisimilitude in the motion of the canvas waves. But the great *tour de force* is the taking of the Bastille, in which, it must be admitted, there is no lack of fire and smoke, crashing of timbers, and general confusion. Mr. Smith's personation of *Fabian*, while indicating an adequate conception of the part, such as it is, exhibited abundance of energy, with perhaps rather too much of attitudinising and grimace. It were desirable to see the actor in some other *role* before pronouncing on his capabilities. Suffice it to say, meanwhile, that on Saturday night he met with a cordial reception.[28]

The *Scotsman* devoted less space to *The Child of the Sun*, saying only that "Mr Smith, in the part of the 'Chevalier de St George,' seems to give considerable satisfaction, though his acting is characterised by excessive energy of declamation, and a superabundance of what may perhaps be best described as posture-making."[29]

Afterward, Morgan Smith went directly to Dundee's Theatre Royal, where he had performed twice before in 1867. For the first week he played mostly the same set of roles he had been acting in

Glasgow and Edinburgh: namely, *The Rising of the Tide*, *The Slave*, *The Child of the Sun*, and *Dred*, but in addition an advertisement on October 4ᵗʰ reported he would appear that evening in *Robert Macaire*, a melodrama in two acts by Charles Selby.[30] This was a piece he had never played before and would never again perform afterwards. The action takes place in a country inn, where two escaped prisoners stop overnight while fleeing. One of them, a skilful pickpocket who robs the other guests, turns out to be the father of an abandoned foundling the innkeeper has raised since infancy. This impudent outlaw, after murdering another guest, is at last apprehended and confesses his true identity while dying in the arms of his poor, neglected former wife, who happens to have taken refuge at the same inn. Improbable coincidences make this a rather silly tale. Morgan Smith was wise to avoid repeating it.

As for his other roles, he was said to have impersonated Fabian "most effectively, and so much to the approbation of the audience that he was several times called before the curtain....At the close Mr Smith briefly expressed his sense of the favour with which he had been invariably received by the Dundee public, and expressed the hope (which is a well-grounded one) that his present engagement might prove as successful as its predecessors."[31] *The Era* agreed that, as Fabian, he "evinced a large degree of dramatic judgment, and was greatly relished" by the audience.[32]

During his second week in Dundee, Morgan Smith finally got an opportunity to appear in *All But Lost; or, The Totem of the Tortoise*, the play that has been written expressly for him by F. Warrington.[33] *The Era* provided a lengthy plot summary:

> The drama is much above the average of the sensational class to which it belongs. The language is simple and natural, and many of the situations are forcible and striking. The scene is laid in Canada, and the period is 1757. Cora, the eldest daughter of Major Herries, a retired British officer, is beloved by Uncas, a young Mohican chief, which love is returned by Cora in her heart, although her pride will not allow her to show her affection for an Indian. Regan Ramond, a French spy and bold adventurer, is also possessed with a passion for Cora, who, understanding his real nature, rejects his addresses with scorn and contempt. He watches his opportunity, and, taking advantage of the

attendance of the Herries party at an Indian festival, he, with the assistance of Magua, an Indian, who is an enemy, though seeming friend of Major Herries, takes the party prisoner and carries off Cora, whom he threatens with the murder of her friends before her face if she does not consent to become his. She entreats for mercy, and he is about to carry her off when he is obstructed by the arrival of Uncas and his friend Hawkseye, a backwoodsman. Uncas defies Ramond to fight a duel, but no sooner do they cross swords than Magua and a party of Indians swoop down and take the Herrie[s]'s party prisoners. The Indian finding Cora will not become his Squaw, is about to put her to death when he is prevented by the arrival of Uncas, who fires at him and wounds him mortally. Regan Ramond then appears and demands Cora from Uncas, who of course refuses. The French commander Montcalm, with a number of soldiers, now arrive (their aid having been besought by Major Herries). Regan Ramond is taken prisoner as a renegade, and, Cora declaring her love for Uncas, all ends happily. Mr Morgan Smith, as Uncas, appeared to great advantage.[34]

What this summary fails to say is that the author of this play, F. Warrington, appears to have been heavily influenced by James Fenimore Cooper's *The Last of the Mohicans*, since he uses many of the characters and situations that can be found in that novel.

The *Dundee Courier* also reviewed *All But Lost*, concentrating primarily on Morgan Smith's handling of the role of Uncas:

The play is of course written to show off to the best advantage the abilities of the coloured tragedian. These are not of the very highest order, and do not entitle him to the same rank in the profession as that which Ira Aldridge occupied; but at the same time Mr. Smith is far from deficient of native talent, and acts with great care and study. We do not wish to consider Mr Smith merely as a *lusus naturae* a coloured tragedian, but to compare him with those whose colour is paler than that of the Children of the Sun. This is the proper test to apply to Mr Smith, and the one which we have no doubt he would prefer to have applied to him. Mr Smith is an actor of some power; he, however, wants fire, and inclines to the melodramatic rather than to the classic in style.[35]

Morgan Smith came on as Uncas four times before taking his benefit on Friday as Othello, a part he "sustained admirably,"[36] playing it "with dignity and grandeur. His delivery of the apology before the Senate was justly admired and applauded."[37] The critic added, "Seldom has the fair Desdemona found a better representative than Mrs Morgan Smith (who specially appeared for this evening); she is blessed with a beautifully clear and well-modulated voice, and is an admirable elocutionist."[38]

To top things off that evening, Morgan Smith went on to play for the first time the role of George Harris, the heroic mixed race slave in Edward Fitzball's adaptation of Harriet Beecher Stowe's *Uncle Tom's Cabin*. This was his third theatrical experiment during his twelve nights in Dundee. Unfortunately, all that was said in the press about this afterpiece was that the various roles in it "were performed in a manner that gave much enjoyment to the audience,"[39] but that at least was a better response than this particular adaptation of Harriet Beecher Stowe's novel received when it was performed at Drury Lane seventeen years earlier.[40] It was then competing with many other versions that were being performed at London theatres at the same time,[41] and reviewers felt that the subject was growing stale.[42] Fitzball "has evidently laboured to make his work as unlike the other versions as possible. It was natural that he should do so; but the best incidents having been already appropriated by skilful hands, the Drury-lane piece differs, unfortunately, from the others in being worse rather than better than they are."[43] He had produced "a species of *capum mortuum* [lit. dead head, i.e., worthless residue] which bears little...resemblance to the original novel."[44] Nevertheless, the *Uncle Tom's Cabin* mania had not yet subsided by 1869,[45] and Morgan Smith may have hoped that this popular racial melodrama might prove to be a rewarding addition to his repertoire. He certainly had the advantage of possessing the right complexion for playing a character like George Harris.

After fifteen days of subsequent inactivity, Morgan Smith opened the first week of an engagement in Aberdeen by playing Fabian, Chevalier, and Gambia to appreciative audiences:

> The entertainments at the Theatre this week have been greatly enhanced by the advent of Mr. Morgan Smith, the coloured

tragedian, in the theatrical world. The engagement of an actor like Mr. Morgan Smith is most welcome, while it was in some respects necessary, and will go far to add to the prestige of the lessee of the Theatre. Mr. Smith has already appeared in the favourite dramas of "The Rising of the Tide; or the Black Doctor of Bourbon," and "The Child of the Sun;" and in both he has met with a flattering reception. His acting is quiet, yet effective, and especially in declamation, of which he is a master. He displays a naturally powerful voice to fine advantage, and invariably calls forth applause. The sable tragedian also invests such a part as that of the "Black Doctor" with an air of realness which it would altogether lose were it rendered by a "pale-faced" actor.[46]

In his second week he enacted Uncas for four nights and then offered a double bill featuring Othello and Dred for his last two nights. Uncas, considered "perhaps his best performance,"[47] was played "in a splendid manner and was loudly applauded at intervals."[48] It "provided good scope for the display of Mr Smith's powers."[49] One commentator thought his impersonation of the Moor of Venice was "deserving of the highest praise,"[50] but another felt that "his voice and expression savoured just a little too much of the Yankee and spoiled what would otherwise have been an exceptionally good representation."[51] Meanwhile, Mrs. Morgan Smith, as Desdemona, "produced a very natural representation of the heroine of the piece."[52] *Dred*, on the other hand, was described as "decidedly of the sensational order, and has little to recommend it."[53]

Morgan Smith spent the rest of November performing Fabian "in a most creditable manner" in Perth for at least two nights,[54] and then playing some of his more traditional roles—Hamlet, Richard III, Othello (with his wife as Desdemona), and Gambia—as well as Stranger, Pizarro, and Dred for a week in tiny Longton (population 6402 in 1871), where he "created a good impression, and good houses have appreciated his efforts."[55]

He continued this winning streak in December "appearing very successfully as Fabian" in Hull for four nights[56] and rounding off the week with Othello on his benefit night which "he played with great ability" and in which his wife "appeared to good advantage" as Desdemona.[57] He also added *Dred* as an afterpiece that evening, and played Richard III on his final night there.

He ended the year with a week in Exeter, where he had been billed long in advance as the "only successor to the late Ira Aldridge,"[58] and where he was now being advertised erroneously as the "great African Tragedian."[59] He started off with two nights as Fabian, "when he made a favourable impression, which was much increased by his *Richelieu* on Wednesday evening."[60] A reviewer for *The Era* wrote that "Morgan Smith has given unmistakable evidence of his talent as a tragedian by his masterly impersonation of the wily Cardinal in Lord Lytton's play."[61] On Thursday he appeared as Rolla, and on Friday he took his benefit under the patronage of several members of the Devon and Exeter Club,[62] playing "with singular success Chevalier [de] St. George. He also recited with power and effect 'How they brought the Good News from Ghent to Aix' and 'The Charge of the Light Brigade.' On Saturday he bid farewell in the character of Gambia."[63]

All in all, it was another good year for Morgan Smith, especially during the fall season. His acting seems to have improved after his marriage, and his wife Harriet had enhanced his success in *Othello* by supporting him as Desdemona. He also appears to have gained greater confidence in his abilities as an actor, having had the courage to try out five new roles in the course of the year. There was still some awkwardness or passivity in his handling of melodramatic scenes of passion, and there continued to be a few complaints about his American accent and unusual mannerisms, but it is clear that audiences responded to his efforts, often applauding heartily and calling him before the curtain to congratulate him on his effective impersonations. After three and a half years in the United Kingdom he was by now being recognized as a professional actor capable of playing a great variety of roles rather well. And his reputation was beginning to spread abroad as well. A Philadelphia paper, noticing his appearances in Scotland, reported an interesting rumor: "It is said he will visit America."[64]

Morgan Smith had toured once in Ireland, once in Wales, twice in London, four times in English provincial towns, and seven times in Scotland. Racial melodramas were now outnumbering Shakespearean plays in his offerings by a ratio of more than two to one, reflecting perhaps the preferences of theatre managers in those venues who may have wished to capitalize on the popularity of his black and mixed race impersonations, especially that of Fabian, the Black Doctor, which he now played more often than any other role.

Endnotes

1   *Derry Journal*, January 6, 1869.

2   *Derry Journal*, January 20, 1869.

3   *The Era*, February 7, 1869.

4   *Staffordshire Sentinel and Commercial and General Advertiser*, February 20, 1869.

5   *Illustrated Sporting and Theatrical News*, April 3 and 10, 1869.

6   *The Era*, April 11, 1869.

7   Palmer (Finlay) Family Tree, Ancestry.com. See also England and Wales, Non-Conformist and Non-Parochial Registers, 1567-1970.

8   *Aberdeen Guardian*, November 13, 1869.

9   The first report of her in this role appeared in the *Arbroath Guide*, September 18, 1869. Before her marriage she may have performed under a stage name, for no actress with the surname of Goldspring can be found on playbills or in the press before 1869.

10   *Northern Advertiser*, November 16, 1869.

11   *The Era*, October 23, 1870.

12   *Wrexham Advertiser*, May 29, 1869.

13   Ibid.

14   *Chester Chronicle*, May 29, 1869.

15   *The Era*, July 4, 1869.

16   "Foreign Show News," *New York Clipper*, August 7, 1869.

17   *The Era*, August 8, 1869.

18   *The Era*, September 5, 1869.

19   *Glasgow Herald*, August 30, 1869.

20   *The Orchestra*, September 3, 1869.

21   Advertisement in the *Glasgow Herald*, August 31, 1969.

22   *The Era*, August 23, 1869.

23   *The Era*, September 12, 1869.

24 Allardyce Nicoll, *A History of English Drama 1660-1900*, 6: 129.

25 For further information on Aldridge in this role, see Bernth Lindfors, *Ira Aldridge, The Last Years, 1855-1867* (Rochester, NY: University of Rochester Press, 2015), 36-40.

26 *Glasgow Herald*, September 2, 1869. For further information on Doyle Wallace, *alias* James Kelly, see "Apprehension of an Impostor," *Glasgow Herald*, September 1, 1869. Posing as the son of an African king, he had persuaded a merchant to give him goods amounting in value to 18 or 19 shillings and to lend him £5 on the pretense of soon expecting a fortune of more than £50,000 to be transferred to his account at the Bank of Scotland in Glasgow.

27 *Arbroath Guide*, September 18, 1869.

28 *Scotsman*, September 20, 1869.

29 *Scotsman*, September 30, 1869.

30 The full title was *Robert Macaire: or, Les auberge des adrets!* (London: J. Duncombe, [1834]).

31 *Dundee Courier*, October 4, 1869; *Northern Warder*, October 5, 1869.

32 *The Era*, October 10, 1869.

33 More than a month earlier, on September 5th in *The Era*, he had once again advertised his eagerness to play this role as well as the lead in a two-act drama now called *Theodore*.

34 *The Era*, October 17, 1869.

35 *Dundee Courier*, October 13, 1869.

36 *Dundee Courier*, October 16, 1869.

37 *The Era*, October 24, 1869.

38 Ibid.

39 Ibid.

40 This was the last of three versions of the play that Fitzball had written for production in London in 1852 at the Olympic Theatre in September, the Grecian Saloon in October, and Drury Lane in December. See Nicoll, *A History of English Drama, 1660-1900*, 5: 368. In his autobiography, *Thirty-Five Years of a Dramatic Author's Life* (London: T. C. Newby, 1859), 261, Fitzball reports that "I was engaged by three managers to write three distinct pieces, which I did to the best of my abilities; indeed, it did not require any remarkable ability, as it was only to select scenes and join them together." However, this method of cutting and pasting scenes together appears to have been mainly what prompted a negative response from critics.

41 Harry Birdoff, *The World's Greatest Hit: Uncle Tom's Cabin* (New York: SW.F. Vanni, 1947), 144, states that "the London stage in December, 1852,

was crowded with eleven different competing dramatizations" of *Uncle Tom's Cabin.*

42   *The Era*, January 2, 1870.

43   *Morning Post*, December 28, 1852.

44   *Morning Chronicle*, December 28, 1869.

45   Birdoff, *The World's Greatest Hit*, 8, says the play continued to be performed for ninety years.

46   *Aberdeen Guardian*, November 6, 1869.

47   *Northern Advertiser*, November 16, 1869.

48   *Illustrated Sporting and Theatrical News*, November 13, 1869.

49   *Aberdeen Journal*, November 10, 1869.

50   *Aberdeen Journal*, November 13, 1869.

51   *Northern Advertiser*, November 16, 1869.

52   *Aberdeen Journal*, November 13, 1869.

53   *Northern Advertiser*, November 16, 1869.

54   *Dundee Advertiser*, November 16, 1869.

55   *Staffordshire Sentinel and Commercial and General Advertiser*, November 27, 1869.

56   *Illustrated Sporting and Theatrical News*, December 11, 1869.

57   *Illustrated Sporting and Theatrical News*, December 18, 1869.

58   *Exeter and Plymouth Gazette Daily Telegrams*, October 23, 1869.

59   *Exeter and Plymouth Gazette Daily Telegrams*, December 13, 1869.

60   *Western Times*, December 17, 1869.

61   *The Era*, December 26, 1869.

62   *Exeter Flying Post*, December 15, 1869.

63   *The Era*, December 26, 1869.

64   *North America and United States Gazette*, November 24, 1869.

8

1870

Before 1869 ended, Morgan Smith placed another announcement in *The Era* advertising his availability for engagements immediately and in the spring:

> MR. MORGAN SMITH (Coloured Tragedian), having returned to town after a most Successful Tour of Four Months in Scotland and England, is prepared to arrange with Managers not producing Pantomimes, or in want of attraction. Also prepared to arrange dates for coming Spring Tour. Has successfully produced the new Sensational Drama of "All But Lost; or Totem of the Tortoise," on last tour, and prepared to produce the new Three Act Drama of "Theodore," with Colman's (the younger) Celebrated Three Act Sensational Play of "The Africans," as produced at Theatre Royal, Covent-garden. Permanent address at all times, care S. May, Esq., Bow-street, Covent-garden[1]

The response was very good, enabling him to keep busy from the middle of January to the end of May with only a few week-long breaks along the way.

He started in Maidstone in the character of Macbeth "for the

159

benefit of Mr. Ellerton, the lessee. The house was crowded in every part, standing room being scarcely obtainable. The personation of *Macbeth* was a deal too exaggerated, and we must see Mr Morgan Smith in other less difficult characters before we pass on hasty opinion upon his dramatic capabilities."[2] He went on to perform as Richard III, Othello (with his wife as Desdemona), and Gambia, but nothing further was said about him.

In Belfast the following week he sustained the character of Gambia for two nights "in an effectively melodramatic manner,"[3] making "a very favourable impression on the audience, and was frequently applauded,"[4] and then played Fabian thrice, combining both roles at his benefit on Friday. *The Era* reported that on Saturday "Mr Smith's representation of Macbeth, although it may have gratified the curiosity of those who came to see a black Macbeth will not add to his fame."[5]

His next stop was at the Queen's Theatre in Dublin, where he "was received with a sufficient degree of favour. His acting of the 'Chevalier [de] St George' [for two nights] was so good as to justify the applause bestowed on him. The piece was one which afforded sufficient opportunity for the display of the actor's talent."[6] The *Dublin Evening Standard* said "He was so warmly received that we have no doubt that his further stay in the city would conduce to his own interest, and promote the satisfaction of lovers of drama."[7] As Gambia two nights later, he also "was most successful in his representation, possessing, in addition to natural qualifications, very considerable histrionic ability."[8] These triumphs led the lessee, George Owen, to insert Morgan Smith, as the Chevalier de St. George, into a popular pantomime entitled "Harlequin Puss in Boots; or, the Princess, the Magician, the Miller's Son, and King Log and the Fairies" for two nights.[9]

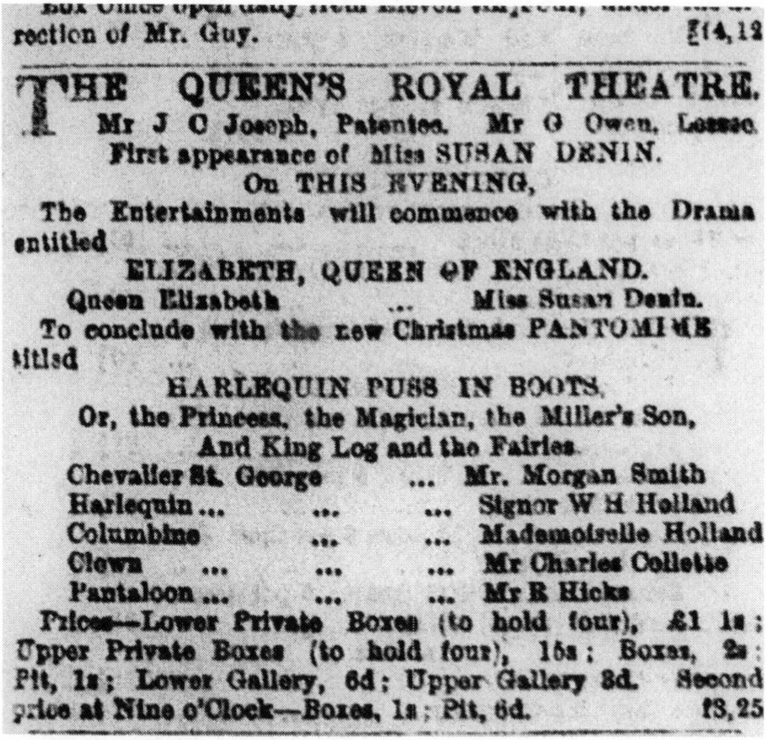
rection of Mr. Guy. [14,12

THE QUEEN'S ROYAL THEATRE.
Mr J C Joseph, Patentee. Mr G Owen, Lessee.
First appearance of Miss SUSAN DENIN.
On THIS EVENING,
The Entertainments will commence with the Drama entitled
ELIZABETH, QUEEN OF ENGLAND.
Queen Elizabeth ... Miss Susan Denin.
To conclude with the new Christmas PANTOMIME titled
HARLEQUIN PUSS IN BOOTS,
Or, the Princess, the Magician, the Miller's Son,
And King Log and the Fairies.
Chevalier St. George ... Mr. Morgan Smith
Harlequin ... ... Signor W H Holland
Columbine ... ... Mademoiselle Holland
Clown ... ... Mr Charles Collette
Pantaloon ... ... Mr R Hicks
Prices—Lower Private Boxes (to hold four), £1 1s; Upper Private Boxes (to hold four), 15s; Boxes, 2s; Pit, 1s; Lower Gallery, 6d; Upper Gallery 3d. Second price at Nine o'Clock—Boxes, 1s; Pit, 6d. [8,25

Figure 18. Advertisement in *Freeman's Journal and Daily Commercial Advertiser* for the Queen's Royal Theatre, Dublin, February 7, 1870. ©British Library Board, 072.91835. Reproduced with permission from the British Library.

When he left Dublin, he crossed the Irish Sea to perform for a week at Whitehaven in Cumbria, where he appeared as Macbeth, Othello, and Richard III as well as Fabian and Gambia. The *Whitehaven News* said the response to his acting was very respectful:

> Mr. Smith's colour is certainly against him [in Macbeth and Richard III], but his rendering of several of the characters in which he has appeared is deserving of higher encomiums than is that of some of his less sable compeers. Mr. Smith, although a Philadelphian by birth, delivers himself with a pure and unaffected accent, and he has evidently taken great pains in the study of his profession.[10]

Before leaving Dublin, he evidently had made an agreement with lessee Owen to return for three more weeks, the first four days of which were devoted to staging the new play that had been written for him, a military drama that got mixed reviews. The *Illustrated Sporting and Theatrical News* was unimpressed:

> The performances each evening have commenced with a new play entitled "The March on Magdala, or the Death of King Theodore." The piece is possessed of little merit, save the fact of Mr. Morgan Smith—from his colour—being peculiarly suited for the part of Theodore, King of Abyssinia.[11]

Freeman's Journal and the *Evening Freeman* also had reservations about the depiction of Theodore:

> We trust, for the honour of human nature, that the authorities were not erring, as English authorities sometimes do, with regard to those who have a difference of opinion with England, and that even Theodore was not as black, morally, as he is represented.[12]

But *The Era* gave the play, and Morgan Smith's part in it, a positive review:

> On Monday Mr. Morgan Smith, the coloured tragedian, made his reappearance in a romantic and sensational play, founded on the events connected with the Abyssinian war, immediately preceding the death of King Theodore, entitled *The March on Magdala; or, the Death of King Theodore*, Mr Smith sustaining the character of the famous King, which he admirably portrayed, and the drama was evidently successful.[13]

This last response drew a letter to the editor from the author of the play:

> MR. EDITOR,—Sir,—Necessarily you can allow only a small space for Provincial criticism; but I think your Dublin correspondent might have stated in his last contribution to your columns that the successful historical play of *The March on Magdala* was expressly written by me for Mr Morgan Smith, and was produced for the first time at the Queen's Theatre, Dublin, on the 21st ult. Trusting that you will kindly insert this in your next issue. I am your obedient servant, F. WARRINGTON.[14]

The play was never published and appears to have been lost, so we can only speculate on how the punitive expedition carried out in 1868 against King Theodore (Tewodros II) by thirteen thousand British and Indian troops against an Abyssinian force of nine thousand was represented.[15] Theodore had imprisoned several missionaries and two representatives of the British Government, and the sizable army sent to rescue them had to traverse four hundred miles across mountainous terrain before arriving at Theodore's fortress at Magdala, where the final battle was fought. The British and Indian army won an impressive victory with only two of their soldiers killed and eighteen wounded, while the Abyssinians suffered the loss of seven hundred killed and twelve hundred wounded.[16] When his fortress was overrun, Theodore committed suicide by shooting himself with a pistol that had been a gift from Queen Victoria.[17]

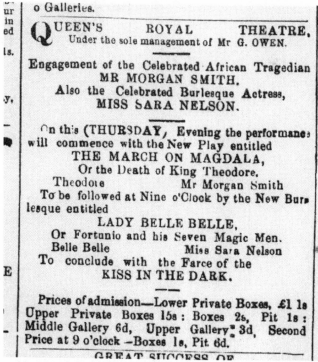

Figure 19. Advertisement in *Commercial Journal and Family Herald* for the Queen's Royal Theatre, Dublin, February 26, 1870. ©British Library Board, General Reference Collection, MFM.M7284. Reproduced with permission from the British Library.

Warrington may have based his play on a 431-page account of the conflict published in 1868 as *The March to Magdala* by G. A. Henty, who had been a war correspondent for *The Standard* at the time. Henty had portrayed Theodore as

> a man of good impulses, and a desire to rule well and wisely, but of a violent temper, and an inordinate pride in his kingly dignity and position... Theodore was a tyrant who had ravaged the whole country, and had murdered thousands of people, including his own near relatives...[He was an] inhuman monster.[18]

This may have been how Morgan Smith had attempted to portray him.

The play would have been of great topical interest because it was being mounted at the very time that Robert Napier, who had led the British Indian army against King Theodore two years earlier, was testifying before a Select Committee of the House of Commons about the Abyssinian expedition.[19] But, according to the *Dublin Advertising Gazette*, after four nights Morgan Smith was directed to turn to other roles, notably to

> "Dred," "Gambia," and..."Fabian" in the "Rising of the Tide," and in each and every part he established himself firmly in the highest estimation of his audiences. All of Mr Smith's impersonations are distinguished by careful study and manly vigour, which will certainly tend to place him in the foremost ranks of his profession.[20]

Toward the end of his second week he also performed the trial scene in *Merchant of Venice*. A critic for *Saunders's Newsletter* noted that

> On Saturday he appeared as Rolla in the tragedy of *Pizaro* [sic], and his acting was in every way well adapted to the various events represented. He is an actor of very considerable ability, and notwithstanding the disadvantages with which an African [sic] must appear before a critical audience of English men or Irishmen, the impression he has produced has been favourable in the extreme. His reading is intelligent and free from rant, and his acting, which is not overdrawn, exhibits some good original points.[21]

In his third week he played Hamlet, Claude Melnotte, Dred, and on his benefit night both Othello and George Harris in *Uncle Tom's*

Cabin. He ended his run on Saturday by appearing in a potpourri of truncated Shakespearean roles: Act 2 of *Macbeth*, the trial scene in *Merchant of Venice*, and, for the first time, the first act of *King Lear*. The *Dublin Evening Standard* summed up his visit by testifying that "his powers in rendering the conceptions of a dramatist are very considerable."[22]

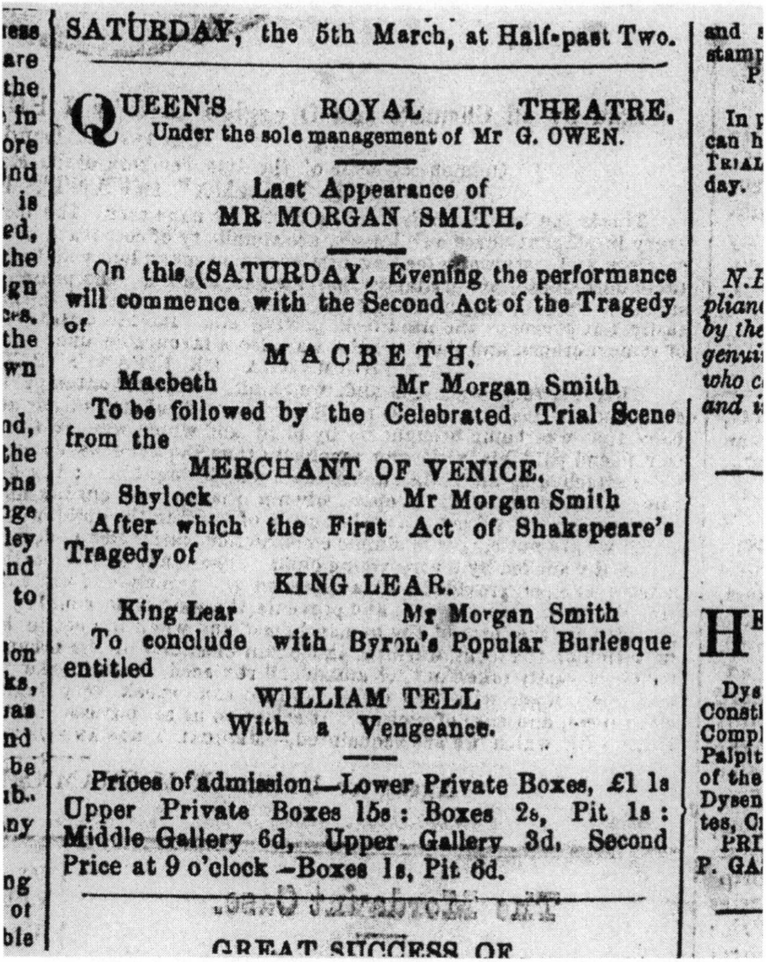
SATURDAY, the 5th March, at Half-past Two.

QUEEN'S ROYAL THEATRE,
Under the sole management of Mr G. OWEN.

Last Appearance of
MR MORGAN SMITH.

On this (SATURDAY, Evening the performance will commence with the Second Act of the Tragedy of
MACBETH.
Macbeth — Mr Morgan Smith
To be followed by the Celebrated Trial Scene from the
MERCHANT OF VENICE.
Shylock — Mr Morgan Smith
After which the First Act of Shakspeare's Tragedy of
KING LEAR.
King Lear — Mr Morgan Smith
To conclude with Byron's Popular Burlesque entitled
WILLIAM TELL
With a Vengeance.

Prices of admission—Lower Private Boxes, £1 1s Upper Private Boxes 15s : Boxes 2s, Pit 1s : Middle Gallery 6d, Upper Gallery 3d, Second Price at 9 o'clock —Boxes 1s, Pit 6d.

GREAT SUCCESS OF

Figure 20. Advertisement in *Dublin Advertising Gazette* for the Queen's Royal Theatre, Dublin, March 12, 1870. ©British Library Board, General Reference Collection, MFM. M8027. Reproduced with permission from the British Library.

Two weeks later Morgan Smith moved on to Birmingham, where his opening performance as Fabian won him a lengthy, enthusiastic endorsement from the *Birmingham Daily Post*:

"Even from our boyish days," when Lacy's theatrical characters were in vogue at one penny plain and twopence coloured, we have been led to set special store by the "coloured drama," and Mr. Morgan Smith, who made his first appearance here last night, in the character of a "coloured tragedian," is well fitted to confirm the traditions of our youth. Certainly no other actor within our experience could have extracted so much entertainment out of such poor materials as fell to his share on this occasion, and though the author may have suffered somewhat in the process the public unquestionably gained. "The Rising of the Tide," as the new production is entitled, turns out to be an old friend with a strange face—the clue to its identity being furnished by the sub-line, or "The Black Doctor of the Isle of Bourbon." It is in fact the old French melodrama of that name, which was played not very long ago at the Theatre Royal, but Mr. Rodgers [the Proprietor] has contrived to impart an air of novelty to it, both by the development of the critical incident which terminates the first act, and supplies the warrant for the new title of the piece, and by the pains he has bestowed upon the spectacular features. Another important innovation is the personation of the benevolent, but not altogether immaculate Black Doctor, *Fabian*, by a "gentleman of colour." In this part, Mr. Morgan Smith has certainly no need of the Prince of Morocco's apology, "Mislike me not for my complexion, the shadowed livery of the burnished sun," inasmuch as his complexion is his most obvious, though not quite his sole, qualification for the character; and even the vagaries of his accent and declamation derive a certain excuse, if not justification, from the evident consanguinity of the speaker with the race whose wrongs he illustrates, in the person of its typical hero. Mr. Morgan Smith, in fact, impersonates the Black Doctor with closer fidelity to nature than would be either possible or desirable to most English actors, and if the result is more realistic than agreeable, truth and the author, and not Mr. Smith, are to blame. As a matter of taste, we might prefer to witness Mr. Fechter's ideal rendering of the part; but in close fidelity to negro nature, physical and rhetorical, there can be no doubt that Mr. Smith's *Black Doctor* is by far the more genuine article. Mr. Fechter simply couldn't, if he would, go into such

166

essentially West Indian convulsions or inarticulate fury as Mr.
Smith displayed last night in all the great "situations." As both
the piece and the part are tolerably familiar to playgoers, we
need not review the performance at length. The social moral
inculcated, viz.—the indebility and wickedness of caste
distinctions among mixed populations—has lost much of its
significance through modern social and political changes, and
especially the liberation of the American Slave States; and the
general morality of the piece is, to say the least, like its literary
merits, very slight. As a spectacle, however, it has its uses, and
these Mr. Rodgers has turned to very creditable account. The
rising of the tide in the closing scene of the first act is very
ingeniously managed, though we think it would be better and
easier to raise the water round the rock than to lower the rock
into the water. Anyhow, the effect on the audience is thrilling,
and their satisfaction with it, judged by their applause, nothing
short of tremendous.[23]

After such a review, Morgan Smith was required to repeat playing
Fabian for the rest of that week.

At about this time, something else was happening that also must
have pleased Morgan Smith. His wife Harriet was back in Norwich,
perhaps at her parents' home, giving birth to her first child, who was
given the name Victor Clarence Goldspring Smith.[24] She now had
three sons to care for, but by the following month she was back on
tour with her husband, playing Desdemona as usual.

Morgan Smith spent his last week in Birmingham playing
Gambia, but at his benefit on Wednesday and again at his last
performance on Saturday, he added an abridged "Theodore; or,
the Fall of Magdala" as an afterpiece.[25] From there, it was on
to Wolverhampton, where he played Othello (with a different
Desdemona), Theodore, Chevalier, and possibly several other
characters during the week[26] before accepting an engagement for six
nights at Northampton, where the press totally ignored him.[27]

Then at Rochdale he performed as Fabian for four nights before
poor audiences[28] until he took his benefit on Friday "appearing to
advantage as Othello," accompanied by his wife who "sustained
very creditably the part of Desdemona. On Saturday *The Slave* was
well played, Mr. Smith enacting the part of Gambia."[29] Afterward, in
Lancaster he commenced a short engagement by playing Macbeth,

Gambia, Shylock and Othello. A critic for *The Era* wrote:

> Mr. Morgan Smith's engagement proving extremely satisfactory
> he was re-engaged for three nights, and on Monday appeared
> as Richelieu in Bulwer Lytton's play of that name....Mr.
> Smith's conception of the crafty minister was marked by much
> intelligence and dramatic power....Tuesday gave us *Dred*, and
> on Wednesday Mr Smith took his benefit, appearing along with
> Mrs Smith in the first act of *King Lear*, a laughable sketch called
> *Domestic Felicity*, and a drama named *King Theodore*.[30]

The title *Domestic Felicity* would at first glance appear to be
a revision of the title of Mark Lemon's farce *Domestic Economy*,
but when Morgan Smith and his wife played it again two months
later, they called it *Conjugal Felicity*, "in which [they] will sustain
their original characters of Mr. Simon Lullaby and Miss [*sic*] Letitia
Lullaby."[31] The identification of the dramatis personae makes it
clear that this was a two-hander written by H. Danvers, who initially
called it *A Comic Scene inculcating and entitled A CONJUGAL
LESSON in One Act*,[32] but it quickly became more commonly known
simply as *A Conjugal Lesson* and remained a popular afterpiece
of the era. In it, Simon and Letitia are a married couple, but she
is annoyed that Simon and his friend Mr Brown frequently go off
to a men's club together until late at night. She decides to sit up
and wait for his return, and when he comes home drunk and sleepy
well past midnight, they quarrel. When he falls asleep, she goes
through the pockets of his overcoat and discovers some unfamiliar
items: money, gloves, a cigar, a scented handkerchief, and a letter
addressed to another woman. She concludes he must be having an
affair and contemplates divorcing him. Then, when he wakes up and
she is asleep, he finds the same articles, and knowing they are not
his, he suspects she has been seeing another man. She awakes, and
they have another quarrel, each blaming the other of infidelity. When
she nods off again, Mr Brown calls through the window asking for
the return of his overcoat, which he had mistakenly exchanged for
Simon's overcoat at the club. Letitia awakes again, and she and
Simon are still at cross purposes until they realize that they had
made erroneous assumptions about one another. In the end they are
happily reconciled.

Although there is a third character in this comedy of errors, he is never seen on stage, and it would have been easy enough to arrange for someone to read his lines when he calls through the window. This was a play that Morgan Smith and his wife occasionally returned to in later years when they performed together in less formal settings than a theatre building.

In the summer months, when theatrical activity generally lessened, Morgan Smith had few opportunities to perform. Toward the end of June he played Gambia for two nights in Bolton,[33] and subsequently he joined a company that Charles Cooke was taking to Douglas, Isle of Man, but this did not materially change his luck. The *Isle of Man Times* reported that

> Notwithstanding the evident fact that the season at the Victoria Hall this summer would be financial a failure, no one expected that it would turn out so disastrously as it has done. The Manager, Mr Cooke, of the Edinburgh and Glasgow Theatres, brought over a good company, and went to considerable expense; but all to no avail; and, with expenses amounting it is said to £60 a week, he struggled on for three weeks, his company playing to 'houses' which did not average twenty shillings a night. On Saturday morning last he left the Island for Liverpool. The result of this sudden departure of the "Manager" was, that the company were left in a destitute condition, but we are glad to say that a benefit given to them on Thursday and Friday resulted in a few pounds being got together for their relief. The owners of the Hall granted the use of the room, and Mr Howell Thomas's band also gave their services.

To this, *The Era* added

> Since the above a benefit was given to Mr Morgan Smith, the coloured tragedian, who came on a starring engagement. The benefit, in which a number of local celebrities gave their services, and which was under Masonic patronage, was not so well attended as could have been wished, but the audience was a highly fashionable one.[34]

During these benefit performances Morgan Smith had recited "How They Brought the Good News from Aix to Ghent" and had teamed up with his wife Harriet to play in the "brilliant fashionable morceau CONJUGAL FIDELITY." Harriet had also pitched in a second time by starring in William Bayle Bernard's comedietta *The Dumb Belle*.[35] Bernard's published play contains a full synopsis of the plot:

> ELIZA, a young lady—rich, handsome, witty and accomplished— is an inmate of the mansion of her uncle, Mr. MANVERS. VIVIAN, who had been the playmate of her childhood and girlhood, had been absent, as an officer, for some six years. He has written to Mr. MANVERS, announcing his return; and in the letter he had mentioned an odd whim that had taken possession of him— he could not bear to hear ladies talk; indeed, he almost wished he could meet with a dumb one. This letter accidentally falling into ELIZA's hands, suggested to her the idea of assuming the character of a deaf and dumb girl, and so punishing VIVIAN for his slur upon the sex, and, perhaps, making him yield to her charms without the least wagging of her "little red rag." Mr. MANVERS, her maid, MARY, and, subsequently SMIRK, VIVIAN's valet, are all let into the secret. On VIVIAN's arrival, MANVERS informs him in a sad tone that ELIZA had the misfortune, a short time before, to be upset from a boat into the lake. Her life was saved, but the shock had deprived her of the power of both hearing and speaking. VIVIAN with difficulty suppresses his joy at finding a beautiful girl, and dumb, too! Here is the very climax of his wishes. Then follows a most amusing series of incidents. VIVIAN, struck with ELIZA's beauty when introduced by his uncle, has his admiration dashed, as if with a shower bath, when ELIZA puts an ear trumpet to her ear, and the uncle tells him that he must shout his compliments, or they will be unheard. This is so ludicrous that VIVIAN begins to wish the lady could speak a *little*. Soon after he hears a lady singing beautifully in the next room, and he falls in love with the unseen vocalist. This lady he is told is a visitor, and he begs to be introduced. Reasons are given why he cannot see her—she being, in fact, ELIZA. Then ELIZA gets up a neat little scheme, by which VIVIAN is led to an arbor, in which SMIRK, disguised as a veiled lady, sits. The young officer, thinking the figure to be that of the sweet singer, is about to kneel and declare his love, but is prevented by the presence of Mr. MANVERS and the rest. VIVIAN excuses himself for neglecting ELIZA by saying that she squinted and had such thick legs. Instantly ELIZA's tongue is loosened, and she gives him as good as he sends. Explanations and apologies follow, which lead to the union of VIVIAN and the DUMB BELLE.[36]

This would have been a highly amusing role for Harriet to play, one requiring quick-wittedness, an agile tongue, and a dumb show.

One of the reasons why the shows at Victoria Hall had not attracted many viewers is that there were a great number of other attractions in Douglas during these weeks. Hengler's Grand Cirque was in town, amateur athletic competitions were being held, as well as horse races, bowling saloons, a flower show, a regatta, and performances by the London Operatic Band.[37] Also, Mr Mercer H. Simpson, lessee of Douglas's Theatre Royal, was

> now receiving that measure of support to which he is undoubtedly entitled, and the result has been that there have been good houses during the week. The performances have been throughout the week very creditable, and the audiences as a [con]sequence been well pleased with the bill of fare with which they have been favoured.[38]

Victoria Hall lost out against such competition.

The benefit performances for Morgan Smith were held in Wellington Hall on July 28th and 29th "under the immediate patronage of the Athol and Tynwald Masonic Lodges, Nos. 1004 and 1212."[39] Morgan Smith may have been singled out for this kind of direct financial support because he and his wife were known to have an ailing four-month-old child, Victor. So worried were the parents about their son that they took the precaution of having him baptized on August 1st,[40] but he died and was buried at St. George's Chapel Yard five days later.[41] The cause of death was reported to have been cholera.[42]

Worse yet, Morgan Smith's eldest son Samuel, born to his former wife Mary Eliza six years and eight months earlier, also died a week later on August 12th and was buried at the same gravesite the following day.[43] His cause of death was said to be "water on the brain."[44] This left Morgan Smith with only one surviving son, Edgar, who was then three years, seven and a half months old, having been the last child born to Mary Eliza.

The loss of two children almost simultaneously must have been devastating. There is no indication where and in what circumstances the distraught parents spent the next six weeks. Late in September, Alfred Parry, who was then running the Theatre Royal in Bilston, a town two miles southeast of Wolverhampton, advertised in *The Era* that he wanted actors "for Completion of Mr Morgan Smith's tour." He specified needing actors and actresses for pantomimes in particular: "FIRST LOW COMEDIAN, Gentlemen for Heavies to share the Load, First Old Man, and Ladies for Responsible Business. Also,...Lady Dancers for Harlequin and Columbine, &c."[45]

There is no record of Morgan Smith appearing in any pantomimes during the rest of the year, but local papers recorded that he did act with Parry's company in Shrewsbury in October, performing an assortment of his customary roles—initially as Gambia, Hamlet, Richard III, Claude Melnotte, Rolla, and Macbeth in his first week,[46] during which he was "awarded immense applause,"[47] and then as Shylock, Othello (with Harriet as Desdemona), Dred, Fabian, Chevalier, and Richelieu the following week.[48] *The Era* also reported that "In *Richelieu* Mr Smith displayed his talents in the difficult part of the Cardinal, and was much applauded. The part of Julie was prettily and effectively rendered by Mrs Smith, a correct and painstaking actress."[49] As a kind of encore, Morgan Smith closed out the season at Shrewsbury by appearing as Mephistopheles in *Faust and Marguerite* on Monday, October 17th.[50] Not a single role had been repeated in his fifteen nights there.

Parry then moved his company to Ludlow (population 9,118 in 1871), where Morgan Smith enacted Othello on Friday, the 21st, in "a very interesting performance, wanting, perhaps, a little toning down, but decidedly intelligent." Also singled out in *The Era*'s review was "Mrs Morgan Smith, whose plaintive and tender acting of Desdemona was highly appreciated."[51]

Three weeks later, after separating from Parry's company, they turned up in Ross-on-Wye, an even smaller town (population 3,724 in 1871) in Hereford about fifty-five miles south of Ludlow where

> On Monday, the 14th inst., Mr Morgan Smith, the colored tragedian, gave an entertainment at the Corn Exchange, assisted by Mrs. Morgan Smith and Mr J. F. Rudge. The performances consisted of a pleasing little comedietta *A Silent Woman*, selections from *Hamlet*, several poems, and terminated with a laughable *morceau*, *Domestic Felicity*. The audience was not numerous, but appeared to enjoy Mr Smith's elocutionary powers.[52]

Rudge had also been in Parry's company and had performed with them in *Richelieu* on October 15th. He now must have provided the voice of Mr. Brown in *Domestic Felicity*. He was also needed to play one of the men in Thomas Hailes Lacy's *A Silent Woman*, which Lacy admitted on the first page of the edition he self-published, was "adapted [*sic*] from a recollection of Mr. Bayle Bernard's 'The Dumb Belle.'"[53] This was a seven-page condensation featuring only three characters: Mr. Sandford, Sandford's daughter Marianne, and Arthur Merton, the suitor who cannot stand talkative women but is tricked into believing that Marianne, after a boating accident, was not only dumb but also deaf. Much of the humor in the condensation, as in the original farce, comes from the interactions of Merton and Marianne, when she, using her ear trumpet, deliberately misinterprets whatever he says. He becomes terribly frustrated by the tedious struggle to converse sensibly in this manner, so when she drops her disguise and reveals that she can still hear and speak normally, he is overjoyed, and they agree to marry. Morgan Smith must have played Merton, with Rudge filling in as Sandford.

This was the kind of light entertainment—a series of short sketches, readings and recitations—that Morgan Smith and Harriet began to offer in small communities when they could find no other work to do in established theatres. As they grew older, it increasingly became a way for them to be able to continue to perform.

This year, with Fabian and Gambia again leading the way, melodramas and romances continued to outnumber Shakespearean plays by about two to one, with a new category—farces—gaining slightly in frequency. *Theodore* and the first act of *King Lear* were also significant new ventures. Morgan Smith performed mainly in England, but he toured parts of Ireland three times as well as once to Wales and once to the Isle of Man. Nine of his stops were at places where he had performed previously, suggesting he was very welcome to return, but he also was invited to appear at seven new sites where he had never been seen before, suggesting perhaps that he had by now acquired something of a reputation as a professional actor. However, the total number of his performances this year was lower than the number given in past years, and this may have been an early sign that he was beginning to have less success in securing engagements.

Endnotes

1   *The Era*, December 26, 1869.

2   *Maidstone Telegraph*, January 15, 1870.

3   *The Era*, January 30, 1870.

4   *Belfast Evening News*, January 26, 1870.

5   *The Era*, February 6, 1870.

6   *Freeman's Journal*, February 2, 1870; *Evening Freeman*, February 2, 1870.

7   *Dublin Evening Standard*, February 7, 1870.

8   *Saunders's Newsletter*, February 7, 1870.

9   *Freeman's Journal*, February 7, 1870.

10 *Whitehaven News*, February 17, 1870.

11 *Illustrated Sporting and Theatrical News*, February 26, 1870.

12 *Freeman's Journal*, February 22, 1870; *Evening Freeman*, February 22, 1870.

13 *The Era*, February 27, 1870.

14 *The Era*, March 6, 1870.

15 There have been many books written about this war. See, for example, Sven Rubenson, *King of Kings: Tewodros of Ethiopia* (Addis Ababa: Haile Sellassie I Univeristy in association with Oxford University Press, 1966), Volker Matthies, *The Siege of Magdala: The British Empire against the Emperor of Ethiopia* (Princeton: Markus Wiener, 2012), Frederick Myatt, *The March to Magdala: The Abyssinian War of 1868* (London: Leo Cooper, 1970), and Percy Arnold, *Prelude to Magdala: Emperor Theodore of Ethiopia and British Diplomacy* (London: Bellew Publishing, 1991).

16 Niall Ferguson, *Empire: How Britain Made the Modern World* (London: Allen Lane, The Penguin Press, 2003), 179.

17 Alan Moorhead, *The Blue Nile* (New York: Harper & Row, 1972), 306.

18 G. A. Henty, *The March to Magdala* (London: Tinsley Brothers, 1868), 6, 222, 390.

19 *Dublin Evening News*, March 3, 1870; *Dublin Evening Mail*, March 5, 1970; *Freeman's Journal*, March 10, 1870.

20 *Dublin Advertising Gazette*, March 5, 1870, and reprinted in the *Commercial Journal and Family Herald*, March 12, 1870.

21 *Saunders's Newsletter*, March 7, 1870.

22 *Dublin Evening Standard*, March 12, 1870.

23 *Birmingham Daily Post*, March 29, 1870. Charles Albert Fechter, an Anglo-French actor, was known for his Shakespearean and melodramatic roles.

24 The exact date of his birth is not known. The only record we have states that his birth was registered "at Norwich June Qtr 1870 4b 161." See the *England and Wales FreeBMD Birth Index, 1837-1915*.

25 See the playbills held at the Library of Birmingham.

26 *The Era*, April 17, 1870.

27 *The Era*, April 24, 1870.

28 *The Era*, May 8, 1870.

29 *The Era*, May 15, 1870.

30 *The Era*, May 29, 1870.

31 *Isle of Man Times and General Advertiser*, July 23, 1870.

32 Published by Thomas Hailes Lacy in London around 1859.

33 *The Era*, June 26, 1870.

34 *The Era*, August 7, 1870. The report from the *Isle of Man Times* was also quoted here.

35 *Isle of Man Times and General Advertiser*, July 23, 1870.

36 [William] Bayle Bernard, *The Dumb Belle: A Farce in One Act*. Chicago: Dramatic Publishing Company, [1841]), 3.

37 *Isle of Man Times and General Advertiser*, August 6, 1870.

38 *Manx Sun*, August 13, 1870.

39 *Isle of Man Times and General Advertiser*, July 23, 1870.

40 *Isle of Man Parish Registers, 1598-1950* (Salt Lake City: Family Search, 2013).

41 *Register of Burials, Parish of St. George, Douglas, Isle of Man.* See also Ancestry.com. Web: Isle of Man Burial Index, 1598-2003.

42 *The Era*, August 21, 1870.

43 *Isle of Man Parish Registers, 1598-1950* (Salt Lake City: Family Search, 2013).

44 *Isle of Man Times and General Advertiser*, August 13, 1870.

45 *The Era*, September 25, 1870.

46 *Shrewsbury Chronicle*, September 30, 1870.

47 *Eddowe's Shrewsbury Journal*, October 5, 1870.

48 *Eddowe's Shrewsbury Journal*, October 12, 1870.

49 *The Era*, October 23, 1870.

50 Ibid.

51 *The Era*, October 30, 1870.

52 *The Era*, November 20, 1870.

53 Thomas Hailes Lacy, *A Silent Woman: A Farce, in One Act* (London: Hailes Lacy, [1835]), 1. John Russell Stephens has reported that "Lacy specialized in buying up copyrights at knock-down prices from impecunious dramatists; but on occasions he assumed copyright without authority." See Stephens, "Lacy, Thomas Hailes (1809-1873)," *Oxford Dictionary of National Biography*, Oxford University Press, 2004; online edn, Jan 2008.

9

1871-1872

Morgan Smith was unemployed for the last seven weeks of 1870, and another week passed before he was called back to perform again at Shrewsbury, where *The Era* confirmed that he had "established himself as a favourite on his first visit a few months ago."[1] He was also a favorite in Wrexham,[2] his next stop, where the *Wrexham Advertiser* reported that he opened as Hamlet and was expected to appear for the next two nights "in a powerful drama written expressly for him,"[3] possibly *Theodore, All But Lost*, or an entirely new play, but instead he came on for three nights as Gambia. A week later the same paper said, "He displayed great power as a tragedian in this piece, and in that part wherein he acknowledges his freedom (purchased by indomitable bravery) he seemed to feel intensely the boon which a poor African slave could scarcely help feeling when the shackles of bondage were snapped off his wrists."[4] On Friday he played Claude Melnotte in *The Lady of Lyons* with Harriet taking the role of Pauline. He also "gave some choice dramatic recitations; and the whole concluded with 'Uncle Tom's Cabin' wherein Mr. Smith appeared as 'George Harris.'"[5]

Then it was off to the Royal Albert Theatre in Landport for twelve nights, the first six of which were to be devoted to "Production of [Morgan Smith's] New Drama by Chas. Daly, Esq., entitled 'War.'"[6] The script of this play has not survived,[7] but a detailed description some of the action in it in a newspaper advertisement gives an impression of what was to be shown:

WAR!

FRANCE AND RUSSIA.

WHEREAS it is well-known to all the world that these two countries, in which thousands of lives are daily sacrificed, the horrors of which no tongue can accurately describe. In order therefore that all classes may see and judge for themselves of this great calamity, the MANAGER of the

ROYAL ALBERT THEATRE, LANDPORT,

Has made a special engagement for the production

On MONDAY NEXT, January 23rd,

Of a new and beautiful dramatic play by C. Daley [*sic*] Esq.,

entitled

WAR!!!

and further to increase the attraction, he has, regardless

of expense, entered…into an engagement for

A FEW NIGHTS ONLY,

with the Great American Colored Tragedian

MR. MORGAN SMITH,

Who will appear Nightly as REUBEN FIDELE.

The piece will be produced on a most elaborate scale,

with especial notice being directed to

The Barricade!—1st Act.

House on the Seine!—2nd Act.

The Prussian Spy!—3rd Act.

and more particularly to

The Attack on the Fortress!—4th Act.

And further, that it may be within the power of all

classes of the community to witness this great spectacle,

THE PRICES OF ADMISSION WILL BE—

Boxes, 1s, 6d. Stalls, 1s. Pit, 6d. Gallery 3d.[8]

Reuben Fidele was said by *The Era* to be "a freed South American slave" in this "new dramatic play (the first time on any stage)."[9] It ran for a week, but on February 1st the *Hampshire Telegraph* reported on a disruption that led to legal action being taken against an unruly member of the audience:

> Two informations were laid down by Mr. William Montague, manager of the Royal Albert Theatre, Lake-road, Landport, and by Mr. Frank Clifford, actor at the above theatre, against a young man named Doudney, for throwing oranges on the stage, and otherwise causing a disturbance....The bench were unanimously of opinion that the offence was not against [Montague] alone but against good-conduct and public order."[10]

Apparently the oranges were not aimed at Morgan Smith. According to *The Era*, he continued in this role the following week until his benefit on Friday, "when he performed Othello, a character well suited to his talent. Mrs. Morgan Smith supported him as Desdemona. Saturday was the last night of Mr. M. Smith's engagement, when he enacted the role of Gambia in the play *The Slave*, concluding each evening with *War*."[11]

When he moved on to Leicester to play Reuben Fidele again, an announcement appeared in *The Era* stating that

> "War."—This Drama, as Played by Mr. MORGAN SMITH with unbounded applause, and written expressly for him in October last by Charles Daly, Esq., having lately been represented (with Mr Smith's permission) with an additional Act (which Act continuing to be played), Mr Morgan Smith has determined to alter the title, and begs to announce that in future this great Drama will be entitled "THE AFRICAN SPY," being an episode of the Franco-Prussian Struggle in Three Acts.[12]

However, a question was raised about how this drama had been advertised:

WHAT is the "complexional part" of the war in France? The question arises upon the perusal of an advertisement in that interesting paper the *Era*, whereby "Mr. MORGAN SMITH, coloured tragedian," announces to managers that he is prepared to produce his new three act drama, written expressly for him, entitled "War," the scenes and incidents of which are laid in France "embracing the features of the present struggle (complexional part)." Mr. MORGAN SMITH evidently resides in some favoured locality where he has not the fear of Mr. INGLE before his eyes, or he would not talk about a drama "embracing the features" of anything, least of all of "a struggle." But, passing that by, which are the "features" of the struggle that have a special claim to be regarded as "complexional?" The "requisitioning" and "the saving" are features we know, and thanks to the extension of telegraphy, we are not wholly unacquainted with the devotional. But which are the 'complexional?" Is it possible that "Mr. MORGAN SMITH, coloured tragedian," thus delicately refers to his own "features?"[13]

As in Landport, Morgan Smith ended his run at Leicester by performing as Othello at his benefit on Friday, at which time he "was listened to and applauded by an attentive auditory. Mr. Morgan Smith's conception of the misguided Moor was a careful performance and gave evidence of much study; and his wife, who represented Desdemona, was most pleasing....Mr Morgan Smith played Gambia, the Slave, [as well as Reuben Fidele] on Saturday to a crowded house."[14]

His next engagement took place at West Hartlepool a month later, when he played his more familiar roles: Gambia, Shylock, Claude Melnotte, Othello (with Harriet supporting him as usual), and Richard III. On his benefit night he added a couple of dramatic recitations: "'Grand Charge of the Light Brigade,' and [Thomas John Ouseley's] feeling and graphic Poem, 'Drink up, have one more," both of which were said, with some exaggeration, to have been "as given by him before the President and Governors of the United States of America."[15]

Figure 21. Playbill of the New Theatre Royal, West Hartlepool, March 24, 1871. DF.WOD/2875. Reproduced with permission from the Tyne & Wear Archives.

Three weeks later he was performing at the Corn Exchange in tiny Earlston (population 1,168 in 1871):

> The great attraction was the acting of Mr Morgan Smith, whose histrionic powers were thought very highly of by competent judges. Unfortunately the company did not succeed in drawing very good houses. On Saturday they wound up with a concert in the Christy Minstrel style, which was very thinly attended also.[16]

Engagements were now getting much more difficult to find, and we do not know how Morgan Smith and Harriet managed to support themselves in the meantime. Their next opportunity to perform may not have come until three months later, when they revisited Dundee. Morgan Smith opened as Gambia, sustaining "the part of the noble-minded slave with his usual power and naturalness,"[17] and the *Northern Warder* and *Dundee Courier* tried to stimulate interest by billing him as the "Greatest Success ever known in Dundee" and "the only Tragedian of Colour on the Universal Stage."[18] To finish the week he went on to play Hamlet, Macbeth, Claude

Melnotte, Richard III, Dred, and on his benefit night both Othello and Chevalier as well as some dramatic recitations.[19]

Four more months may have passed before another opportunity arose, this time at the Prince of Wales Theatre in Glasgow, where Morgan Smith had appeared two years earlier. The *Glasgow Herald* welcomed him back:

> [He] began a seven nights' engagement in this theatre on Saturday night, when he was warmly received as *Richard III* by a good house. Last night the play produced was "Othello," and the audience, though scanty, were not niggard of their applause. Mr Smith, of course, supported the leading *rôle* of the dusky and hot-blooded lover, and, by the careful and energetic character of his delivery, showed that his qualifications for the part are something more than skin-deep. His action is always dignified, and not unfrequently effective, while his delivery of the more impassioned passages, although too often marred by outbursts of that rant which delights the gallery, is spirited and dramatic....This evening Mr Smith will make his appearance as *Shylock*, and on the following night as *Gambia.*[20]

The *North British Daily Mail* added that

> As Shylock, Mr Smith displayed histrionic talent of a high order, his conception of the character being marked by considerable breadth and vigour. In the earlier scenes, and notably in that when the Jew resolves upon his artful scheme, the acting was especially good, and called forth abundant expression of approbation on the part of the audience.[21]

Toward the end of the week Morgan Smith took his benefit, and the *Glasgow Herald* remarked that

> The entertainment provided was certainly lengthy enough to satisfy the most ardent lover of the drama, comprising as it did "The Rising of the Tide," in five acts, and "Dred," the latter professing to be a representation of slave life. Mr Smith appeared in both pieces. Between the dramas he recited Tennyson's "Charge of the Light Brigade" in a very unimpressive manner and a temperance poem, "Drink up, have one glass more."[22]

There is no verifiable record of any additional performances by Morgan Smith in the remaining six weeks of 1871, though it is entirely possible that he and Harriet may have occasionally found employment in a few small towns.

The new year got off to a more promising start, albeit initially in rather small venues. In Brighouse (population 12,814 in 1871), about thirty miles northeast of Manchester, Morgan Smith and Harriet "appeared in some of Shakespeare's best and other popular plays, to crowded houses" during the second week of January.[23] From there they moved to Macclesfield, a larger town (population 59,339 in 1871) about 20 miles south of Manchester, where he performed as Macbeth, Shylock, Rolla, Count Walbourg, Othello (no doubt with Harriet's help), and Fabian. "In the various *roles* in which Mr Morgan Smith has appeared during the week connoisseurs have pronounced him an excellent and talented *artiste* in the line he takes. He has been several times called before the curtain. The place has been well patronised."[24]

However, at the end of his second week there, an incident occurred that attracted attention in the press. Here is the account that appeared in *The Era*:

A TRAGEDIAN IN A FIX.—The Manager of the Macclesfield Theatre a fortnight ago engaged the services of Mr. Morgan Smith, a coloured gentleman and actor of no mean repute. On Saturday, the 27th ult., the last day of his stay in Macclesfield, he sent over to Mr. Samuel Ackroyd's, Chester-gate, tailor, for a few pairs of trousers to select from. The parcel was sent, and a pair was selected and paid for, and the remaining pairs were returned. The impression of Mr. Ackroyd's assistant was that instead of one pair being kept there had been two. This caused Mr. Ackroyd to demand the alleged missing pair. Mr. Smith strongly asserted his innocence, and was naturally indignant that such a false accusation should be made against him. Mr. Ackroyd was positive two pairs had been kept instead of one, and threatened Mr. Smith with the police. The threat was carried out, and Mr. Smith accompanied the police to the police-station, followed by a large crowd of people. Mr. Smith demanded that a search should be made at his lodging. Accordingly the police searched every nook and corner and everything belonging to him, but no trousers could be found. Mr. Smith was accordingly released from the custody of the police, and performed his *role* in *Othello* the same evening. We learn that the matter will not

183

rest here as Mr. Smith has placed the matter in the hands of a solicitor, and is determined that Mr. Ackroyd shall answer for his most unwarrantable and unjustifiable conduct.[25]

At Warren's Theatre in Carmarthan (population 12,915 in 1871), Wales, the following week, Morgan Smith, according to further reports in *The Era*,

> made his first appearance here on Monday [January 29th] in the character of Hamlet. He met with a most enthusiastic reception from a crowded house, which testified its appreciation of his acting by frequent bursts of applause....The remainder of the week we had *The Merchant of Venice*, *The Stranger*, *Othello*, and *The Slave*. The leading parts have been sustained by Mr Morgan Smith in a vigorous and artistic manner. The Theatre has been crowded during his stay, and the performances have given great satisfaction.[26]

> Mr Morgan Smith, the coloured tragedian, completed his engagement here on the 3d, when he played Gambia in the drama called *The Slave*. His rendering of the part was highly picturesque, and gave great delight to a well filled house. Mr Smith has made many friends here, not only on account of his talent as an actor, but for his gentlemanly behaviour on all occasions.[27]

Then a month passed before he landed a contract for two weeks at the Alexandra Opera House in Sheffield (population 162,271 in 1871), a town large enough to enable him to repeat several of his most popular roles. He played Gambia five times, Chevalier de St. George thrice, Fabian twice, and gave single performances as Shylock, Hamlet, and Dred on other nights. The *Sheffield Daily Telegraph* praised all of his performances, saying as Shylock, "his acting showed that he had given the character a careful study."[28] And his performances as Fabian and the Chevalier prompted the comment that "so good acting has not often been seen on the boards of the Alexandra."[29] But it was his appearance as Hamlet on his benefit night that excited the most interest:

> For the Prince of Denmark to be played by a man of colour, seems at first to upset the very idea of him who was the glass of fashion and the mould of form; but after seeing Mr. Smith on the

stage it can be said that the assumption of the character by him does not really appear so incongruous after all. In the dialogues, especially those with Polonius and the Queen Mother, Mr. Smith was exceedingly effective, and rendered the text in a very clear and intelligent manner; but the beauty of the soliloquies was somewhat marred by his broken accent and by a slight tendency to "saw the air too much." His Hamlet, however, on the whole, was very enjoyable....Mr. Smith afterwards recited "The Charge of the Light Brigade."[30]

Another month passed until he was invited back to Macclesfield to play a variety of roles for nearly two weeks. *The Era* said in these he was very successful. On Friday, April 12th, at a benefit for manager Brinsley Sheridan, "the part of Shylock [was] ably sustained by Mr. Morgan Smith," and "On Saturday Mr. Smith appeared in the drama of *Dred*. On both occasions there was a very large audience. On Monday was introduced *Pizarro*. A capital exponent of the principal part was found in Mr. Smith."[31]

On Saturday [April 20th] was placed upon the stage Shakespeare's tragedy of *Macbeth*, the title-*role* being portrayed by Mr M. Smith, the coloured tragedian....On Monday, for the benefit of Mr Morgan Smith, was produced the French drama of *Chevalier* [*de*] *St. George*. Mr. M. Smith was a true exponent of the part of St. George, and the Countess was represented by Mrs. Morgan Smith, who appeared for this night only. [In addition,] Mr. Smith addressed the audience in a very proper speech, referring to the false charge lately made against him, and for which he the previous Saturday had obtained the paltry sum of £5 damages—but even that was sufficient to vindicate his character.[32]

This outcome of his court case concerning a missing pair of trousers was discussed at some length in *The Era*:

A Coloured Tragedian Charged with Felony

On the 20th January last it will be remembered Mr Morgan Smith, the coloured tragedian, was charged by Samuel Ackroyd, tailor and draper Chestergate, Macclesfield with having stolen a pair of trousers, value 18s, an account of which unfounded charge appeared in this journal. Mr Smith, of course, instituted proceedings against his accuser, and the matter was entered at the Queen's Bench. The case, however, was sent down to Macclesfield to be tried before Joseph St. John Yates, Esq., Judge of the County Court, and came on for hearing on Saturday last. Mr Jordam and Mr Richardson, barrister, of Manchester, instructed by Mr T. Cooper, solicitor, Congleton appeared for the plaintiff, and Mr. Addison and Mr. Yates (son of the Judge), instructed by Mr J. Barclay, was for the defendandt [*sic*]. The damages were laid at £500. The counsel for the plaintiff detailed the circumstances of the case, pointing out that his client was a gentleman of no mean education and refinement; that he was an accomplished member of an American University and an actor of good repute; that he had been subjected to a gross indignity upon the responsibility of the defendant, and concluded by asking the Jury to compensate him for having been the victim of so disgraceful and unfounded a charge. The plaintiff, his wife, the police, and other witnesses having deposed to the facts of the case.

Mr. Addison addressed the Jury for the defence, describing the case as a paltry one; pointing out the improbability of a respectable young man like his client making such a charge without some grounds for his suspicion, and contending that five pairs of trousers were taken to the plaintiff's lodgings, and only three were returned, one pair having been paid for, and the other being missed. In support of this theory he called the defendant's apprentices.

The judge summed up, remarking to the Jury that the only question they would have to decide was whether there had been a felony committed, and if there had, had it been committed by the plaintiff. A deal had been said by the learned counsel for the defendant respecting the calling of the plaintiff; that, he said, had nothing to do with the case; there were as respectable men in the dramatic profession as in any other walk-in-life, and the plaintiff, although he was a man of colour, had as much right to receive justice at the hands of an English bar as an Englishman.

The Jury retired to consider their verdict, and in a little over ten minutes entered into court, and on the Foreman being asked by the Registrar whether they had considered their verdict, said they had, and found a verdict for the plaintiff—£5 damages.[33]

Morgan Smith, pleased to have been exonerated, inserted his own statement about the case in *The Era*:

A CARD

Mr. MORGAN SMITH begs to announce to his many friends, Readers of *The Era*, and all those who feel an interest in the Drama, and Professionals, the highly-successful ending of his action against Samuel Acroyd [*sic*], Draper, of Macclesfield, in the matter of the article appearing in *The Era* in the early part of February last, entitled "A Tragedian in a Fix." This Action, instituted in the Queen's Bench, was tried at Macclesfield, simply from my inability and Indisposition to request Two Friends to place their bonds in the Court for from One to Five Hundred Pounds each. The Jury, after being absent about ten minutes, found that no felony had been committed, that the goods were never "brought," and gave me £5 damages, placing all cost on the defendant, who, I am told by my Solicitor, will have to pay some £105. It will be gratifying to my friends to know as regards the small figure of damages. But for the fact (universally) expressed in this town of the marked features of the Jury, it being asserted that such a Jury were never before called together, the figure of damages would have been far greater. There is but one expression in the town, and that is of derision and disgust for the contemptible smallness of the estimate. As far as I am concerned and my many kind friends this verdict, which carries with it wanton error, palpable prejudice, because of my Profession and foreign line with a far more grave feature, as is proud a record and result of the villainous action as I desire. Money never being my object; my character, which has stood unstained for Thirty-nine years, all.

MORGAN SMITH,
Tragedian, and only recognized Coloured legitimate Artist in the world.[34]

This prompted further discussion of the matter in a number of papers,[35] most notably *The Orchestra*:

"King Solomon was a worthy peer," says Shakespeare, who further informs us what his Majesty's trousers cost him. Five shillings is certainly not an exorbitant sum to pay for this article of clothing in these days, however it may have struck the royal customer of the House of Blois. But Othello's trousers would have cost him still less, if the statement of Samuel Ackroyd, tailor and draper of Macclesfield, could be believed. This bold outfitter charged Othello, (through his representative, Mr. Morgan Smith, coloured tragedian) with having stolen a pair of trousers, value 18s. Mr. Morgan Smith, being acquitted of the charge, brought an action against the tailor, and laid his damages at £500, from which the jury struck the two ciphers and found for the plaintiff. Mr. Smith's counsel pointed out that his client was a gentleman of no mean education and refinement; that he was an accomplished member of an American University and an actor of good repute. A conflict of feelings experienced by Mr. Morgan Smith on procuring the verdict—his delight at being justified by the jury, and his disgust at not getting more than £5—finds curious illustration in "a card" which he has since made public in the theatrical organ.

[Here follows a reprinting of Morgan Smith's entire statement in *The Era*.]

The last sentence is unique, and says much for the teaching at American universities. But what *does* Mr. Morgan Smith mean when he says, "It will be gratifying to my friends to know as regards the small figure of damages?" Does he seriously mean that his friends will be glad to learn that he did not get more? or is he speaking ironically? or does the latter clause belong to the next sentence? There is another mystery, which we implore him to elucidate. He says that the damages would have been greater "but for the marked features of the jury." We are most anxious to know about these marked features. Was it their noses? Or were the jury pock-marked? Or did they all horribly squint? It is most important that Mr. Morgan Smith should complete our information on this point, because it if can be ascertained that jurymen who have marked features are prone to take a lower estimate of the plaintiff's case than other and ordinary jurymen, a very interesting psychico-physiological discovery will have been reached. We fancy that the marked features of the Macclesfield jury must have been their mouths, which resembled the mouths of Cheshire cats. We infer this, because Mr. Morgan Smith concludes by alluding to their "palpable prejudice because of my profession and foreign line, with a far more grave feature." That is it, then. Mr. Smith is a man of serious and earnest countenance, and these grinning jurymen were prejudiced against him because of his gravity. If he had worn a smile like Mr. Tenniel's tomcat in "Alice in Wonderland," their sympathies would have been touched and their verdict augmented.

Upon leaving Macclesfield, if the near absence of verifiable records can be believed,[36] Morgan Smith appears to have been out of work in established theatres for two and a half months until he secured an engagement in Warrington, a small town (population 29,894 in 1871) in Cheshire midway between Manchester and Liverpool, where *The Era* recorded that "a very cordial reception greeted him. He chose for his *debut Macbeth*, and if applause proves success, then Mr Smith was very successful....Mr Smith appeared as Hamlet on Tuesday. *Pizarro* was performed on Wednesday and *The Black Doctor* on Thursday."[37] On Friday, "Mr. Smith appeared as 'Othello'—a part well suited for him—and Mrs. Smith as 'Desdemona.' There was a good house, and Mr. Smith would no doubt reap a substantial benefit. On Monday night 'The Merchant of Venice' will be produced; and the 'Child of the Sun' on Tuesday; the performance each evening terminating with 'Dred.'"[38] He also managed to squeeze in a performance of Richard III on Saturday, July 30th.[39]

Thereafter it becomes difficult to trace Morgan Smith's movements and activities with any certainty because he was playing in places so small that they had no newspapers of their own and remained outside the range of *The Era*'s coverage of provincial theatre circuits. For instance, in early December he reported "having concluded Fourteen Consecutive Weeks at Mexborough,"[40] a hamlet (population 4,316 in 1871) about seventeen miles northeast of Sheffield. During this interval he had received an invitation in September to appear as a leading man at a theatre in Nantwich (population 6,673 in 1871), another village in Cheshire about eighteen miles west of Stoke-on-Trent and about twenty-seven miles southwest of Macclesfield,[41] but we do not know if he was able to accept an engagement there.

The only hard evidence we have of him performing in November is a brief account of his appearance for six nights at the Theatre in

Runcorn (population 30,534 in 1871), thirty miles east of Liverpool, the first three nights of which were spent playing Macbeth ("very successful"), Rolla, and Count Walbourg ("gaining the hearty applause of the audience").[42]

He ended the year impersonating Hamlet and Count Walbourg on December 30-31 at the Victoria Theatre in West Hartlepool (population 21,110 in 1871) in a dramatic company run by W. C. Dews. Harriet also joined this company as a co-equal star. Her first assignment was to play Ophelia in *Hamlet* and then Mrs. Haller opposite Morgan Smith as Count Walbourg in *The Stranger* on New Year's Eve.[43]

The total number of his known performances dropped significantly during this biennium, but actually it might have grown had there been published evidence on his activities in the fourteen weeks he spent in Mexborough. All we know from the limited data available is that melodramas continued to outnumber Shakespearean plays, and one new military drama written for him had been performed, but two others that he had commissioned and paid for, *All But Lost* and *Theodore*, were no longer being played. Morgan Smith was finding a lack of interest in these speculative investments.

Endnotes

1   *The Era*, January 15, 1871.

2   *Wrexham Advertiser*, January 14, 1871.

3   Ibid.

4   *Wrexham Advertiser*, January 21, 1871.

5   Ibid.

6   *The Era*, January 22, 1871.

7   It should not be confused with T. W. Robertson's *War: A Drama in Three Acts* (New York and London: Samuel French, n.d.), which opened a week earlier at London's St. James Theatre but with a different cast of characters. It is described at some length in Nicoll, *A History of English Drama, 1660-1900*, 5: 129-31

8   *Portsmouth Times and Naval Gazette*, January 21, 1871.

9   *The Era*, January 29, 1871.

10   *Hampshire Telegraph*, February 1, 1871.

11 *The Era*, February 12, 1871.

12 Ibid. In *The Era*, June 30, 1872, Daly advertised that in addition to having sold his play *The African Spy* to Morgan Smith, he had written and sold plays to a number of other actors and theatre managers. Morgan Smith had opened at Leicester on Saturday, February 11, by playing a melodramatic role he never repeated: Hassan in Matthew Gregory Lewis's *The Castle Spectre; or, Ormond the Pirate*. See the *Leicester Chronicle*, February 11, 1871.

13 *Exeter and Plymouth Gazette*, February 3, 1871. *The Era* had inserted the advertisement in its issue of June 22, 1871.

14 *The Era*, February 26, 1871.

15 See the playbills held in the Robert Wood Collection, Theatre and Entertainments Section, at the Tyne and Wear Museum, Newcastle-upon-Tyne.

16 *Berwickshire News and General Advertiser*, April 18, 1871.

17 *Northern Warder*, July 18, 1871.

18 Ibid. *Dundee Courier*, July 18-20, 1871.

19 *Northern Warder*, July 21, 1871.

20 *Glasgow Herald*, November 14, 1871.

21 *North British Daily Mail*, November 17, 1871, quoted in *The Era*, November 26, 1871.

22 *Glasgow Herald*, November 18, 1871.

23 *Huddersfield Chronicle and West Yorkshire Advertiser*, January 13, 1872.

24 *The Era*, January 21, 1872.

25 *The Era*, February 4, 1872. A version of this account was carried in other papers as well.

26 Ibid.

27 *The Era*, February 11, 1872.

28 *Sheffield Daily Telegraph*, March 2, 1872.

29 *Sheffield Daily Telegraph*, March 9, 1872.

30 Ibid.

31 *The Era*, April 21, 1872.

32 *The Era* April 28, 1872.

33 Ibid.

34 Ibid.

35 *The Orchestra*, May 3, 1872. See also the reports in the *Cheshire Observer*, April 27, 1872; *Morpeth Herald*, April 27, 1872; *Fife Herald*, April 25, 1872;

and *Isle of Man Times*, April 27, 1872.

36 An exception was the report in the *Todmorden & District News*, June 14, 1872, recording that two days earlier in Hebden Bridge (population 3,666 in 1871), near Halifax, Mr. and Mrs. Morgan Smith gave "an entertainment in St. George's Hall, consisting of dramatic readings, &c. The audience was of a very limited character a few short of twenty persons being present. The readings and impersonations were creditable and the few who were present appeared pleased."

37 *The Era*, July 21, 1872.

38 *Warrington Examiner*, July 20, 1872.

39 *The Era*, July 28, 1872.

40 *The Era*, December 8, 1872.

41 *The Era,* September 22, 1872.

42 *The Era,* November 17, 1872.

43 See the playbill in the Robert Wood Collection, Theatre and Entertainments Section, at the Tyne and Wear Museum, Newcastle-upon-Tyne.

10

1873-1874

M organ Smith and Harriet remained with W. C. Dews's troupe for two weeks, performing a different play every night. Most of these featured characters Morgan Smith had acted many times before—Chevalier (in the same romantic play but retitled *Caste! or, The Bondmen Brothers*) as well as Richelieu, Dred, Macbeth, Fabian, and Gambia—but in each of them Harriet now took the leading female role. They also appeared in four plays in which there is no record of their having acted in before, but it is possible they may have worked up these roles in the fourteen weeks they were in Mexborough. Indeed, the demands of performing in such a tiny town for several months may have forced them to develop a more diversified repertoire rather quickly, for local audiences might have been unwilling to sit through frequent repetitions of the same limited set of plays. What was true there, apparently was also true of West Hartlepool, even though it was five times larger than Mexborough.

Flowers of the Forest, A Gipsy Story by John Baldwin Buckstone[1] was the first new melodrama to be attempted by Morgan Smith and Harriet while in West Hartlepool. He played Ishmael, also known as the Wolf, a Gypsy who hates Englishmen, and she played his

Figure 22. Playbill of the Victoria Theatre Royal, West Hartlepool, January 1-2, 1873. DF.WOD/3044. Reproduced with permission from the Tyne & Wear Archives.

daughter Cynthia, who had fallen in love with Alfred, an Englishman suspected of killing Captain Lavrock in a duel. However, the Captain had actually been shot there by a young Gypsy boy whom he had horse-whipped the day before. Alfred is tried for the murder, but when Cynthia discovers who the true killer is, she reveals this to the court, so Alfred is set free and the boy is sentenced to death. Her father, unhappy with this turn of events, threatens to shame and disown her unless she will kill Alfred. Instead, she commits suicide.

This turns out to be a rather odd kind of melodrama because much of the action focuses on a group of comic characters—a fortune teller, a thief, and an auctioneer—who play minor roles in the main plot but have more to say than the principals. When originally produced at London's Adelphi Theatre in 1847 with Madame Celeste as Cynthia, the play was hailed as "triumphantly successful,"[2] abounding "in striking situations, adapted to the peculiar qualities of the leading performers,"[3] but the *Morning Post* complained that "we do not so much object to...comic excrescencies *per se*, but when they have no earthly connection with the drama, they tend to destroy the sympathy and outrage the probability."[4] Critics also felt that the play was far too long, lasting almost four hours, "a time unprecedented for the representation of a three act drama."[5] The version performed in West Hartlepool twenty-six years later was shorter, several minor players having been removed from the cast of characters.

Morgan Smith and Harriet next came out in Morris Barnett's *The Serious Family*,[6] a farce about a husband and wife whose home life has been disrupted by her domineering mother who, with a puritanical companion, has enforced a strict code of pious morality that does not permit the couple to enjoy even the smallest pleasures. As a consequence, the husband begins secretly to seek recreation elsewhere. When one of his fun-loving Irish friends comes to visit and sees the damage that has been done to the marriage by this holy interference, he succeeds in freeing them from such tyranny and returning them to a more wholesome way of life.

Allardyce Nicoll, commenting on nineteenth-century farces, noted, "Heavy contrasts were beloved. Take your hypocritical Puritans (a stage mother-in-law and an Aminadab Sleek) and show a good-natured husband, yearning for brighter things, in their toils, and your farce—in this instance *The Serious Family*...by Morris Barnett—is done."[7] When the play was originally performed at London's Haymarket Theatre in 1849 with Buckstone in the role of the sanctimonious Aminadab Sleek, it was described as "one of those light, sparkling, and very amusing pieces...with strongly humourous situations, well drawn characters, and a company in every respect suited to carry them off as briskly as possible."[8] Another reviewer agreed, saying, "The comedy is full of smart sayings and bustling doings: the situations are excellent, and the acting as perfect as possible."[9] Morgan Smith played the harried husband and Harriet the confused wife in this delightful satirical sketch.

The third new play was John Tobin's *The Honey Moon*,[10] in which Morgan Smith appeared as Duke Aranza and Harriet as his proud, headstrong wife Juliana, whom he tames in a manner resembling that in Shakespeare's *The Taming of the Shrew*.[11] After their marriage, his ploy is to pretend to be a poor peasant living in a modest cottage, not in a palace, and upon spending a month there she learns to appreciate a simpler style of life with a man she comes to admire and obey. This was another very popular play in its day, and Morgan Smith would have had opportunities to see it performed many times in Philadelphia with different visiting stars playing the Duke.[12] A comedy such as this also gave Harriet an interesting new role to play as a woman who is transformed by her marriage.

The final new venture for the co-stars during their initial fortnight in West Hartlepool was *Rob Roy MacGregor*,[13] Isaac Pocock's adaptation of Sir Walter Scott's novel featuring a real historical figure, a member of a proscribed clan who in bitterness had become a dangerous outlaw bravely leading a band of Highlanders in skirmishes against their British and Scottish enemies. In the novel and in the play he was not a ruthless avenger but a seeker after justice who struggled to right wrongs. A song in the play links him with the English archetype of the good outlaw:

> A famous man is Robin Hood,
>> The English ballad singers' joy;
> But Scotland has a thief as good—
>> She has her bold Rob Roy
> A dauntless heart Mcgregor shews,
>> And wonderous length and strength of arm;
> He long has quell'd his Highland foes,
>> And kept his friends from harm.

> *Chorus.*
> A famous man, &c.[14]

Pocock follows Scott's plot fairly closely, so Rob Roy is pitted against a young villain who has allied himself with British Forces and stolen family funds belonging to his uncle and cousin. Judging from the cast list, the version of the play that Morgan Smith performed appears to have focused on battle scenes and other highly melodramatic events in which Rob Roy displays his valor and swordsmanship. Harriet meanwhile played Helen Macgregor, Rob Roy's feisty wife.

Afterward, *The Era* noted that their engagement with W. C. Dews's company was extended for at least another four and a half weeks, the first of which presented additional challenges:

> The resources of the hard working little company under Mr.
> Dews's management have this week been taxed to their fullest
> extent. Commencing on Monday with *The Colleen Bawn*, they
> have during the week produced *The Beggar's Petition*, *The
> Octoroon*, *All that Glitters is Not Gold*, and *Romeo and Juliet*.
> Each piece has been carefully and, upon the whole, creditably
> represented.[15]

Four of these five plays are not known to have been previously
performed by Morgan Smith and Harriet, and it would have been
difficult for them to have mastered the lines in all of them in a single
week. They may have played at least some of them in Mexborough.

The Colleen Bawn; or, The Brides of Garryowen[16] was a
relatively new drama that had been originally produced in New
York in 1859 and was brought out at London's Adelphi Theatre the
following year and again in 1864. At its debut in London

> The play was performed for three hundred and sixty nights
> consecutively—at that time "one of the longest runs on record."
> "When I wrote 'The Colleen Bawn,'" says the author, "I
> invented the Irish drama. It was original in form, in material, in
> treatment, and in dialogue."[17]

It starts as a drama about differences in social class. Hardress
Cregan, a well-educated young gentleman from a formerly wealthy
family, has fallen in love with Eily O'Connor, a poor, uneducated
"fair-haired girl" (a "Colleen Bawn") and has secretly married her
without telling his mother, who wants him to marry a rich heiress in
order to save his family from ruinous debt. This places Hardress in
a very difficult dilemma, and in a moment of despair he mentions
to Danny Mann, his loyal servant, that he wishes he could get rid of
Eily. Danny mistakenly assumes this to be an assignment for him,
so he attempts to drown her in a lake. She is rescued by Myles-
na-Coppalleen, a good-hearted rogue who manages to survive as
an outlaw by poaching, smuggling, and stealing horses. In the end,
Hardress, who is on trial for Eily's murder, is cleared of the charge
when Myles arrives with her at court and the husband and wife are
reunited.

Boucicault based his melodrama on a famous murder that

Figure 23. Playbill of the Theatre Royal, Hartlepool. DF.WOD/ Hartlepool, February 6-8, 1873. Reproduced with permission from the Tyne & Wear Archives.

had taken place in Limerick in 1819,[18] but he changed the details to give it a romantic resolution. He also populated the play with colorful characters, a good many of whom, including Myles and Eily, played by Morgan Smith and Harriet, speak and sing with a rich Kerry brogue. There is much homespun humor, some of it resting on a weakness for alcohol, a national Irish cliché. William Winter recalled in a memoir that Boucicault called *The Colleen Bawn*

> a "Sensation Drama," and then and thus he invented the name that ever since has been used to designate the class of dramas dependent on thrilling situation intensified by means of striking mechanical effect. "Sensation," he once said to me, "is what the public wants, and you cannot give them too much of it."[19]

According to an introduction in an early edition of *The Beggar's Petition; or, A Father's Love and a Mother's Care* by George Dibdin Pitt,[20]

> This Drama, which will be found Unequalled in Pathos, Effect, and Situations of Thrilling

Interest, is taken from a Subject hitherto overlooked by Dramatic Authors....in which are all the materials for a Domestic Drama—the Farmer losing his Land by ill success and the rapacity of the Landlord—the Seduction of his Daughter by a Wealthy Villain—his being reduced to Acts of Mendicity—his begging at the Gates of the Proud and Unfeeling, and having to suffer the taunts of the "Pampered Menial"—Losing his Wife, the "Partner of his Cares"—and his pathetic appeal to the feelings of the humane—all of which is embodied in a Three Act Drama—embracing the events of a Beggar's Life—each Act being an Era—the vacancies between the Acts comprising Ten Years in each. To draw Life as it truly is—depicting the good and bad passions of the human heart—their operations on the Rich and Poor—to excite the hearty laugh at Folly and Eccentricity—and cause the tear to flow at the distress of the good, is the true purpose of the Stage.

This melodrama does indeed contain all these events, most of which are experienced by a farmer and his wife, Robert and Matilda Brightwell, played by Morgan Smith and Harriet, who are impoverished and denied assistance over a span of thirty years. Occasional comic relief of a rather ridiculous sort is provided by silly minor characters whose eccentricities are absurdly farcical. This was not a play that drew life as it truly was. Everything was exaggerated.

The Octoroon; or, Life in Louisiana[21] was another sensation drama by Dion Boucicault in which Morgan Smith portrayed Salem Scudder, the Yankee overseer of a plantation, perhaps in whiteface, and Harriet assumed the role of Zoe, a beautiful octoroon beloved by her father, the former owner of the plantation, who freed her in his will. George Peyton, his nephew, has inherited the estate, parts of which have been purloined by a corrupt previous overseer, Jacob M'Closky, who has designs on obtaining the rest of the plantation, which has fallen into debt and is about to be auctioned off. All the slaves living there are be sold too, including Zoe, whose status as a free person is in question due to faulty records. The villain is attracted to her and wants to buy her, but she and George have fallen deeply in love, even though they are aware that it would be illegal in Louisiana for a white man to marry an octoroon.

M'Closky kills a young slave in order to gain access to a mail bag the boy is carrying that contains legal papers from England indicating that the plantation is no longer in debt, but the murder is captured on film in a camera that overseer Scudder has set up. This evidence, discovered shortly after M'Closky has purchased Zoe, proves that he is guilty of the crime and is about to be punished for it by his captors. Zoe, in the meantime, not knowing of his arrest and preferring death to enslavement, decides to commit suicide by taking poison, which leaves George utterly devastated.

There are striking melodramatic moments in this drama, not only the murder and suicide, but also the scene where George and Zoe declare their love for one another, as well as the heartbreaking scene at the slave auction. The first published edition of the play contains five acts, but Morgan Smith and Harriet performed in a version with only four acts, which concluded with the explosion of a steam ship carrying M'Closky away. The unmasking of the villain by means of a camera was reputed to be the first time this device had been used on the stage.[22]

Boucicault wrote the play while he was living and working in the United States. It opened at the Winter Garden in New York on December 5, 1859 and had its London debut at the Adelphi on November 18, 1861, when Boucicault "did not hesitate to make the play more commercially attractive by substituting a happy ending in which Zoe lived to marry George."[23] Such a miscegenetic resolution would have been unacceptable in the United States, especially at a time when racial tensions were rising in advance of the civil war. Some commentators felt that Boucicault's treatment of American life in that period was fair: "He solved the difficult problem of portraying Southern life on the stage without offending Southerners or overheating truculent Northerners, and he combined truth with picturesqueness."[24] "There were various opinions as to which way the play leaned—whether it was Northern or Southern in its sympathy. The truth of the matter is, that it was non-commital. The dialogue and characters of the play made one feel for the South, but the action proclaimed against slavery, and called loudly for its abolition."[25] Considering Morgan Smith's earlier commitment to the abolition movement in Philadelphia, it must have been bracing for him to take a role in a play that dealt squarely with slavery in the American South.

All that Glitters is not Gold by Thomas and J. M. Morton[26] is a comedy dealing with social and economic issues affecting attitudes toward marriage. A review of the first London performance in 1851 summarized the plot succinctly:

> The scene is laid in a Bristol cotton factory, the wealthy owner of which, Mr. Plum,…has two sons; the elder, Stephen,…having a decided taste for cotton spinning, superintends the factory, and falls deeply in love with one of the *employees*, a young girl named Martha Gibbs….The younger son, Frederick,…marries a young patrician, [Lady Valeria Westendleigh], who has laid herself open to misconstruction with regard to the attentions of a former admirer, a fashionable rake, but is shielded by Martha, who is ignominiously dismissed on suspicion of being the really guilty person. At this point, an *eclaircissement* occurs, and all ends happily, the would-be seducer being summarily "warned off the premises," the wife pardoned for his involuntary offence, and the young girl made happy by being united to her employer's son.[27]

The father is delighted that Frederick decides to marry the daughter of a real Earl, for this will raise the social standing of the family, perhaps enabling him to become the grandfather of a peer of the realm. At the same time, and for much the same reason, Mr. Plum is alarmed to hear that Stephen is intending to marry a poor girl with no family connections of any significance. He insists that she undergo a three-month trial to prove herself worthy. The villain in this piece is a young baronet, Sir Arthur Lassell, who declares his love for both women and also makes overtures to Lady Valeria's mother, hoping to seduce them all. Martha saves the day by exposing Lassell's perfidy, and she and Stephen, the virtuous working-class pair who value neither wealth nor social position, make plans to marry. Morgan Smith and Harriet played this happy couple.

By doing so, they also proved their versatility as professional performers by undertaking in rapid succession a variety of new roles set in distinctive Irish, Scottish, African American, and British societies. And they ended the week by appearing as Romeo and Juliet in Shakespeare's Italian romance, even though both were by now considerably older than those lovers, each being forty years old.

The following week W. C. Dews moved his company from West Hartlepool to Hartlepool, a larger town (population 39,970 in 1871), where audience expectations apparently were much the same. The bill of fare at the theatre changed every night for the next three and a half weeks, and Morgan Smith and Harriet ended up co-starring in twenty different plays in twenty nights, most of them selections from his established repertoire but now also including the six pieces they had introduced in West Hartlepool as well as two others, *Ingomar the Barbarian* and *Father, Come Home*, in which they may never have appeared before.

Ingomar, the hero in Maria Lovell's translation of Friedrich Halm's *Der Sohn der Wildnis*,[28] was the noble leader of a barbaric band of Allemani, who has captured Polydor, a poor Greek tradesman, and is holding him for ransom. Polydor's beautiful daughter Parthenia frees her father by offering to take his place as Ingomar's captive. Ingomar, a misogynist, believes women are

Vain, foolish playthings, only born to bear

And serve; to eat and drink;

To squat among the cattle, feed the children;

To oil their hair, and look at themselves in brooks.[29]

Nonetheless he falls so deeply in love with Parthenia that he pays her ransom and follows her back to her town with the intention of giving up his warlike ways and becoming a civilized Greek so he can marry her. When he is asked to lead the Greeks against his own countrymen, however, he refuses to do so and intends to rejoin his former band, even if it means losing his ladylove. Parthenia wishes to leave with him, but she cannot because she and her parents have been enslaved by a wealthy former suitor of hers to whom her father is in debt. At that point Ingomar offers to become a slave in their place, sacrificing his own freedom for theirs, but all ends happily when the leader of the Greek community steps forward to pay Polydor's debt. The beauty and the barbarian are thus reunited,

Two souls with but a single thought,

Two hearts that beat as one.[30]

Morgan Smith was already practiced in playing roles that required both a rugged toughness and a romantic tenderness, so he might have been adept at representing a character who changes from a hardened misogynist to a soft-hearted lover without losing any of his noble, manly bearing. One can understand why he might have been attracted to a melodrama that would have enabled him once again to prove that he was capable of portraying a complex individual, a man of many moods and contrasting characteristics.

Father, Come Home, a temperance drama by William Pratt originally called *Ten Nights in a Bar-room*,[31] takes place in a country inn where men gather to drink, argue, fight, and even kill one another while drunk. Joe Morgan is one of this dissipated crowd until the innkeeper throws a glass at him that strikes his young daughter, who is begging him to come home. The girl dies from her injury, and Joe promises his wife that he will give up drinking. Ten years later he is shown to have remained true to his pledge and consequently to have become a model citizen of his town. Actually, the Morgans—with Morgan Smith as Joe and Harriet as his wife—play only a small part in this moral melodrama. Much of the focus is on the unruly patrons at the bar whose drunkenness provokes violence. The drama ends with both husband and wife sermonizing on the curse of alcoholism. Morgan Smith and Harriet could have learned their limited roles rather quickly.

Unfortunately, except for one brief mention in *The Era*,[32] there was no press coverage of what they performed during their seven and a half weeks in West Hartlepool and Hartlepool.[33] A collection of playbills at the Tyne and Wear Museum in Newcastle-upon-Tyne provides the few details that are available. Even less was said about Morgan Smith's engagement for six nights in Coventry in mid-March.[34] It was not until he arrived in Southport at the end of that month that he began to receive attention again, this time from the *Southern Witness*:

MORGAN SMITH AT THE BIJOU THEATRE

The only actor of colour on the universal stage made his *debut* before a Southport audience on Monday night, appearing in Shakespeare's masterpiece of "Hamlet." Mr. Smith's impersonation of the spirited Prince, whose aim in life is to be revenged for the murder of his father, is not a wonderful representation. A great fault in those actors who attempt to play "Hamlet" is the detestable rant which is often infused into the character, and Mr. Smith is in my opinion one of these. In the more sober passages of this great play Mr. Morgan Smith appeared to far greater advantage, and his speech to the players and "O that this too, too solid flesh would melt," were given in a manner deserving great praise. Mr. Smith's "Hamlet" was on the whole a creditable performance, and if he would not only let his calm judgment get the better of his "rant," his Prince of Denmark would be greatly improved....On Tuesday "Ingomar" was produced. "Snapper" delights in giving praise where praise is due, and he was agreeably surprised and pleased by the impersonation of the sturdy outlaw. Mr. Smith as Ingomar seemed perfectly at home in the part, which he certainly did not in "Hamlet"...."Hamlet" was again the attraction on Wednesday, and last evening "The Merchant of Venice" was announced to be played. To-night Mr. Morgan Smith takes his benefit, when "Othello" will be produced. Mrs. Smith will make her first and only appearance as Desdemona, and doubtless Othello will prove a great attraction. The character of the jealous Moor will of course be played by Mr. Smith.

Snapper[35]

SNAPPER returned with further commentary a few days later:

THE BIJOU THEATRE ROYAL

On Friday evening Mr. Morgan Smith took his benefit at the little house in Portland-street, when he appeared in Shakespear's well known and highly appreciated tragedy of "Othello." The jealous Moor, who by the wily intrigues of his supposed friend, "Iago,"...is led to hate her whom he once loved, was of course played by Mr. Smith, who gave a fair rendering of the character, the only fault being his disposition to "rant," throughout the entire play. Mr. Smith might easily overcome this defect by a little calm consideration, and his "Othello" would then be highly commendable....Mrs. Morgan Smith acted well as "Desdemona"....On Saturday the occupants of the gallery had their night, Mr. Smith taking his farewell as "Dred," in the play of that name. "Robert Macaire" concluded the performance.[36]

A few weeks later he was in Neath, South Wales, playing Hamlet, Othello, and five of his melodramatic roles.[37] He also received an invitation to perform in Barnsley,[38] but there is no proof that he accepted it. His big break for the year came a month later when he was recruited to perform for the first time at London's Surrey Theatre.

His debut there was welcomed with enthusiasm by the reviewer for *The Era*:

> Mr Morgan Smith (the coloured tragedian) is the novelty which Miss Virginia Blackwood has introduced at her Theatre for the past week, and his position on the bill is, no doubt, a great reason for such a large attendance of visitors as has greeted him. His entrance on the stage last Saturday as Richard III was the signal for a hearty greeting, and on each dropping of the curtain he received an imperative summons to reappear. It was not, perhaps, a very fortunate selection that *The Slave* was chosen for his second appearance, as, although, in the character of Gambia, he delivered himself well of the text, and trod the stage with skilful confidence, the drama was scarcely an adequate test of his numerous powers. Still, it gave him an opening for displaying some capital points, among which are good reading, unexaggerated action, a clear, powerful voice, a correct memory, and an intelligent apprehension of dramatic requirements. Seizing such points which are sure to tell, he yet avoided making too much of them; and his natural delivery and accompanying deportment secured him a reception which few coloured tragedians can boast of.[39]

A week later *The Era* noted that he continued to perform as Gambia twice more before switching to other roles:

> MR MORGAN SMITH'S BENEFIT.—The engagement of the above-named gentleman, truthfully described as a coloured tragedian, has proved a very successful one at the Surrey, and to the ability of the actor, as much as to the novelty of seeing a member of the dark-skinned race upon the boards in the legitimate drama, may be attributed so pleasant a result. On Friday evening the performance was for the dusky "star's" benefit, and the occasion attracted a crowded audience. *Othello* was the play selected, the *beneficiaire*, of course, sustaining the title *role*, for which Nature has eminently fitted him. Mr Smith laboured under the

disadvantage of hoarseness, but he nevertheless managed to give an extremely good reading of the character, and to gain the repeated applause of his audience. The drawback to which we have alluded was most perceptible in the great scene of the play in which the jealous Moor and his scheming "lieutenant" have so fierce an encounter; but, throughout, it was evident Mr Morgan Smith is an intelligent student and an apt illustrator of England's greatest dramatist....Mrs Morgan Smith was Desdemona.[40]

This was clearly a very successful run in which Morgan Smith was reported to have earned "four special calls nightly" from large audiences.[41] His drawing power may have helped to relieve some of the financial pressure on the Surrey Theatre, which at that very time was facing bankruptcy proceedings:

COURT OF BANKRUPTCY, MAY 20.

(*Before Mr. Registrar* ROCHE, *sitting as Chief Judge.*)

IN RE G. W. WOOD

Mr. THEODORE LUMLEY applied on behalf of certain creditors for the appointment of a receiver under a petition of liquidation file in March last by George William Wood, of 124, Blackfriar-road, lessee and manager of the Surrey Theatre. The meeting of creditors now stands adjourned, and inasmuch as proceedings were pending against the debtor and the nightly receipts at the Surrey Theatre were large, the performances being well attended, it was necessary that a receiver should be appointed. The debtor had returned his liabilities at 4,100*l.*, and stated that he had placed theatrical property which had cost him 1,200*l.*, and was worth 700*l.* in the theatre.

His HONOUR appointed Mr. W. L. C. Browne, accountant, 25, Old Jewry, receiver.[42]

The favorable publicity Morgan Smith received for his performances at the Surrey Theatre may have persuaded Mrs. Sara Lane, the sole proprietor of London's Britannia Theatre in Hoxton, to engage him for two weeks during the summer to play Gambia for the first week and then to play Rolla in *Pizarro* the second week, interrupted only by a benefit performance as Othello with Harriet supporting him as Desdemona.[43]

His first week was reviewed in the London press only once, this being a very brief notice in the *Weekly Dispatch*:

BRITANNIA

Mr. Morgan Smith, the African [*sic*] tragedian, is at present at this theatre in the romantic drama of "The Slave; or, the Revolt in Surinam." As may be imagined, Mr. Smith is eminently adapted by Nature to figure as the dusky hero of the piece, and although exception may be taken at certain details of his acting, yet he appears already to have become a favourite with the audience, and was called before the curtain to receive the testimony of their favour.[44]

His second week there was ignored by the press.

Morgan Smith and Harriet rejoined W. C. Dews's company in West Hartlepool for two weeks to appear "in a selection of high-class plays, including *Ingomar, Hamlet, Macbeth, Romeo and Juliet,* and various other pieces, the principal characters in which he has impersonated in a highly satisfactory manner" with his wife's assistance.[45]

At the end of that run, Morgan Smith announced in *The Era* that he was disengaged,[46] but this yielded only a few invitations from theatres in small towns: Newton Abbott (population 12,137 in 1871),[47] Barnstaple (population 11,272 in 1871),[48] and Crownpoint in Glasgow.[49] He did appear for a few nights at the Exchange Hall in Grantham (population 18,369 in 1871) at the end of September[50] before moving on to Barnstaple in North Devon, where he was seen as Rolla, Othello, Macbeth, Richard III, and other plays over a span of two weeks.[51]

Mr. Montague deserves all praise for the enterprise he has thrown into his engagements with the public at the ever-popular Grecian Hall. Not only had he retained the full strength of the attractive company with which he opened, but two additions have been made to it—one as we stated last week, Mr. Morgan Smith, justly styled "the eminent coloured tragedian"; and the other Mr. Alfred Parry....Mr. Smith's colour is unimpeachable; so also is his character for clever, artistic, and withal stirring and passionate acting....In "Othello" Mr. Smith's great abilities developed themselves with great advantage to him—his pronunciation was, considering his nationality (for negroes find an insurmountable difficulty in the oft-recurring labials of the English language), marvelously correct and clear; his acting touching in the extreme, and his whole demeanor that of a gentleman and a finished artiste. As "Desdemona" Mrs. Smith won rapturous applause....Last night Mr. Montague produced to a good house "Richard III," with Mr. Smith in the title *role*.[52]

Montague then took him on tour to Newton Abbott in East Devon, where he performed in mid-October.

Mr. Montague's Dramatic Company has this week proved attractive at the Corn Exchange, owing to the appearance of Mr. Morgan Smith, the coloured tragedian. Mr. Smith on Monday appeared to advantage in the difficult part of Hamlet, which he performed with a degree of truthfulness and animation which drew upon him the encomiums of the audience, and installed him a public favourite. As the Barbarian on Tuesday, and Gambia the slave on Wednesday, he was equally successful; and on Thursday, as Othello, his acting was most creditable, rewarding those who favoured him with a visit.[53]

Morgan Smith continued to perform there with Montague's company until at least the second week in November,[54] but there is no evidence of him appearing anywhere else for the rest of the year. Indeed, for the next six months Morgan Smith and Harriet appear to have remained unemployed or at best invisible as practicing performers. There is no record of them appearing in any of the metropolitan or provincial theatres that were routinely monitored in the pages of *The Era*. Morgan Smith also stopped advertising that he was disengaged and available for future engagements. We do not know what accounts for this. Perhaps they had fallen ill or had suffered an accident of some kind. Or perhaps they had decided to take a break from constant traveling in order to attend to the education of their son Edgar, who was now seven years old.[55]

It was not until the middle of May 1874 that they started to reappear, and thereafter all their activities for the next four months took place in small towns in Cornwall, where they returned to a form of entertainment that did not require a theatre or a supporting cast of players. A renewed experiment of this kind was first tried in Fowey (population 7,209 in 1871). For the next six weeks such engagements were recorded in the *Royal Cornwall Gazette*:

> Mr. Morgan Smith (a coloured man from America) with the assistance of his wife, who is a very superior white woman, gave a grand drawing room entertainment on Monday last, at the Town Hall. The most forcible illustration was that which showed how ridiculous a man does make himself while in a state of inebriety, (*voz* [sic] *et praeterea nihil* [a voice and nothing more; sound without sense]) not only before his wife, but also the general public. Other theatrical representations followed and were much appreciated by the audience which was considerable.[56]

Two days later they repeated their show:

> Mr. and Mrs. Morgan Smith, the former of whom is a coloured gentleman, gave another drawing-room entertainment on Wednesday last, at the Town Hall, by special request. The programme consisted of farces and songs, which were loudly applauded by the audience, which was very select.[57]

At the beginning of June they appeared for a single night in Grampound, an even smaller town (population 4,907 in 1871) fifteen miles away where the size of their audience was again disappointing:

> On Monday last the town was favoured with the presence of Mr. and Mrs. Morgan Smith, an actor and actress of considerable ability. The entertainment, although scantily attended, was a great success, and gave entire satisfaction.[58]

At miniscule Roche (population 1,863 in 1871) four weeks later and only eleven miles away, their success was such that they were invited to repeat it:

> Mr. Morgan Smith, the coloured tragedian with Mrs. Smith, is now traveling in Cornwall, visited this place last week and delighted a very enthusiastic audience with many clever and amusing impersonations. So pleased were the people with the entertainment that Mr. Smith was engaged to appear again at the Foresters' Fete on Wednesday last.[59]

At the end of August, in preparation for a two-night stand in Penzance, a larger town (population 10,414 in 1871), Morgan Smith placed an advertisement in the *Cornish Telegraph* in an attempt to draw audiences:

LECTURE HALL, PENZANCE.

FRIDAY AND SATURDAY, AUGUST 28 AND 29,

FOR TWO NIGHTS ONLY.

Mr. and Mrs. MORGAN SMITH'S

UNIQUE DRAWING-ROOM ENTERTAINMENT.

MR. MORGAN SMITH (the only acknowledged coloured artiste in Great Britain) having passed, successfully, the press of London eight times, together with the press of Edinburgh, Glasgow, Dublin, Belfast, and Cardiff; and with hearty commendation, the press and public of Cornwall; and having visited every part of the United Kingdom, begs to announce, in conjunction with

Mrs. MORGAN SMITH

(acknowledged by press and public as one of the most talented artistes and elocutionists of the present day,) that they will give the above entertainment, consisting of HIGH-CLASS DRAWING-ROOM selections; selections from Shakespeare, and the great poets, affording

TWO HOURS OF GENUINE FUN AND WIT,

Some of the attractions of which are indicated by posters and programmes.

Several of the selections have had a most extended run in London and New York.

Doors open at 7:30; entertainment at 8 o'clock.

A few reserved seats (2s 6d) can be had of Miss Allsop, Stationer, 20, Clarence-street.

First seats, 2s, second do., 1s; third do., 6d.

Carriages can be ordered for 10 o'clock.[60]

They earned another good review and were called back for a third night, even though not many people had turned out to see them perform earlier:

MR. AND MRS. MORGAN SMITH gave a very clever and intelligent entertainment in the Lecture Hall, Penzance, on Friday evening, repeated it on Saturday evening, and again on Monday evening.

> Mr. Smith (a coloured gentleman) and his wife, are exceedingly
> clever artistes, both in acting and recitation; and the hearty and
> continued applause of small but appreciative and respectable
> audiences testified to this. A couple hours of genuine edification
> and amusement, without any approach to vulgarity, were well
> spent in their company. Mr. Smith's rendering of "The Charge
> of the Light Brigade" was exceedingly well done; and Mrs.
> Smith was equally successful in giving the pathetic piece,
> "Little Jim."[61]

By the time they arrived in Truro, a much larger town
(population 41,722 in 1871), to perform for two nights the following
week, Morgan Smith was so upset by the poor turnout on the first
night that on the second night he lost his temper and scolded the
tiny audience that had assembled. The *Cornish Weekly News and
Advertiser* carried the story.

> To perform to bare stools and chairs must always be far from
> satisfactory, but especially must this be the case when one is
> fully conscious of the merits of one's own performance. This
> state of things compelled Mr Morgan Smith, on Tuesday
> evening, in the course of a little speech to a very little audience,
> to say he was disgusted with Truro. He pitied the depraved
> taste of the inhabitants, who could not appreciate such a high-
> class entertainment as his, and in return he asked pity for the
> man who catered for the public amusement. They were so hard
> to please. Mr Morgan Smith announces himself as "the only
> acknowledged coloured artiste" and in conjunction with Mrs
> Smith, who is one of the "fair" sex (not the "coloured" sex), he
> gives a "unique drawing room entertainment." If every man in
> the world got his deserts, Mr Smith ought certainly to have had
> better audiences, but the public taste may be capricious as well
> as depraved; and when he next visits Truro, if he should ever
> have the courage to do so, we hope he will find taste has altered;
> and that he will obtain the patronage he so well deserves.[62]

Clearly this was a difficult way to earn a living. Morgan Smith
and Harriet no doubt gave a number of additional drawing-room
entertainments of this sort at other towns in Cornwall before and
during these months, and though they were skilled performers
who pleased those who came to see them, they repeatedly failed to
attract large crowds. Inevitably, on September 20th *The Era* carried

an advertisement stating that "MR. MORGAN SMITH, Coloured Tragedian (after an extended Tour through the West of England), prepared to arrange dates. Address, as usual, care of S. May, Esq, 35, Bow-street, Covent-garden, London, W. C."[63]

The ad yielded quick results. Within a week he had a contract for twelve nights at London's Elephant and Castle Theatre in Southwark, where *The Era* said he made an excellent impression with his spirited performance in the first week:

> A great attraction has been provided here during the week in the engagement of Mr Morgan Smith, the coloured tragedian, whose name must be tolerably familiar to the majority of our readers. He has appeared with the most gratifying success in the *role* of Gambia in the old romantic drama entitled *The Slave*, and at each performance he has gained the repeated plaudits of the large and admiring audiences which have assembled. A good attendance appears to be the rule at this establishment just now, and Mr Freeborne, the Manager, is undoubtedly securing success where his predecessors have met with little else than failure. The secret, we suppose, is to be found in liberal catering and judicious engagements, and in securing Mr Morgan Smith another trump card has been played, and the tastes of the patrons of the establishment have been hit to a nicety. Transpontine playgoers never fail to appreciate a good stirring play, appealing strongly to their sympathies. Such a play is *The Slave*. They are sure to evince a strong liking for an actor with a vigorous style of elocution and one who is impassioned in action as well as speech. Such an actor is Mr Morgan Smith. By nature fitted physically for the *role* we have indicated, he has also many mental qualities which enable him to give it adequate and effective interpretation, and the impersonation ought to meet with great favour wherever and whenever it is introduced. There is one scene in the play in which Mr Morgan Smith is seen to wonderful advantage. We allude to that in which, reminding Zelinda, the Quadroon beauty, of the risk he has run and the dangers he has encountered for her sake, and in the rescue of her infant from a terrible death, he offers her his love, only to find that love rejected and a hated rival given the preference. He seizes her child and would do it harm, but its pretty face and innocent prattle disarm his wrath, while later on with his rival in his power we see his better nature gain the victory, and Gambia giving a blessing where he had threatened something

worse than a curse. In these episodes of the play, and, indeed, throughout, Mr Morgan Smith was more than equal to the task set before him, and, as we have hinted, he was deservedly the recipient of the warmest of plaudits and of repeated calls before the curtain.[64]

In the second week he appeared twice each night, first as Chevalier de St. George and then as Dred, before ending his run on his benefit night with a performance of Othello. However, Harriet was not included in the cast in any of these plays, except possibly *Othello*.[65]

In Oldham a month later Morgan Smith opened with a performance of Macbeth that impressed a local journalist:

> An eloquent critic once said, "The history of Macbeth is like that of Hamlet, a story of moral poisoning," and every time one sees either only tends to confirm that remark. From the moment the subtle power of ambition take hold of Macbeth, which ultimately culminates in his own defeat and death, the moral disease is presented vividly before us, and it requires an artist of no mean order to realize the high intellectual picture of the conscience-stricken Thane. None but a master hand can delineate the slowly-culminating vengeance of Providence which follows the regicide from the moment of his committal of the crime. Mr. Morgan Smith, the coloured tragedian, succeeded in presenting a careful and well-studied portraiture. He threw an earnestness into his acting which at once showed forth the artist.[66]

He followed with representations of Chevalier, Claude Melnotte, Othello, and Richard III, but again Harriet supported him as Desdemona only on his benefit night.

The same pattern held afterward when Morgan Smith rejoined W. C. Dews's company for two weeks in Coxhoe (population 3,059 in 1871), not far from Hartlepool and West Hartlepool. During his first week he led off by playing Richelieu, Claude Melnotte, and Fabian without Harriet's assistance. In the second week he appeared as Shylock, Gambia, Ingomar, and Chevalier without her, but on his benefit night he teamed up with her in a production of *Honey Moon* in which she had been given top billing as Juliana. In the afterpiece he played Dred without her assistance, and on his final night he took the role of Robert Brightwell in *The Beggar's Petition* with another actress playing opposite him as Matilda Brightwell.[67]

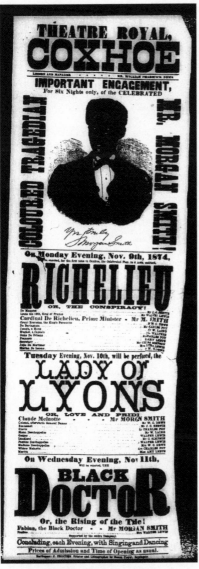

Figure 24. Playbill of the Theatre Royal, Coxhoe. DF.WOD/Coxhoe, November 9-11, 2874. Reproduced with permission from the Tyne & Wear Archives.

He ended the year by performing in Sutton-in-Ashfield for six nights, where he "gave great satisfaction,"[68] followed by twelve nights in Tunstall and six nights in Gloucester,[69] about which newspapers said nothing.

However, some remarks made by Auguste Creamer, the manager of Gloucester's Theatre Royal, in a letter to the editor of the *Gloucester Mercury* on December 19th, Morgan Smith's last day performing there, reveals some of the difficulties that Creamer and other provincial theatre managers were facing when attempting to cater to the tastes of a disinterested public:

THE STATE OF THE DRAMA

Sir,—As the manager of the Gloucester Theatre I cannot allow a letter under the above heading in your issue of the 5th inst., to pass without a few words in defence of my management. The first night I had the honour of addressing a Gloucester audience I briefly stated that I would place on the stage the class of drama the

214

public required, and if my artistes failed to gain the favour of my patrons I would discharge them and engage others. Both my promises I have kept; and, in order to test the tastes of the lovers of the drama, I tried the standard comedies, such as "She Stoops to Conquer," "Honeymoon," "Still Waters Run Deep," &c., and the attendance was so poor that I lost money each night. I next tried the "sensation" drama, with some success. I mounted them with good scenery and properties, yet the patronage was not of a nature to lead me to believe that the "sensational" was what the public required. I then engaged "stars," but lost money week after week….I now propose presenting to my patrons a series of legitimate dramas, supported by acknowledged artistes, and if the works of the immortal Shakespeare, Lord Lytton, and Knowles fails to "draw" good houses I shall accept with great reluctance the opinion freely expressed by my brother managers throughout the provinces that "Gloucester is a truly bad theatrical city." In concluding this hurried letter, I must say I've but one thought, and that was and is to place the Theatre in its true position as an institution and a public educator. I have not shocked the audiences by engaging "Can Can" dancers, or any objectionable performers; I have made repeated changes in my company to render it worthy of the beautiful temple of the drama in which they appear; and if I had been favoured with crowded houses, I've no doubt each piece would have given satisfaction, for there is nothing more depressing to an artiste than to perform to empty seats. Trusting you will find room in your valuable journal for this defence of my management,

I am, Sir, yours respectfully,

AUGUSTE CREAMER

Theatre Royal, Gloucester.[70]

Apparently, not even a "star" as accomplished as Morgan Smith was able to fill the empty seats at this theatre.

Morgan Smith had performed in a number of new roles while he and Harriet were members of W. C. Dews's company, but they seldom repeated these characters in the months that followed. Theatre managers elsewhere tended to prefer placing him in popular melodramas or in Shakespearean tragedies full of melodramatic scenes. He and she also had fewer opportunities later to perform in anything other than *Othello* or in light, drawing-room entertainments. Consecutive engagements were becoming exceedingly difficult to find.

Endnotes

1   John Buckstone Baldwin, *Flowers of the Forest, A Gipsy Story* (London: National Acting Drama Office, [1847]).

2   *Illustrated London News*, March 13, 1847.

3   *Bell's Life in London and Sporting Chronicle*, March 14, 1847.

4   *Morning Post*, March 12, 1847.

5   *Illustrated London News*, March 13, 1847. See also *Bell's Life in London and Sporting Chronicle*, March 14, 1847, and the *London Daily News*, March 12, 1847.

6   Morris Barnett, *The Serious Family: A Comedy in Three Acts* (New York: S. French, [185-?]).

7   Nicoll, *A History of English Drama, 1660-1900*, 4:131.

8   *Bell's New Weekly Messenger*, November 4, 1849.

9   *Lloyd's Weekly Newspaper*, November 11, 1849.

10   John Tobin, *The Honey moon: A Comedy in Five Acts, as Performed at the Theatres, New York and Drury Lane: from the Prompt-book by Permission of the Managers* (New York: David Longworth, at the Dramatic Repository, Shakespeare-Gallery, 1807).

11   Nicoll, in *A History of English Drama, 1660-1900*, 4:164, notes that the play also bears some resemblance to parts of Shakespeare's *Twelfth Night, Romeo and Juliet, Henry IV*, and Beaumont and Fletcher's *Rule a Wife and Have a Wife*.

12   Among those who played this role in Philadelphia theatres between 1860 and 1865 were J. E. Murdock, J. W. Wallack, E. L. Davenport, and L. E. Shewell.

13   Isaac Pocock, *Rob Roy Macgregor: or, Auld Lang Syne* (London: Oxberry, 1820).

14   Ibid., 40.

15   *The Era*, January 19, 1873.

16   Dion Boucicault, *The Colleen Bawn: or, The Brides of Garryowen. A Domestic Drama in Three Acts* (London: Thomas Hailes Lacy, [1865]). The *Northern Echo*, January 15, 1973, and the *South Durham Herald*, January 18, 1873, reported that after the performance of this play in West Hartlepool, W. C. Dews

and Morgan Smith presented a cruet stand to the conductor of the orchestra in celebration of his recent marriage.

17   W. Davenport Adams, *A Dictionary of the Drama* (London: Chatto and Windus, 1904), 311.

18   For details, see Nicholas Daly, "The Many Lives of Colleen Bawn: Pastoral Suspense," *Journal of Victorian Culture*, 12:1 (2007): 1-25, and Eugene McNulty, "The Cultural Afterlife of the Colleen Murder: From Crime Scene to Law Scene," *New Hibernia Review*, 20:2 (Summer 2016): 98-114.

19   William Winter, *Other Days: Being Chronicles and Memories of the Stage* (New York: Moffat, Yard and Company, 1908), 130.

20   George Dibdin Pitt, *The Beggar's Petition; or, A Father's Love and a Mother's Care: A Drama in Three Acts* (London: Thomas Hailes Lacy, [1850]), 2.

21   Dion Boucicault, *The Octoroon; or, Life in Louisiana* (New York: Samuel French, [1859]). See also Dion Boucicault, *The Octoroon* ([Whitefish, MT]: Kessinger Publishing, [2004]).

22   Richard Fawkes, *Dion Boucicault: A Biography* (London: Quartet Books, 1977), 107.

23   Robert Hogan, *Dion Boucicault* (New York: Twayne, 1969), 75.

24   Townsend Walsh, *The Career of Dion Boucicault* (New York: Dunlop Society, 1915), 65.

25   Joseph Jefferson, who played Scudder in New York, as quoted by Fawkes, *Dion Boucicault*, 108.

26   Thomas and J. M. Morton, *All that Glitters is not Gold* (New York and London: Samuel French, n.d.).

27   *Globe*, January 14, 1851.

28   Maria Lovell, *Ingomar the Barbarian*, French's Standard Drama 89 (New York: T.H. French; London: Samuel French, n.d.). Friedrich Halm was a pseudonym of Baron Eligius Franz Joseph Münch-Bellinghausen.

29   Ibid., 20.

30   Ibid., 65.

31   William Pratt, *Ten Nights in a Bar-Room: A Temperance Drama in Five Acts* (New York and London: Samuel French, n.d.), was based on a novel by Timothy Shay Arthur entitled *Ten Nights in a Bar-Room and What I Saw There* (Boston: L.P. Crown, 1854).

32   *The Era*, January 19, 1873.

33   During this interval an advertisement placed in *The Era* on January 20, 1873 from the manager of a theatre in Burnley invited Morgan Smith to "please send terms" for an engagement there, but there is no evidence that he did so or that he later performed there.

34 An advertisement in *The Era* on March 16, 1873, says he was there, but no reviews have been found.

35 *Southern Witness*, April 4, 1873. See also a briefer review in *The Era*, April 6, 1873.

36 *Southern Witness*, April 8, 1873.

37 *The Era*, April 27, 1873.

38 Ibid.

39 *The Era*, May 25, 1873.

40 *The Era*, June 1, 1873.

41 Ibid.

42 *The Times*, May 21, 1873, reprinted in *The Era*, May 25, 1873.

43 See the announcements in *The Times* and *The Era* on June 22 and 29, 1873.

44 *Weekly Dispatch*, June 29, 1873.

45 *The Era*, August 10, 1873. The playbills in the Robert Wood Collection, Theatre and Entertainments Section at the Tyne and Wear Museum in Newcastle-upon-Tyne reveal that on August 5th they had also appeared in *Caste; or, The Child of the Sun*, as Chevalier de St. George and the Countess of Preste.

46 Ibid.

47 *The Era*, August 31, 1873.

48 Ibid.

49 *The Era*, September 7, 1873.

50 *The Era*, September 28, 1873

51 *North Devon Herald*, September 25, 1873.

52 *North Devon Herald*, October 2, 1873.

53 *The Era*, October 19, 1873.

54 *The Era*, November 2, 1873.

55 Edgar had been born to Morgan Smith's first wife Mary Eliza on December 31, 1866.

56 *Royal Cornwall Gazette*, May 23, 1874

57 *Royal Cornwall Gazette*, May 30, 1874.

58 *Royal Cornwall Gazette*, June 6, 1874.

59 *Royal Cornwall Gazette*, July 4, 1874.

60 *Cornish Telegraph*, August 26, 1874.

61 *Cornish Telegraph*, September 2, 1874.

62 *Cornish Weekly News and Advertiser*, September 12, 1874.

63 *The Era*, September 20, 1874.

64 *The Era*, October 4, 1874.

65 Ibid.

66 *Oldham Evening Chronicle*, November 3, 1874. See also *The Era*, November 8, 1874.

67 See the playbills in the Robert Wood Collection, Theatre and Entertainments Section, at the Tyne and Wear Museum in Newcastle-upon-Tyne for these details.

68 *The Era*, December 6, 1874.

69 See the advertisements in *The Era*, November 22, 1874.

70 *Gloucester Mercury*, December 19, 1874. Creamer was responding to a letter to the editor written by an anonymous "Lover of the Drama" about the poor acting in a production of *East Lynne* staged weeks earlier, Before Creamer had taken over management of the theatre, there had been complaints about the "meretricious and trashy performances [there], none of which seem to have been profitable, either in the pecuniary or any other sense." See the *Gloucester Journal*, August 1, 1874, and October 17, 1874.

11

1875-1877

Morgan Smith had hoped to begin a tour of Scotland in January 1875,[1] but he apparently received no offers from theatre managers there to do so. Instead, he and Harriet may have continued to present drawing-room entertainments in small towns in England, where they attracted no attention in the press, or they may have suspended touring altogether. Indeed, for the next nine months they appear to have been doing something else, for only once was Morgan Smith mentioned in a local paper as having performed at Chesterfield's Theatre Royal, starting on April 26th:

> Mr. B. Kelly has provided a rich and unique treat for the people of Chesterfield and district, for the ensuing week, in securing Mr. Morgan Smith, the celebrated coloured tragedian, who will give one of his remarkable impersonations each evening. This gentleman is a negro of the purest blood, and displays a histrionic talent, which approaches, if it does not actually reach to the height of genius. His "Othello" is a marvelous piece of acting, "the greatest legitimate triumph for years" as the *Times* termed it a few years since. And the same may be said of his other characters—critics being divided as to which is his masterpiece. The people of Chesterfield will have an

opportunity of judging for themselves during the week when he will perform his favorite round of characters, the particulars of which may be seen in our advertising columns. We trust that crowded houses will greet the great African [*sic*] actor—the legitimate successor of Ira Aldridge, whom he much resembles both in personal appearance and masterly acting.[2]

This engagement lasted for two weeks, until May 7th,[3] but nothing more is known of it.

In September he was invited to apply for a position at Paisley's Theatre Royal, where the manager was attempting to recruit "First-Class Dramatic Stars,"[4] but he was not able to accept this invitation until the following March.[5]

Morgan Smith finally returned to the stage on October 11th at London's Elephant and Castle Theatre by taking a new role, that of banker Barton Walgrave, in L. W. Harleigh's *Thirty Thousand Pounds; or, The Dread Secret*, which was being played for the first time ever, having been billed as a "new and stirring drama."[6] Unfortunately, according to *The Era*, it turned out to be far from that, for it

> managed to levy a very heavy and almost insupportable tax upon the patience of the large audience assembled to witness it. The drama is the work of Mr. L. W. Harleigh, who has evidently mistaken his vocation, and who has most decidedly misjudged the tastes of such audiences as assemble here. Long, dull, prosy speeches are to them an abomination, and with these the new drama is overburdened. "Then he will talk—good gods! How he will talk," remarks one of the characters in Nathaniel Lee's *Alexander the Great*, and a similar observation may be applied to the most prominent personages introduced by Mr. Harleigh. Every one of them acts too little and talks too much. That we do not exaggerate in speaking of the exercise of patience to which we and all present were subjected, and that the author has accomplished his task in very clumsy fashion, will readily be believed when we say that the first act—the piece is in prologue and two acts—is arranged in no fewer than nine scenes, and that it occupied just upon two hours! The story has little about it that is original, and it appears to have been suggested by that of the well-worn drama *The Streets of London*. Captain Fairweather here becomes Captain Gilbert Halford. Suspecting the stability

222

of the bank of a certain Barton Wallgrave he demands his deposit of £30,000, prior to his departure on a long voyage. The banker does a bold stroke of business by murdering his customer, thus securing a handsome fortune and gratifying his revenge at the same time, for in years gone by the Captain has been his successful rival for the hand and heart of Constance Grantley. The Captain is supposed to be drowned; his estates are seized by the banker, whose advances are repelled with scorn by the widow; the latter and her children are reduced to want; the Captain's son Percy by a curious chain of circumstances becomes tutor to the daughter of his father's murderer; falls in love with her; suspects the banker of foul play; is consigned to a lunatic asylum, and ultimately proves victorious in unmasking the villain, laying his detestable deeds open to the light of day, and recovering from him the fortune—*plus* interest—which he has so shamefully appropriated. We thus summarize the plot, for we have no desire to weary our readers with the many of details of a story which wearied us, and which caused many among the audience to audibly yawn. Mr Morgan Smith, the coloured tragedian, was especially engaged for the *role* of Barton Wallgrave, the banker, and we may give him credit for his powers of memory, as exhibited in a part overweighted with almost interminable speeches.[7]

Meanwhile, Morgan Smith's agent, Samuel May, in the same issue of *The Era* in which this harsh review appeared, was describing the play as an "immense success" and stating that he was "now prepared to treat for the production of this play through the Author, L. W. Harleigh, Esq."[8] Perhaps Harleigh had written it for Morgan Smith or at least had him in mind as the right actor to play the villainous banker in his financial melodrama. However, there is no record of Morgan Smith replaying this role anywhere else.

Before his first week at the Elephant and Castle ended, he was playing Gambia, and in his second week he went on to appear in such familiar roles as Shylock, Chevalier, and Othello. His performance of the latter was singled out for praise in *The Era*, for this was

a character in which his talent, combined with natural advantages, enabled him to appear with fair success. If asked wherein Mr Morgan's [*sic*] ability is most conspicuous, we should say it was in scenes of impulse and passion. Possibly the very temperament of his race tended to such a result. Certainly it was in passages requiring vehemence and intensity that his acting told best with the audience. For instance we could not help thinking that the speech to the Senate would have been better if the actor has possessed greater flexibility of voice, and so also in the pathetic "farewell," in which the soldier so regretfully speaks of war and its pomp and glory. Here, although the speeches were well delivered, greater variety would have improved them; but, where Othello, gradually worked upon by crafty Iago, lashes himself into a perfect storm of jealous rage, any peculiarities of the actor and anything like stiffness gave way under the earnestness with which he delineated the deep feelings of the hero. The result was in these scenes most unqualified success, and Mr Morgan Smith was called before the curtain and greeted with unstinted applause. We put aside the questions of race and training. What is good is good, whether we find it in a Hindoo, a Chinese, or a native of Fiji. Happily such narrow prejudices have passed away, and we were glad to perceive the audience listening with attention and giving the performer fair play. There were no more interruptions than there would have been if a white man had appeared as Othello. We must not omit to compliment Mr Morgan Smith upon the tenderness and warmth of feeling displayed in the scenes with Desdemona, a part which, as played by Miss Marie Henderson, received its due importance throughout the play....It was amusing to watch the audience throughout the night. At first they were restless and somewhat noisy; but gradually, as they felt the subtle spell of Shakespeare's genius influence them, they scarcely knew how or why, the house became quiet, and in some of the best speeches even the most exuberant of the gods listened intently and applauded vociferously.[9]

In November Morgan Smith appeared for a week at the New Albion Theatre in Poplar, East London, playing an assortment of his favorite characters—Shylock, Rolla, Gambia, Dred, and Othello, with Harriet supporting him as Desdemona.[10] The following week he repeated the same repertoire at the Greenwich Theatre, and then moved on to Cardiff, where he opened for two nights as Gambia in *The Slave,* "a play which makes no very great demand on high histrionic ability," and where "Mr Morgan Smith's colour adds considerably to the effect of the performance."[11] He then played

Richelieu for two nights,[12] enacted Othello with Harriet's assistance at his benefit on Friday,[13] and concluded the week by impersonating Rolla and Dred in a double bill.[14]

After leaving Cardiff on December 5th, Morgan Smith suffered a "severe accident" of some kind.[15] However, he had recovered sufficiently to be able to appear at Jennings Theatre in Aberdare on January 3, 1876. His roles there included Claude Melnotte, Hamlet, Shylock, and Othello before he moved on in subsequent weeks to theatres in Dowlais, Merthyr, and South Wales, where he continued to play a combination of his usual roles.[16] When he reached Macclesfield at the end of January, he impersonated Gambia, Shylock, Hamlet, and possibly others in his standard repertoire.[17]

Nothing further was heard of him until he turned up at Paisley for six nights toward the end of March to play three of his Shakespearean roles—Hamlet, Shylock, and Othello—as well as four of his melodramatic roles—Gambia, Ingomar, Fabian, and Dred.[18] He also revived a role he had not performed since 1873—Charles Torrens in *The Serious Family*. The *Glasgow Herald* said, "The attendance during the week was very good, and Mr Smith, a painstaking actor, received every evening at the hands of the audiences frequent and hearty acknowledgments of his ability."[19]

Morgan Smith and Harriet remained in Scotland for the next few months, performing at first at the Palace of Varieties in Perth and the Theatre in Hawick in April and conducting drawing-room entertainments in Earlston in May and in Stow in June. The Earlston event was poorly attended:

> Mr and Mrs Morgan Smith occupied the Corn Exchange here on Saturday and Monday evenings, and performed their "unique drawing-room entertainment." Saturday night was a failure so far as an audience was concerned; on Monday night the attendance was much better, but still far below what was to be expected.[20]

The three performances in Stow, eleven miles from Earlston, drew small audiences initially, but attendance improved on the third night. A brief review provides information on what was performed:

> The programme consisted of three humorous selections, entitled "The Fascinating Widow; or Who Shall Win?" "A Husband in

Clover," and "After the Party." The characters were sustained by Mr and Mrs Smith very truthfully, causing a good deal of mirth, and eliciting hearty rounds of applause. Mrs Smith also gave "Little Jim, the Collier's Dying Child," with good effect; and Mr Smith (who is a man of colour) showed that he was not only a master of our language, but of the art of elocution in his reciting of the piece entitled "Beautiful Snow."[21]

"The Fascinating Widow; or Who Shall Win?" appears to have been a condensation of John Till Allingham's "Who Wins? or, the Widow's Choice," which originally had eight characters,[22] but somehow Morgan Smith and Harriet got rid of six of them and still managed to preserve essential elements of the farcical plot, which revolves around a contested inheritance. A wealthy man has died, leaving £50,000 and a will specifying that the money should go to his niece, a widow, on condition that she marry a cousin, one of whom is a poor poet, the other a prosperous merchant. If both wish to marry her, the matter is to be settled by a roll of the dice. If the widow refuses to marry one of them, the inheritance is to be split by the rejected cousins. If they refuse to marry her, she shall inherit all the money. The poet wins at dice, but, having been deceived into believing the widow to be ugly, he sells her for a thousand pounds to the avaricious merchant. But he has already made a promise to marry another woman and therefore is disqualified from marrying the widow. Having thus been abandoned by both men, she decides to marry the poet and share with him the full inheritance.

It may be difficult to imagine how negotiations between these three colorful characters could be represented adequately in a dramatic vehicle involving only two of them. The most likely solution may have been to tell the tale entirely through interactions between the widow and the poet, who often speaks and sings his lines in rhymed verse. When the farce was originally performed at Covent Garden in 1808, it was described in the *Morning Chronicle* as

> a broad farce, interspersed with songs, and it is at times very droll and comical. The clearness and rapidity with which the most whimsical jingle of words comes off the tongue of [the poet], shows the value of articulation. A song of his at the conclusion of the first act was of this nature, extremely

difficult to the performer, and yet was delivered with a voice so intelligible that not a word was lost....[The widow], in a song of rage, looked like a butt of beer bursting—it was all vapour and noise, but the look and the sputter are irresistibly laughable.[23]

Morgan Smith and Harriet could have a lot of fun with material of this kind, which resembled silly songs in a Gilbert and Sullivan operetta.

A Husband in Clover was a French comedietta adapted by Herman Charles Merivale[24] that had first been performed at London's Lyceum Theatre on December 26, 1873. The *Morning Post* said,

The plot, which is of the slightest construction, turns upon the different notions of connubial bliss entertained by a fond couple only recently married....The clever rendering of the sparkling dialogue, which abounded in strokes of humour, reflects great credit on the adapter. It seems that Horace [the husband] having a horror of "a placid life, without any storm or ripple," has in an unguarded moment entered that sentiment in his private journal, which, having fallen into the wife's hands, arms her with the means of tormenting the writer. As a woman of spirit, these means she uses unsparingly to his utter discomfiture by assuming a variety of characters suitable to the occasion, and eventually he is only too glad to confess that a placid life is the summit of human happiness.[25]

"After the Party" another French comedietta that had been adapted by George Roberts and was originally performed at the St. James Theatre in London on June 2, 1862 under the title *Forty Winks*,[26] was summarized a few days later in the *Morning Advertiser* as follows:

A certain lady, *Mrs. Honiton*, ... has had a grand party, and being overcome by her exertions drops to sleep; and waking at a quarter past four in the morning she hears a snoring, and finds to her horror that a middle-aged gentleman...is asleep behind her curtains. It turns out that he too had been overwearied by a day of travel and had snatched his *Forty Winks*. Unwilling to arouse the suspicions of a watchful admirer who lives opposite, she makes a bargain with *Mr. Poppyfield* to stop until the front door is opened for the milk, when he can pass out unobserved. But how to fill up the time till seven o'clock in the morning, is the difficulty. The lady makes up a sort of couch for the gentleman, and retires; and he, more selfish than gallant, makes a nightcap of his handkerchief and is soon snoring again. The lady, seized with the sudden idea that he is a burglar in disguise returns, and finds the gentleman eating a supper which he has collected from the fragments of the previous night's repast. Notwithstanding all their caution, the opposite *Paul Pry* sees them, and *Mr. Poppyfield* is so indignant that he challenges him, and to vindicate the lady's character, himself offers her marriage, and is accepted.[27]

Such amusing two-handers were farces of a kind in which Morgan Smith and Harriet evidently excelled.

They appear to have remained in Scotland through the summer. In late August, from a base in Glasgow, Morgan Smith advertised that he was "disengaged" and "prepared to settle dates for [an] Autumn Tour."[28] However, nothing came of this, and for the next five months he was ostensibly out of work, at least in proper theatres. The next time we hear of him is in a notice published in *The Era* in the middle of January 1877:

NOTICE TO MR. MORGAN SMITH.—If the portion of his Wardrobe left with Mr. Nicholson is not sent for within Twenty-one days from this date, Saturday, January 13th, 1877, it will be sold to defray expenses incurred with Mr H. De Ville. Address, Mr H. DE VILLE, care of Mr W. Nicholson, Painter, High-street, New Mexborough, Yorkshire.[29]

Two weeks later, Morgan Smith announced in *The Era* that he was ready to begin performing again:

MR. MORGAN SMITH, Coloured Tragedian, begs to announce he resumes his Profession, GLOBE THEATRE, GLASGOW, February 5th. Mr. Morgan Smith avails himself of this opportunity to express his acknowledgements to Mrs W. Sidney, T. H. Glenney, W. E. Wynn, A. St. Nicholas, and M. Glenroy, Esqs., for offers of Engagement, and shall now be happy to treat for future dates. Address as above; or, at all times, care of Mrs Sam May, 35, Bow-street, Covent-garden, London, W. C.[30]

The lessee and manager of Glasgow's Globe Theatre was now August Creamer, who had employed Morgan Smith in Glasgow in December 1874, when his theatre there was facing hard times. Perhaps he was instrumental in persuading Morgan Smith to resume touring. Among the other theatre managers the actor acknowledges in his announcement was Mrs. W. Sidney, the wife of the former lessee and manager of Glasgow's Prince of Wales Theatre, who had hired him to perform there in November 1871. She too must have remembered the impression he had made as a performer earlier.[31]

The Era reported that Morgan Smith's six nights at the Globe Theatre were

> witnessed by fairly numerous and appreciative audiences. On Monday and Wednesday he appeared as Macbeth...Mr. Auguste Creamer, with his accustomed versatility, sustaining the dual *role* of Macduff and Hecate. *The Merchant of Venice* was the *piece de résistance* on Tuesday, Mr Smith of course playing Shylock and Mr Creamer Gratiano. *Pizarro* was produced on Thursday with the "Star" in the part of Rolla.[32]

Nearly three weeks later Morgan Smith was in Belfast, where he opened as Rolla, a role in which the *Belfast News-Letter* claimed his acting was

> in every way well adapted to the various events represented. He is an actor of very considerable ability, and notwithstanding the disadvantages with which an African [*sic*] must appear before a critical audience of Englishmen or Irishmen, the impression he has produced has been favourable in the extreme. His reading is intelligent and free from rant, and his acting, which is not overdrawn, exhibits some good original points.[33]

Next he appeared as Gambia, a performance endorsed by the *London and Provincial Entr'acte*:

> Mr. Smith, as is well-known, is the only coloured gentleman on the stage, and this phenomenal singularity, perhaps, somewhat affects the public patronage he obtains. Be this as it may, however, his masterly pourtrayal of the noble qualities of "a man and a brother," on this occasion, and the admirable support which the regular company afforded him, secured for the performance the lusty applause of a fairly-filled house.[34]

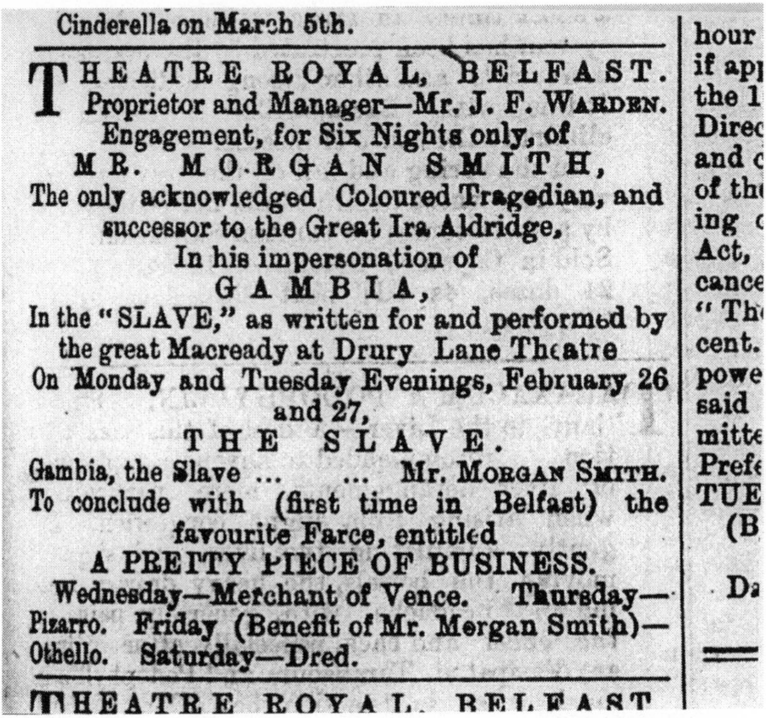

Cinderella on March 5th.

THEATRE ROYAL, BELFAST.
Proprietor and Manager—Mr. J. F. WARDEN.
Engagement, for Six Nights only, of
MR. MORGAN SMITH,
The only acknowledged Coloured Tragedian, and
successor to the Great Ira Aldridge,
In his impersonation of
GAMBIA,
In the "SLAVE," as written for and performed by
the great Macready at Drury Lane Theatre
On Monday and Tuesday Evenings, February 26
and 27,
THE SLAVE.
Gambia, the Slave ... ... Mr. MORGAN SMITH.
To conclude with (first time in Belfast) the
favourite Farce, entitled
A PRETTY PIECE OF BUSINESS.
Wednesday—Merchant of Vence. Thursday—
Pizarro. Friday (Benefit of Mr. Morgan Smith)—
Othello. Saturday—Dred.

THEATRE ROYAL. BELFAST

hour
if ap
the l
Direc
and c
of th
ing c
Act,
cance
" Th
cent.
powe
said
mitte
Pref
TUE
(B

Da

Figure 25. Advertisement in the *Belfast Evening Telegraph* for the
Theatre Royal, Belfast, February 26, 1877. ©British Library Board,
072.9167. Reproduced with permission from the British Library.

The *Belfast News-Letter* was also favourably impressed:

Mr. Smith, being a coloured man, possesses facilities for a
natural performance of the character Gambia which a tragedian
of a white complexion could not possibly avail himself of.
His effective impersonation last evening drew forth frequent
indications of approval, and we have no doubt that there will be
a numerical increase in his audiences every night till "crowded
houses" reward the effort of his superior histrionic powers. Few
tragedians have appeared on our local boards preceded by better
or more reliable recommendations of merit than Mr. Smith. In
his tour through England last year he received from the press the
most favourable notices, and although we have had but a single
opportunity of observing his acting, we have not the slightest
doubt that he will be found worthy of even greater praise than
has yet been bestowed on him.[35]

However, the *Northern Whig* expressed a different opinion of him in this role:

> What the genius of Macready achieved in the title part, and what the lamented Ira Aldridge could have made it, are beyond the reach of Mr. Smith's ability. He is never able to lift it above the level of common melodrama, or to impart to it that artistic grace which might render it acceptable to a cultivated assemblage. Mr. Smith's acting is not bad of its kind, and his elocution might be worse; but in neither is he worthy to be called, as the playbills announce him to be, the "successor to the great Ira Aldridge." He will always attract a number of the more curious portion of the public, because a coloured "man and brother" is a *rara avis* on the stage; but, when judged by the standard applied to actors of the first rank, it must be said that he fails to impress his audience with any idea of his competency in the higher walks of the histrionic art.[36]

His next role was Shylock, which was also somewhat controversial, the *Belfast Morning News* finding it satisfactory though derivative:

> There are but two scenes in the play where the Jew has got anything very special to do, and in both Mr. Smith acquits himself with much more than average ability. The more important of the scenes is the trial in the last act, where the avaricious wretch insists on his pound of flesh. Mr. Smith breaks no fresh ground. He follows the beaten track, content to imitate, too unambitious to attempt to lead. But he has evidently given much attention to the study of the part. His style of reading is pleasing, and, while his acting is free from anything like tameness, there is a quiet composure both in his manner and bearing which is in perfect keeping with the settled determination of the Jew to have his bond. The attendance was small, which may be accounted for in some measure by the extreme coldness of the weather. Mr. Smith is a coloured man—the only one now on the stage. There is not much of a negro caste in his countenance, which exhibits signs of intelligence not found in every white man; and when called before the curtain at the close of the play last evening he bowed his acknowledgment of the complimentary plaudits of the audience with something of the grace of a Sullivan.[37]

But the *Belfast Evening Telegraph* disagreed:

> His impersonation of the relentless Jew, taken as a whole, was

a fair performance; yet running all through the piece there was an evident want of tragic power. Mr. Morgan Smith is an able artist, and is possessed of undoubted histrionic ability, but he lacks the power necessary to make him "tell" in a character such as Shylock.[38]

Nothing was said about his performance on Friday as Othello, in which Harriet supported him, nor was there any comment on his appearance as Dred on Saturday.

In April he performed for two weeks at the Alhambra Theatre in Musselburgh,[39] then in May for six nights at the Gaiety Theatre in Crook,[40] and in June at the Theatre Royal in Croydon,[41] but none of these engagements were discussed in the press. It was not until he returned to Elephant and Castle Theatre in London in July that we begin to receive scraps of news about the plays in which he now performed: Gambia and Chevalier the first week, Macbeth, Chevalier, Duke Aranza, Fabian, and Othello the second week.[42]

On July 22nd *The Era* carried an announcement that

MR. JAMES GUIVER, late of Drury-lane and Princess's Theatres, having concluded an arrangement with the above celebrated actor [Mr MORGAN SMITH, Coloured Tragedian] for a Provincial and Foreign Tour, will be glad to hear from Managers desirous of engaging him. Address, 108, Royal-road, Kennington-park, London, S.E.[43]

But nothing became of this.

Then in August a critic for the *Pall Mall Gazette* remarked on summer being an odd time in the theatrical calendar:

There is a "silly season" in the theatrical world as in the larger community of which it forms a part; and this epoch of folly has now fairly set in upon the London stage. Its signs are uniform and unmistakable. It is the silly season which brings in the "coloured tragedian" and the "performing dogs;" it is the spirit of the time which incites the itinerant "dramatic company" who would fail to secure an audience when London is full to try their luck there when it is comparatively empty; it is, lastly, the silly season which transfers the "great success" of the provincial or transatlantic stage to the boards of a metropolitan playhouse, to be condemned by an audience quite large enough to express disapprobation and too small to be leavened by indulgence.[44]

Perhaps Morgan Smith's appearance at the Elephant and Castle was thought to be representative of this "silly season," and it certainly did not help him secure additional engagements in London or elsewhere afterwards. The last we hear of him performing anywhere in the rest of 1877 is in October at the Royal Lyceum in Rochester, where "the audiences have been very thin indeed; on Thursday last there were but thirteen in the house, twelve in the gallery, and one in the pit."[45] A turnout like this must have been very discouraging to Morgan Smith, perhaps prompting him to consider whether he should continue to attempt to pursue a career on stage.

Endnotes

1 See his advertisement in *The Era*, November 1, 1874.

2 *Derbyshire Times and Chesterfield Herald*, April 24, 1875.

3 *Derbyshire Times and Chesterfield Herald*, May 1, 1875.

4 *The Era*, September 19, 1875.

5 *Paisley Daily Express*, March 20, 1875.

6 *The Era*, October 17, 1875.

7 Ibid.

8 Ibid.

9 *The Era*, October 24, 1875.

10 *The Era*, November 7, 1875.

11 *Western Mail*, December 1, 1875.

12 *Western Mail*, December 2, 1875.

13 *Western Mail*, December 3, 1875.

14 *South Wales Daily News*, December 4, 1875.

15 This was reported in *The Era* on January 9, 1876 with no further details provided.

16 See his advertisements in *The Era* on January 9 and 30, 1876.

17 *The Era*, February 6, 1876.

18 See the bills published in the *Paisley Daily Express* from March 18 to 25, 1876.

19 *Glasgow Herald*, March 27, 1876.

20 *Southern Reporter*, May 25, 1876.

21 *Southern Reporter*, June 15, 1876.

22 John Till Allingham, *Who Wins? or the Widow's Choice* (London: M'Gowan, 1808). A later edition was published as *The Widow; or Who Wins?* (London: John Cumberland, n.d.)

23 *Morning Chronicle*, February 26, 1808.

24 Herman Charles Merivale, *A Husband in Clover* (London and New York: Samuel French, 1873).

25 *Morning Post*, December 27, 1873.

26 W. Davenport Adams, *A Dictionary of the Drama* (London: Chatto and Windus, 1904), 542.

27 *Morning Advertiser*, June 6, 1862.

28 *The Era*, August 20, 1876.

29 *The Era*, January 14, 1877.

30 *The Era*, January 28, 1877.

31 According to the *London and Provincial Entr'acte*, November 11, 1876, Samuel May, Morgan Smith's former agent, had died on November 5, 1876, so his widow became Morgan Smith's new agent.

32 *The Era*, February 11, 1877.

33 *Belfast News-Letter*, February 26, 1877.

34 *London and Provincial Entr'acte*, March 3, 1877.

35 *Belfast News-Letter*, February 27, 1877.

36 *Northern Whig*, February 27, 1877.

37 *Belfast Morning News*, March 1, 1877.

38 *Belfast Evening Telegraph*, March 1, 1877.

39 *The Era*, April 8, 1877.

40 *The Era*, May 13, 1877.

41 *The Era*, June 10, 1877.

42 *The Era*, July 8, 1877.

43 *The Era*, July 22, 1877.

44 *Pall Mall Gazette*, August 16, 1877.

45 *London and Provincial Entr'acte*, October 13, 1877. This news was reprinted in *Reynolds's Newspaper* in London on October 21, and even made its way across the Atlantic to be repeated in a Chicago paper, the *Inter Ocean*, on November 17, 1877, which drew the unhappy conclusion that Morgan Smith was "starving in England."

12
The Last Years, 1878-1882

I n 1878 Morgan Smith decided to stop seeking engagements at established theatres. Instead, he and Harriet chose to perform their drawing-room entertainments only occasionally and ordinarily just on long weekends stretching from Saturday through Monday. It was not until five months had passed that they were seen again in such a situation, this time in a two-night stand in mid-March at Coventry, where it was said that "the gentleman, who is known as the coloured tragedian, showed considerable ability, and was ably assisted by the lady."[1]

A week later they were in nearby Atherstone (population 14,390 in 1881) giving "their versatile and literary entertainment to a very respectable audience in the Corn Exchange....The principal parts of the entertainment were 'A Living Couple,' 'The Dumb Belle,' and 'After the Ball's Over,' in which the acting was particularly good."[2] "The Living Couple" cannot be traced, but *The Dumb Belle* may have been either a version of Thomas Hailes Lacy's *The Silent Woman* that they had performed at Ross-on-Wye in November 1870 or perhaps a version of the farce by Bayle Bernard[3] upon which Lacy had modeled his sketch. "After the Ball's Over" may have been George Roberts's *After the Party* (also known as *Forty Winks*) under a new title.

They gave more entertainments on the two nights they spent at the Town Hall in Hinckley (population 17,406 in 1881) in early April, but "on each occasion very few attended."[4] They had no better luck later in April at the Town Hall in Lutterworth (population 17,407 in 1881): "There was but a small attendance, although the entertainment was of a high-class character."[5]

We next hear of them six months later in the hamlet of Billingborough (population 1,189 in 1881), where in the Horbling School-room they "gave one of their popular entertainments to a small but appreciative audience, on Friday night, the 25th [October] ult. A similar entertainment was announced to be given in the Public Hall on Monday night last, but owing to the very small attendance, the performance was postponed until the following evening, when but a limited number were present: all were, however, very satisfactorily entertained."[6] Seven weeks later, toward the end of December, Morgan Smith gave a different kind of entertainment at the White Hart Auction-room in Spalding (population 22,962 in 1881) by offering "readings from Shakespeare and several well known poets. There was only a limited audience, but it is due to say that his readings were admirable and certainly deserving of better support."[7]

All these entertainments were held in the neighboring counties of West Midlands, Warwickshire, Leicestershire, and Lincolnshire, so he and Harriet must have been living somewhere in the area. There were no trips taken to faraway places such as Scotland, Ireland, or even London. Apparently they had taken up other forms of work to support themselves that year.

They continued to do so for most of 1879. In June, Morgan Smith alone was invited to perform "a round of Shakespearian characters" at Scarborough's Theatre Royal, where his friend T. H. Glenney was the manager. Glenney was one of those who had offered to help him find engagements when he had resumed performing in Glasgow in February 1877. Glenney evidently was making good on his promise to do so, even though he must have been aware that Morgan Smith was by now living in semi-retirement. Perhaps he wanted to encourage him to return to the theatre world. In Scarborough, the bill of fare for the week included *Hamlet, Richard III, Macbeth, Lady of Lyons,* and *Othello,* and the performances went well: "Much satisfaction [was] expressed by appreciative audiences."[8]

In September both Morgan Smith and Harriet were invited to perform at the Gaiety Theatre in Barnsley, a fairly large town (population 78,603 in 1881) in Greater Manchester. The Gaiety Theatre had an energetic proprietor, Ben Walker, who had turned it into a thriving enterprise:

> The alterations and improvements at this place of amusement have rendered it a really commodious and attractive Theatre, and the public have shown their appreciation of the efforts of the Proprietor by crowding the place nightly. During the last fortnight Morgan Smith, the coloured tragedian, with Mrs Morgan Smith, and two old Barnsley favourites in the persons of Mr and Mrs Stoddart, have appeared in several favourite pieces.[9]

The Stoddarts were old friends. Morgan Smith had performed with Mr. Stoddart for a week in June 1867 at Barrow-in-Furnace, and he had acted with both husband and wife in May 1870 at Lancaster. Now they all were performing together before audiences larger than any Morgan Smith and Harriet had seen for more than a year.

In November the theatre manager of the Drill Hall in Keighley was trying to recruit actors, actresses, and a scenic artist to support Morgan Smith,[10] but there is no record of him appearing there afterward. All but one of his engagements in the last half of the year had taken place in parts of Yorkshire, and in December he made it known that he was disengaged and could be reached through the post office in Bingley, Yorkshire. He and Harriet evidently had moved north, and were again prepared to seek re-entry into the professional theatre world.

However, they were no longer in great demand. The first offer they received didn't come until August, but it was for two weeks at a major playhouse, the Theatre Royal in Leeds. Morgan Smith performed for the first three or four nights as Dred, and then impersonated Fabian, Gambia, and Rolla for the rest of the run.[11]

"The pieces have been remarkably well mounted, and have given great satisfaction. Mr and Mrs Smith have been frequently recalled, and the applause throughout has been genuine and hearty."[12]

Morgan Smith's last known performance in 1880 occurred in early November at the Star Theatre in Ashton-under-Lyne, where he played Iago in a production of *Othello*. There was no mention of Harriet participating in this play.[13]

In January 1881 the manager of the Stourbridge theatre fourteen miles west of Birmingham was advertising for "a STAR or NOVELTIES, Two good Swordsmen, with Dogs, or anything new." He asked, "Will Morgan Smith please write?"[14] There is no evidence that the manager received a response, possibly because Morgan Smith by that time may have given up acting altogether.

Nearly the last we hear of him this year is in October when the *Barnsley Chronicle* announced he was back:

> A coloured gentleman, Mr. Morgan Smith, who is well-known as a delineator of Shakespeare, gave readings in St. George's Schoolroom, on Friday night last, and also on Monday night. Mr. Smith, who gave his recitations in most graphic style, was much applauded by his audience.[15]

He repeated this kind of entertainment in Barnsley two months later:

> MR. MORGAN SMITH (coloured) will give his Dramatic Entertainment and Reading on Thursday, 22nd Dec., 1881, at 8 p.m. Prices 2s and 1s. This is really a first class entertainment and worthy of patronage.[16]

This may have been his swan song.

In early March the manager of the Adelphi Theatre in Liverpool, who was looking for a "LEADING LADY, for Easter, and Stars for present dates," said he would be "Glad to hear from Mr Morgan Smith,"[17] but by then Morgan Smith was in no condition to reply. A few days later the *Sheffield Daily Telegraph* reported that he was dying:

> Many of my readers will remember a "man of colour" named Morgan Smith, who at one time lectured on "Shakespeare" in various parts of the country. Smith was also a tragedian of some repute, but his colour kept his *repertoire* of characters somewhat select. As a matter of fact he was confined to Othello.

Smith is now *in extremis*. On a sick-bed at Lowfield, utterly prostrated, without any hope of ever earning a livelihood again, the poor fellow and his faithful wife—who married him much as Desdemona married the Moor, for the perils he had undergone— are making a gallant fight against starvation. All the money they have coming in is 8s. a week earned by their boy. Morgan Smith is himself too proud to appeal to anyone, and if he lives may possibly resent this reference. Fellow-Masons have helped him already—freely and generously, as Masons always do. If others care to assist a man of colour to die comfortably, Mr. Superintendent Gill, of the West Riding Constabulary, will see that their aid reaches that shadowed home at Lowfield.[18]

And on March 22nd he died:

Poor Morgan Smith, to whom reference was made last week, died yesterday. He was a man of much ability and high spirit, and not a few of my friends have told me they have often listened to his Shakespearean lecture with mingled pleasure and profit. It is some consolation to know that the allusion I made last week was—to quote the words of one who ought to know in a letter I received last evening—"the means of her receiving generous pecuniary assistance from a few friends in her time of need."[19]

His death certificate stated that he died of pneumonia at age 49, having been ill for three weeks.[20] The news spread quickly in the British press, the *Morning Post* noting that he was "little known in London, but popular in the provinces," an apt summary of his career.[21] *The Era* added that he was "deeply mourned by his dearly-beloved, sorrowing widow and his son, and greatly regretted by a large circle of friends in both countries."[22] The *New York Clipper* picked up the story a few weeks later and provided further details on what he had managed to achieve:

Samuel Morgan Smith, a colored tragedian, died March 22, at his residence in Sheffield, England, aged 49. He left a widow and one son, besides a large crowd of friends. He was an American, and went to England about seventeen years ago, when Ira Aldridge, a colored actor, was in the zenith of his fame. Mr. Smith was kindly received by the British public, and played there successfully for a number of years; but, we think, he had been in retirement for some little time past.[23]

This was reprinted in a number of American papers, including some addressed to African-American readers.[24]

He had started mainly as a Shakespearean actor, with Othello, Shylock, Hamlet, Macbeth, and Richard III as his principal roles, but he had also frequently played black characters in two of the most popular racial melodramas of his day—Gambia in *The Slave* and Fabian in *The Black Doctor*. As the years passed, he gradually expanded his repertoire to well over forty roles in which he played a wide variety of black and white heroes and villains. This made it possible for him to perform a different role every night for two or three weeks without repetition, if called upon to do so. Such flexibility and versatility gave him opportunities to tour as a star with a few acting companies that moved from town to town in a provincial circuit, but he also accepted short-term engagements that were secured for him by an agent in London or by his own efforts at advertising his availability for employment in *The Era*.

His had certainly been an unusual career, but at least he had had a chance to perform as a professional actor on stage in Britain, an opportunity denied him in the United States because of his race. Following in the pioneering footsteps of his more famous predecessor, Ira Aldridge, he had set out by boldly leasing a theatre in Gravesend and hiring a company of British actors and actresses for a month to support him in a dozen roles, none of which he had acted previously in America. This was followed by brief engagements in Birmingham and London, and then an extensive tour of the provinces that kept him fully employed for more than five years. Indeed, by billing himself as a successor to Aldridge, he found it easier in these early years to secure more engagements than Aldridge himself had been able to secure at a comparable period in his life. Aldridge, to increase his appeal as a foreign actor, chose to pretend to be a native-born African at a time when England was debating the abolition of slavery, but Morgan Smith, coming to the same part of the world after the American Civil War, was proud to identify himself as an African American. He suffered some serious personal setbacks, including the loss of his first wife and two sons, but he found love and support by marrying a British actress who frequently performed with him in venues large and small. In his last years he also had some success in farcical roles enacted in tandem with his wife before small provincial audiences. Several plays had been written for him, but these proved to be less popular than those in his standard repertoire. By the mid-1870s he began to find it increasingly difficult to find enough work to keep himself productively occupied, and in his last five years he must have been forced to supplement his income by other means. His health, perhaps aggravated by a severe accident he suffered at the end of 1875, also appears to have gradually started to decline, leading to his death at a relatively early age.

Yet he had had enough success, especially in his early years as a performer, to have made a name for himself in his chosen profession. He was not one of big stars of his time, but he was certainly in demand at many theatres in his heyday and continued to be so sporadically even in his declining years.

Errol Hill, who wrote *Shakespeare in Sable*,[25] a classic account of black Shakespearean actors, concluded in one of his essays on him that

> Morgan Smith was no Ira Aldridge. One might say that he lacked that spark of genius which is reserved for the very few whom the gods love. He had neither Aldridge's range nor power. He did not perform in foreign countries of Europe, as Aldridge did, with companies speaking their native tongue while he spoke in English. He received no awards from crowned heads. Yet he was a superior performer, a talented and painstaking actor of intelligence, a careful elocutionist devoid of rant and exaggeration whose personal and artistic life was governed by a sure sense of taste, good judgment, and proper deportment.[26]

This is a fair assessment of what Morgan Smith was able to achieve in his sixteen years as an itinerant actor in Britain, a profession he never would have been allowed to enter and practice in the United States of America.

Endnotes

1   *The Era*, March 24, 1878.

2   *Coventry Herald*, March 29, 1878. All references to population statistics for 1881 are drawn from the *Census of England and Wales*, Vol. 2 (London: George E. B. Eyre and Spottiswoode, 1883).

3 Bayle Bernard, *The Dumb Belle* (Chicago: Dramatic Publishing Company, n.d.).

4 *Leicester Chronicle*, April 13, 1878.

5 *Leicester Chronicle*, May 4, 1878; *Rugby Advertiser*, May 4, 1878.

6 *Grantham Journal*, November 2, 1878.

7 *Lincolnshire Chronicle*, December 27, 1878.

8 *The Era*, June 22, 1879.

9 *The Era*, October 25, 1879.

10 *The Era*, November 2, 1879.

11 See the advertisements in the *Leeds Express*, August 10-20, 1880, as well as a notice in the *London and Provincial Entr'acte*, August 21, 1880.

12 *The Era*, August 22, 1880.

13 *The Era*, November 7, 1880. This was described as a "return visit," so he must have appeared here some time earlier.

14 *The Era*, January 8, 1881.

15 *Barnsley Chronicle*, October 15, 1881.

16 *Barnsley Chronicle*, December 17, 1881.

17 *The Era*, March 11, 1881.

18 *Sheffield Daily Telegraph*, March 16, 1882.

19 *Sheffield Daily Telegraph*, March 23, 1882.

20 General Register Office, Register of Death of Samuel Morgan Smith in the Sub-district of Ecclesall Bierlow in the County of York, DYD 809213.

21 *Morning Post*, March 27, 1882.

22 *The Era*, March 25, 1882.

23 *New York Clipper*, April 15, 1882.

24 See, e.g., the *Cincinnati Daily Gazette*, April 22, 1882, and the *Colored Patriot* of Topeka, Kansas, May 7, 1882.

25 Errol Hill, *Shakespeare in Sable: A History of Black Shakespearean Actors* (Amherst: University of Massachusetts Press, 1984).

26 Errol Hill, "S. Morgan Smith: Successor to Ira Aldridge," *Black American Literature Forum*, 16 (1982): 135.

Appendixes

Appendix A:
Itinerary

1866
London, Gravesend 660521-616
Birmingham, Prince of Wales 660806-11
London, Olympic 660825-919
Leicester 661022-27
Rochester 661105-10
Northampton 661112-17
Kilmarnock 661119-1201
Paisley 661203-08
Coatbridge 661210-15
Carlisle 661217-29

1867
Worcester 670114-19
Hartlepool 670121-26
Dundee 670128-209
Bradford 670211-16
Aberdeen 670219-23
Hanley 670225-302

Tredegar 670304-16
Cardiff 670318-23
Darlington 670401-06
North Shields 670408-13
Hartlepool 670415-16
Middlesborough 670417
Wrexham 670506-11
Kendal 670513-18
Wigan 670603-08
Barrow-in-Furness 670610-15
Bolton 670617-22
Aberystwyth 670624-29
Lancaster 670701-06
Stockport 670715-20
Great Grimsby 670729-803
Margate 670826-670903
Belfast 670909-14
Dublin 670916-21
Arbroath 670925-28
Rochdale 671007-12 (canceled due to death of Morgan Smith's
    wife on October 6th)
Barnstaple 671021-26
Rochdale 671028-1102, 671107-11
Birkenhead 671112-20
Great Yarmouth 671125-30
Dundee 671202-14
Dunfermline 671216-21

1868
Kidderminster 680113-18
Cheltenham 680203-08
Leeds 680224-29
Dewsbury 680302-07
Kidderminster 680309-14
Jarrow-on-Tyne 680316-21
Sunderland 680327-28
Wakefield 680330-404

Newcastle-upon-Tyne 680407-08
Wishaw 680413-18
Blackburn 680420-25
Stockport 680427
Wishaw 680506-16
London, Marylebone 680526
Preston 680622-26
London, Pavilion 680627-703
Margate 680820-22
Ipswich 680831-905
Aberystwyth 680907-08
Wrexham 680914-16
Oswestry 680917-18
Wrexham 680919
Dublin 680921-1003
Wrexham 681010
Swansea 681012-24
Cardiff 681026-31
Tunbridge Wells 681109-14
Hastings 681207-19

1869
Londonderry 690104-22
Port Glasgow 690201-06
Hanley 690215-20
Northampton 690329-403
Wrexham 690524-29
Stockton-on-Tees 690531-605
London, Royal Alfred 690710-16
London, Sadler's Wells 690804
Glasgow 690828-911
Arbroath 690914-16
Edinburgh 690918-1001
Dundee 691002-15
Aberdeen 691101-13
Perth 691115-16
Longton 691122-27

Hull 691206-11
Exeter 691213-18

1870
Maidstone 700112-18
Belfast 700124-29
Dublin 700201-08
Whitehaven 700214-19
Dublin 700221-312
Wrexham 700314-19
Birmingham 700328-409
Wolverhampton 700411-12
Northampton 700425-29
Rochdale 700502-07
Lancaster 700516-19, 700523-25
Bolton 700620-21
Douglas, Isle of Man 700728-29
Bilston 700925
Shrewsbury 701003-17
Ludlow 701021
Ross-on-Wye 701114

1871
Shrewsbury 710109-14
Wrexham 710116-20
Landport 710123-204
Leicester 710211-18
West Hartlepool 710320-25
Earlston 710410-15
Dundee 710717-22
Glasgow 711111-18

1872
Brighouse 720108-13
Macclesfield 720115-27
Carmarthen 720129-203
Sheffield 720226-309

Macclesfield 720412-22
Hebden Bridge 720612
Warrington 720715-23
Mexborough ca. 720903-ca. 1208 (14 weeks)
Runcorn 721111-16
West Hartlepool 721230-31

1873
West Hartlepool 730101-11
Hartlepool 730120-215
Coventry 730317-22
Southport 730331-405
Neath 730421-26
London, Surrey 730517-24
London, Britannia 730623-705
West Hartlepool 730728-805
Grantham 730918-19
Barnstaple 730922-1004
Newton Abbot 731013-16, 731103-08

1874
Fowey 740518-20
Grampound 740601
Roche 740629-701
Penzance 740828-31
Truro 740907-08
London, Elephant and Castle 740926-1009
Oldham 741102-07
Coxhoe 741109-21
Sutton-in-Ashfield 741123-28
Tunstall 741130-1212
Gloucester 741214-19

1875
Chesterfield 750426-507
London, Elephant & Castle 751011-23
London, New Albion 751108-13

Greenwich 751115-20
Cardiff 751129-1204

1876
Aberdare 760103-06
Dowlais 760110
Merthyr Tydfil 760117
South Wales 760124-29
Macclesfield 760131-202
Paisley 760318-25
Perth 760417-22
Hawick 760424-29
Earlston 760520, 760522
Stow 760608-9, 760612

1877
Glasgow 770205-10
Belfast 770226-303
Musselburgh 770402-14
Crook 770514-19
Croydon 770609
London, Elephant and Castle 770630-714
Rochester 771008-13, 771118

1878
Coventry 780316, 780318
Atherstone 780325
Hinckley 780406, 780408
Lutterworth 780429-30
Billingborough 781025, 781029
Spalding 781220

1879
Scarborough 790616-20
Barnsley 790922-1004
Keigley 791110-15

1880
Leeds 800809-21
Ashton-under-Lyne 801101-05

1881
Barnsley 811007, 811007, 811222

Appendix B: Venues

Aberdare 760103-06
Aberdeen 670219-23, 691101-13
Aberystwyth 670624-29, 680907-08
Arbroath 670925-28, 690914-17
Ashton-under-Lyne 801101-05
Atherstone 780325
Barnsley 790922-1004, 811007, 811010, 811222
Barnstaple 671021-26, 730922-1004
Barrow-in-Furness 670610-15
Belfast 670909-14, 700124-29, 770226-303
Berwick-upon-Tweed 710410-15, 760520-22
Billingborough 781025-29
Bilston 700925
Birkinhead 671112-20
Birmingham 660806-11, 700328-409
Blackburn 680420-25
Bolton 670617-22, 700620-21
Bradford 670211-16
Brighouse 720108-13

Cardiff 670318-23, 681026-31, 751129-1204
Carlisle 661217-29
Carmarthen 720129-203
Cheltenham 680203-06
Chesterfield 750426-507
Coatbridge 661210-18
Coventry 730317-22, 780316, 780318
Coxhoe 741109-21
Crook 770514-19
Croydon 770609
Coventry 780316-18
Darlington 670401-06
Dewsbury 680302-07
Douglas, Isle of Man 700728-29
Dowlais 760110
Dublin 670916-21, 680921-1003, 700201-08, 700221-312
Dundee 670128-209, 671202-14, 691002-15, 710717-22
Dunfermline 671216-21
Earlston 710410-15, 760520, 760522
Edinburgh 690918-1001
Exeter 691213-18
Fowey 740518-20
Glasgow 690828-911, 711111-18, 770205-10
Gloucester 741214-19
Grampound 740601
Grantham 730918-19
Great Grimsby 670729-803
Great Yarmouth 671125-30
Greenwich 751115-20
Hanley 670225-302, 690215-20
Hartlepool 670121-26, 670415-16, 730120-215
Hastings 681207-19
Hawick 760424-29
Hebden Bridge 720612
Hinckley 780406, 780408
Hull 691206-11
Ipswich 680831-905

Jarrow-on-Tyne 680316-21
Keigley 791110-15
Kendal 670513-18
Kidderminster 680113-18, 680309-14
Kilmarnock 661119-1201
Lancaster 670701-06, 700516-19, 700523-25
Landport 710123-204
Leeds 680224-29, 800809-21
Leicester 661022-27, 710211-18
London, Britannia 730623-705
London, Elephant and Castle 740926-1009, 751011-23, 770630-
    714
London, Gravesend 660521-616
London, Marylebone 680526
London, New Albion 751108-13
London, Olympic 660825-919
London, Pavilion 680627-703
London, Royal Alfred 690710-16
London, Sadler's Wells 690804
London, Surrey 730517-24
Londonderry 690104-22
Longton 691122-27
Ludlow 701021
Lutterworth 780429-30
Macclesfield 720115-27, 720412-22, 760131-202
Maidstone 700112-18
Margate 670826-27, 680820-22
Merthyr Tydfil 760117
Middlesbrough 670417
Musselburgh 770402-14
Neath 730421-26
Newcastle-on-Tyne 680407-08
Newton Abbot 731013-16, 731103-08
North Shields 670408-13
Northampton 661112-17, 690329-403, 700425-29
Oldham 741102-07
Oswestry 680917-18

Paisley 661203-08, 760318-25
Penzance 740828-31
Perth 691115-16, 760417-22
Port Glasgow 690201-06
Preston 680622-26
Rochdale 671007-12 (canceled due to death of Morgan Smith's
    wife), 671028-1102, 671107-11, 700502-07
Roche 740629-701
Rochester 661105-10, 771008-13, 771118
Ross-on-Wye 701114
Runcorn 721111-16
Scarborough 790616-20
Sheffield 720226-309
Shrewsbury 701003-17, 710109-14
South Wales 760124-29
Southport 730331-405
Spalding 781220
Stockport 670715-20, 680427
Stockton-on-Tees 690531-605
Stow 760608-9, 760612
Sunderland 680320-21
Sutton-in-Ashfield 741123-28
Swansea 681012-24
Tredegar 670304-16
Truro 740907-08
Tunbridge Wells 681109-14
Tunstall 741130-1212
Wakefield 680330-404
Warrington 720715-23
West Hartlepool 710320-25, 721230-31, 730101-11, 730728-805
Whitehaven 700214-19
Wigan 670603-08
Wishaw 680413-18, 680506-16
Wolverhampton 700411-12
Worcester 670114-19
Wrexham 670506-11, 680914-16, 680919, 681010, 690524-29,
    700314-19, 710116-20

Appendix C: Repertoire

Key

a = act
sc = scene
? = precise date uncertain
?? = role uncertain

After the Ball's Over (??) 780325

After the Party (Mr. Poppyfield) 760608, 760609, 760612

All But Lost; or, The Totem of the Tortoise (Uncas) 691011, 691012, 691013, 691014?, 691108, 691109, 691110, 691111

All that Glitters is Not Gold (Stephen Plum) 730116, 730212

The Beggar's Petition; or, A Father's Love and a Mother's Care (Robert Brightwell) 730108, 730114, 730130, 741121

The Black Doctor (Fabian) 661107, 661124, 661205, 661214, 661222, 670116, 670202, 670205, 670207, 670216, 670223, 670302, 670318, 670322, 670323, 671209, 671210, 671214,

680229, 680923, 680924, 681019, 681020, 681022, 690218?, 700215, 700228, 700316, 700502, 700503, 700504, 700505, 720120, 720304, 720305, 720718, 730107, 730203, 730426, 741111, 760325, 770713, 800814, 800817; also billed as *The Rising* [or *Turning*] *of the Tide; or, the Fated Lovers* 690710, 690712, 690713, 690714, 690715, 690716, 690828, 690831, 690901, 690902, 690903, 690904, 690906, 690907, 690908, 690909, 690910, 690911, 690918, 690920, 690921, 690922, 690923, 690924, 690925, 690930, 691002, 691004, 691005, 691006, 691007, 691101, 691102, 691103, 691106, 691115, 691116, 691206, 691207, 691208, 691209, 691213, 691214, 700126, 700127, 700128, 700301, 700303, 700328, 700329, 700330, 700331, 700401, 700402, 701012?, 711117, 800818

The Castle Spectre (Hassan) 710211

The Chevalier de St. George (Chevalier) 670208, 670221?, 670802, 671213, 680227, 680228, 680624, 681023, 691217, 700317, 700412?, 710721, 720306, 720307, 720309, 720422; also billed as *The Child of the Sun; or, The Bondmen Brothers* 680925, 680930, 681015, 690927, 690928, 690929, 691008, 691009, 691104, 691105, 700201, 700203, 700207, 700208, 700308, 701014?, 720723, 741003, 741005, 741006, 741008, 741104, 741119, 751020, 751117, 751118, 770707, 770711, 770712; also billed as *Caste; or, The Bondmen Brothers* 730102, 730805

The Colleen Bawn; or, The Brides of Garryowen (Myles-Na-Copaleen) 730207

Domestic Felicity (Simon Lullaby) 700525, 701114; also billed as *Conjugal Felicity*, 700728, 700729

Dred, a Tale of the Dismal Swamp (Dred) 690911, 691001, 691009, 691112, 691126?, 691210, 691213, 700226, 700310, 700524, 701011?, 710722, 711117, 720302, 720413, 720722, 730104, 730201, 730405, 730424, 730524, 741003, 741004, 741005, 741006, 741008, 741120, 751113, 751120, 751204, 760325, 770303, 800810, 800811, 800812

The Dumb Belle (Vivian) 780325

The Fascinating Widow; or, Who Shall Win? (Iambic Extempore, Esq.) 760608, 760609, 760612

Father, Come Home; or, Ten Nights in a Barroom (Joe Morgan) 730211

The Flowers of the Forest; or, A Gypsy's Story (Ishmael Wolf) 730101, 730204

Hamlet (Hamlet)   660606, 660919, 661025?, 661108, 661204, 661211, 661217, 661221, 670114, 670121, 670128, 670129, 670211, 670225, 670401, 670408?, 670506, 670513, 670612, 670617, 670730, 670827, 670913, 670920, 670921 (a3), 670927, 671112, 671127, 671202, 671203, 671216, 680204?, 680303?, 680327, 680622, 680907, 680916, 681002 (a3), 681016 (a3), 681030, 681212?, 690106, 690201, 690215, 690401, 691122, 700307, 700315, 701004, 701007, 701114 (scenes), 710116, 710718, 720129, 720308, 720423, 720716, 721230, 730127, 730331, 730402, 730421, 730729?, 731013, 760104, 760202?, 760320, 790616

Harlequin Puss in Boots (Chevalier St. George) 700207, 700208

The Honey Moon (Duke Aranza) 730109, 730122, 741120, 770713

A Husband in Clover (Horace) 760608, 760609, 760612

Ingomar, the Barbarian (Ingomar)   730123, 730401, 730728?, 731014, 741118 , 760322

The Iron Chest (Sir Edward Mortimer) 671118, 671119, 680312, 680625, 681015

King Lear (Lear) 700312 (a1), 700525 (a1)

The Lady of Lyons (Claude Melnotte) 660525?, 660611, 660809, 670125, 670507, 671024, 671219, 680206?, 680914, 680917, 700309, 701006, 710120, 710322, 710720, 730120, 741105, 741110, 760103, 790619

A Living Couple (??) 760608, 760609, 760612

Macbeth (Macbeth)   660604, 670124, 670204, 670206, 670213, 670613, 670731?, 670911, 671129, 680203, 680311, 680423, 680905 (a5), 681002 (a2), 681029, 681217, 690203, 690524, 690525, 700112, 700129, 700214, 700312 (a2), 700314, 700516, 701008?, 710323, 710719, 720115, 720420, 720715, 721111, 730106, 730129, 730804, 730927, 741102, 741103,

770205, 770207, 770710, 790618

The March on Magdala; or, The Death of King Theodore (Theodore) 700221, 700222, 700223, 700224; also billed as *King Theodore; or, the Taking* [or *Fall*] *of Magdala*, 700318, 700406, 700409, 700412?, 700525

Merchant of Venice (Shylock)   660608, 660613, 660807 (a4), 660910, 660911, 660912, 660913, 660914, 661023, 661106, 661120?, 661207, 670115, 670123, 670208, 670212, 670220, 670226, 670508, 670514, 670518, 670610, 670801?, 670917, 670926, 671023, 671127, 671203, 671217, 680113?, 680228, 680310, 680831, 680908, 681002 (a1, sc3), 681014, 681028, 681211?, 690105, 690202, 690402, 690527, 690531, 690915, 700304 (a4), 700312 (a4), 700518, 701010?, 710321, 711114, 720116, 720131, 720301, 720412, 720722, 730403, 741116, 751019, 751021, 751108, 760105, 760201?, 760321, 770206, 770228

Obi; or, Three-Fingered Jack (Karfa)   681017, 681019

Octoroon (Salem Scudder)   730115, 730128

Oronooko (Oronooko)   660601?

Othello (Othello)   660521, 660523, 660529, 660616 (a3), 660806, 660825, 660827, 660828, 660829, 660830, 660831, 660904, 660906 (a3,4,5), 661022, 661105, 661119, 661203, 661210, 670126 (a3), 670129, 670201, 670215, 670219, 670301, 670320?, 670416, 670510, 670515, 670614, 670619, 670729, 670802 (a3,4,5), 670826, 670909, 670916, 670919, 670921 (a3), 670925, 671028, 671126, 671203, 671204, 671206, 671220, 680114?, 680207?, 680224, 680302?, 680314?, 680328, 680408, 680420, [680506], 680820, 680904, 680915, 680918, 680921, 681012, 681013, 681026, 681207, 690104, 690205, 690216?, 690402, 690528, 690910, 690916, 691001, 691015, 691112, 691113, 691126, 691210, 700117, 700217, 700311, 700318, 700411, 700506, 700519, 701011?, 710202, 710217, 710324, 710721, 711113, 720119, 720127, 720202, 720719, 730124, 730404, 730425, 730523, 730704, 730730?, 730926, 731016, 741009, 741106, 750426, 751022, 751112, 751119, 751203, 760106, 760324, 770302, 770714, 790620

Othello (Iago) 670912, 671106, 671120, 671206, 680922, 681027, 801101

Pizarro (Rolla) 680905, 681003, 681017, 681031, 681215, 690403, 690529, 691127, 691216, 700305, 701007?, 720117, 720415, 720717, 721112, 730121, 730422, 730630, 730701, 730703, 730705, 730925, 751109, 751110, 751204, 770208, 770301, 800817

The Revenge (Zanga), billed as *El Moresco* 680926, 680930

Richard III (Richard) 660609, 660615, 660616 (a5), 661117, 661122?, 661206, 670119, 670209, 670228, 670511, 670803, 670914, 670921 (a5), 670928, 671205, 671221, 680115?, 680205?, 680309, 680425, 681002 (a5), 681010, 681031?, 681214, 690206, 690219?, 690403, 690804, 690914, 691124, 691211, 700115, 700219, 700319, 701005, 710325, 710722, 711111, 720420 (a5), 720720, 730125, 730517, 730101, 741107, 790617

Richelieu (Richelieu) 660810, 661109, 670122, 670130, 670214, 670509, 670611, 680313?, 680421, 681010, 690204, 690220?, 690331, 691215, 700523, 701015?, 730103, 730210, 741109, 751201, 751202

Rob Roy (Rob Roy Macgregor) 730110, 730131

Robert Macaire; or, Auberge des Adrets! (Robert Macaire) 691004, 730405

Romeo and Juliet (Romeo) 690120, 720424, 730117, 730806

The Serious Family (Charles Torrens) 730108, 730205, 760322

A Silent Woman (Arthur Merton) 701114

The Slave (Gambia) 660607, 660808, 660811, 661024, 661110, 661121?, 661208, 670117, 670126, 670131, 670209, 670227, 670318, 670321?, 670415, 670618, 670910, 671130, 671207, 671211, 671218, 680225, 680226, 680229, 680407, 680408, 680422, [680506], 680526, 680623, 680627, 680629, 680630, 680701, 680702, 680703, 680901, 680928, 680929, 681024, 681216, 690217?, 690330, 690906, 690906, 690907, 690908, 690909, 690925, 690927, 690928, 690929, 691006, 691007,

691106, 691123, 691218, 700118, 700124, 700125, 700128, 700205, 700217, 700225, 700404, 700405, 700406, 700409, 700507, 700517, 700620, 700621, 701003, 710117, 710118, 710119, 710204, 710218, 710320, 710717, 711115, 710213, 720203, 720226, 720227, 720228, 720229, 720302, 730111, 730208, 730423, 730519, 730520, 730521, 730522, 730524, 730623, 730624, 730626, 730627, 730628, 731015, <u>740926</u>, 740928, 741117, 751016, 751018, 751111, 751115, 751116, 751129, 751130, 760131, 760318, 770226, 770227, 770303, 770702, 800816, 80019

The Stranger (Count Walbourg) 680919, 690526, 691125, 720118, 720201, 721113, 721231, 730206

Uncle Tom's Cabin (George Harris) 691015, 700311, 710120

War (Reuben Fidele) 710123, 710124, 710125, 710126, 710127, 710128, 710204, 710213, 710214, 710215, 710216, 710218

£30,000; *or, the Dread Secret* (Barton Wallgrave) 751011

Appendix D: Supporting Performers

Adams, Miss C. 680225, 680226, 680228, 280229

Aickin, Miss Elinor 670128, 670129, 670201, 670209, 730331, 730401, 730402, 730404

Allen 760103

Alleyne, W. 680831

Allwood, Thomas 770227, 770228, 770303

Andrews 691211

Angel, Miss F. 670916, 670918, 670919, 670920, 670921

Anton, Holmes 691213, 691214, 691215, 691216

Appleby 670128, 670209

Arnold, H.C. 730331, 730402

Ashe, Miss Clarissa 790616, 790617, 790618, 790619, 790620

Ashton, Gordon 700411

Ashton, H.G. 680914, 680915, 680916

Ashton, Mrs H.G. 680914, 701003

Atkinson, Miss 660825, 660827, 660828, 660829, 660830, 660831

Austin, Miss 660919

Avern, Miss 670209

Baker, H. 670211, 670212, 670213, 670214, 670215, 670216, 751115, 751116

Bannister 680421

Barnes 740926, 740928

Barnett 720715, 720722

Barnett, Miss Emma 660825, 660827, 660828, 660829, 660830, 660831, 660904, 660906

Barrett 720715, 720722

Barrier 680526

Bashall, Joe 670801

Bauer 730517, 730523

Beaufort, G.H. 730331, 730402

Beaufort, Miss Ellen 670617, 670618

Beckett, F. 671023, 671024

Bell, Edward 661105, 661109, 661110

Bell, Miss Emily 661109, 661110

Bell, Percy 691213, 691214, 691215, 691216

Bell, R. 730623, 730624, 730626, 730627, 730628, 730630, 730701, 730703, 730705

Bellair, Miss E. 720722, 720723

Bellair, Miss M. 730623, 730624, 730626, 730627, 730628, 730630, 730701, 730703, 730705

Belverstone, J. 691011, 691012, 691013, 691015

Bennet, C. 691206, 691207, 691208, 691209, 691210, 691211

Bennett, T.B. 660825, 660827, 660828, 660829, 660830, 660831, 660904, 660906, 660910, 660911, 660912, 660913, 660914

Bennett, Miss A. 680831

Benson, Miss Carrie 680328

Benson, Miss E. 670415

Bentley, Miss Annie 671203, 671209, 671210

Berand, Miss Rose 680627

Bertie, J.C. 741109, 741110, 741117, 741118, 74119, 741120, 741121

Bertram, Miss Kate 720308

Best, F. 681026, 681027, 681028, 681029, 681030, 681031

Best, Mrs F. 681028, 681029, 681031

Beveridge, J.D. 670909, 670910, 670913

Bidson, J. 710323

Bigwood 730623, 730624, 730626, 730627, 730628

Bisson, James 691215, 691216

Bisson, Mrs James 680627, 680629, 680630, 680701, 680702, 680703, 691213, 691214

Blackwood, Miss Emilie 730517, 730519, 730520, 730521, 730522, 730523, 730524

Bloom 691206, 691207, 691208, 691209

Blyde 670920

Blythe, George 690828, 690830, 690831, 690901, 690902, 690903, 690904, 690906, 690907, 690908, 690909, 690910, 690911

Bond 661105, 661109, 680225, 680226, 680227, 680228, 280229

Booth, T. 660919

Booth, Miss 720308

Bosworth 680113, 680114, 680115

Bradley, P. 680225, 680226, 680228, 280229

Brady 690828, 690830, 690831, 690901, 690902, 690903, 690904, 690906, 690907, 690908, 690909, 690910, 690911

Bramah, Miss Marie 680328

Branch, Mrs 751115, 751116

Brennan, Miss Maude 691101, 691102, 691103, 691106, 711113

Brooklyn, Joseph

Brooks 730517, 730519, 730520, 730521, 730522, 730523, 730524

Brown 670124, 680225, 680226, 680229, 700404, 700405, 700406, 700409, 740926, 740928

Browning 691211

Brunelli, Miss Teresa 790616, 790617, 790618, 790619, 790620

Brunton, Watty 680526, 740926, 740928, 741003, 741005, 741006, 741008

Buchanan, J. 670916, 670917, 670918, 670919

Burchell, Miss Clara 681026, 681027, 681029, 681030, 681031

Burdett, Miss Agnes 660914

Burke 671118, 671119

Burnand 671118

Burney, Miss May 691213, 691214, 691215, 691216

Burns, Miss 670213

Burton, Mrs 670211, 670215, 670216

Burton, Mrs E.W. 670910, 670913

Butler 751115, 751116

Butler, J.H. 670729, 670801

Buxton, Mrs 751115, 751116

Campbell, Miss Isabel 790616, 790617, 790618, 790619, 790620

Cardon, Miss Marian 700228, 700301, 700303

Carr, Miss Carrie 691210, 691211

Chailes 730121

Chapman, Charles 751011, 751022

Charles, G.F. 670121, 670124, 670125, 670126, 670415, 670416

Charleton, Mrs Rose 680831

Chester, Harry 670211, 670213, 670214

Clarence 720115, 720116, 720117, 720118, 720119, 720120

Clare, Miss 751011

Clarke, C.A. 660521, 660523, 660529, 661105, 661106, 661107, 661109, 661110

Clarke, Mrs C.A. 660521, 660523, 660529, 661105, 661106, 661107, 661109, 661110, 751115, 751116

Clarkson, J.L. 681028, 681029, 681030, 681031

Clavering, Miss B. 730519, 730520, 730521, 730522, 730524

Clifford 730517

Clifford, Harry G. 660806, 671120, 680921, 680922

Clifton 730519

Collard, Miss Bessie 670212, 670213

Collens, W.J. 660825, 660827, 660828, 660906, 660919

Collett, John 680627, 680629, 680630, 680701, 680702, 680703

Colling 710320, 710322, 710323, 710325

Colville, W. 730728, 730729, 730730, 730731, 730801, 730802, 730804, 730805, 730806, 730807, 730808, 730809

Coneanen, E. 700124

Conliffe, Miss 710323

Conway, Miss Annie 730728, 730729, 730730, 730731, 730801, 730802, 730804, 730805, 730806, 730807, 730808, 730809

Cook, J. 690201

Cooke, Charles 690911

Cooke, Fred 671204, 671206, 691101, 691102, 691103, 691106, 711113

Cornwell 730519

Corri, Master 710325

Corri, Master N. 710325

Corri, Rupert 710320, 710321, 710322, 710323, 710324, 710325

Cosnett 680113, 680114, 680115, 680310

Coutts 720722, 720723

Coveney, Miss 730623, 730624, 730626, 730627, 730628

Cowdery 660825, 660827, 660828, 660829, 660830, 660831, 660904, 660906, 660919, 680627

Craddock, Miss Louisa 670123, 670124

Craig, James 660906

Creamer, Auguste 720308, 770205, 770207

Creswell 700404, 700405, 700406, 700409, 730517, 730519

Curtis 690906. 690907, 690908, 690909

Dalton, H. 660829, 660830, 660831, 660904, 660906, 660910, 660911, 660912, 660913, 660914

d'Alvéra, Miss Marie 681020?

Daly 700404, 700405, 700406, 700409

Daly, Miss 700404, 700405, 700406, 700409

Daly, Miss Celia 730109, 730113, 730114, 730115, 730116, 730117, 730122, 730128, 730207

Daly, Tim 691011, 691012, 691013

Dampier 660806

Davies 670209

Dearle, T. 700411

De Foe, Tom 721230, 721231, 730101, 730102, 730103, 730104, 730106, 730107, 730109, 730110, 730111, 730120, 730121, 730122, 730123, 730124, 730125, 730127, 730128, 730129, 730130, 730131, 730201, 730203, 730204, 730206, 730207, 730208, 730210, 730211

Delevanti, A. 680113, 680114, 680115, 680309, 680310, 710320, 710321, 710322, 710323, 710324

Delaville, Miss 660910, 660911, 660912, 660913, 660914

Doyne, J.H. 680526

Dugarde 660919

Duncan 670925

Edmunds, E. 700404, 700405, 700406, 700409

Edwards 701015, 730101, 730121, 730204

Edwards, Miss 701015

Egan, Miss M.A. 670121, 670123, 670125, 670126

Ellerton, George 700112

Elliott, C. 670213, 670216

Elliott, W. 680225, 680226, 680227, 680228, 280229

Ellison 670617

Emery, F. 670617

Emery, John 680526

English 730926

Ennis, J.W. 690104, 690105, 690106, 690120

Eversleigh, Miss Claire 730331, 730402, 730404

Eyre, Miss Claire 700328

Eyre, Miss Emilie 700328, 700329, 700330, 70031, 700401, 700402, 700404, 700405, 700406, 700409

Falconer, C. 680309, 680310

Farren, Miss E. 660910, 660911, 660912, 660913, 660914

Faulkner, Miss 670610, 670611, 670612, 670613, 670614, 670615

Fenton, Harry 661109, 661110

Ferrass 740926, 740928, 741003, 741005, 741006, 741008

Ferris 680309, 680310

Fiddes, Miss Madge 670415

Finch, Jones 751119

Fisher, Miss 661211

Fitzchapman 671023, 671024

Fitzdavis, Edward 660608, 660611, 660615, 660616

Fitzgerald, Miss L. 740926, 740928, 741003, 741005, 741006, 741008

Fitzjames 690919

Fletcher 691101, 691102, 691103, 691106, 691108, 691109, 691110, 691111, 691112, 691113

Flockten, C.P. 670909, 670913

Foote, Miss Bessie 670211, 670213, 670214, 691113

Foote, Miss Rose 670212, 670216, 691101, 691102, 691103, 691106, 691108, 691109, 691110, 691111, 691112, 691113, 700502, 700503, 700504, 700505

Forde, Miss Emily 680627, 680629, 680630, 680701, 680702, 680703

Forde, Miss Maggie 690906. 690907, 690908, 690909

Forrest, C. 690201

Forrester, Will 710320, 710321, 710325

Fossette, B. 740928, 741003, 741005, 741006, 741008

Fowler, Edward 660608, 670909, 670913

Foy, Charles 741109, 741110, 741117, 741118, 74119, 741120, 741121

Foy, Mrs. Charles 741117, 741118, 74119, 741120, 741121

Francis, James 680627

Francis 661105, 661109, 661110

Franks 660825, 660827, 660828, 660904, 660906, 660910, 660911, 660912, 660913, 660914, 660919

French 680627, 680629, 680630, 680701, 680702, 680703

French, Miss E. 740926, 740928, 741003, 741005, 741006, 741008

Fuéll, J.C. 691002, 691004, 691005, 691006, 691007, 691011, 691012, 691013

Fyson, Sydney 751011, 770707, 770710, 770711, 770712, 770713, 770714

Gallagher, J. 690201

Garden 680328

Gardiner, Miss Maggie 790616, 790617, 790618, 790619, 790620

Garrett 671023, 671024

Geary, S. 680225, 680226, 680227, 680228, 280229

Giddings, Miss 760103

Gilbert, W.H. 680526

Gill 690710, 690712, 690713, 690714, 690715, 690716

Glennie, Miss 731001

Glynn, Miss Marie 690918, 690920, 690921, 690922, 690923, 690924, 690925, 690930

Goddard, G.W. 690915, 690916, 700217, 700218, 700219

Goddard, Miss 670925

Gofton, E. 720415, 720715, 720722, 720723

Gordon 690919, 740926, 740928, 741003, 741005, 741006, 741008

Gordon, Miss Nelly 691213, 691214

Gordon, W. 691015

Goudge, Miss 691210

Goudge, Miss 691210

Grace, Edmund 670415, 670416

Gray, Miss Lizzie 660521, 660523, 660529, 660608, 660609, 660611, 660613, 660615, 660616, 690915,

Green, John 670121, 670123, 670124, 670125, 670126, 700411

Green, Sydney 680921, 680922

Greenwood, T. 730728, 730729, 730730, 730731, 730801, 730802, 730804, 730805, 730806, 730807, 730808, 730809

Griffiths, Miss C. 740926, 740928, 741003, 741005, 741006, 741008, 751011

Griffiths, Miss Clara 680627

Grisdale, Walter 751019, 751021

Groves, Miss 700404, 700405, 700406, 700409

Guiver, James 721230, 721231, 730101, 730102, 730103, 730104, 730106, 730107, 730108, 730109, 730110, 730111, 730120, 730121, 730122, 730123, 730124, 730125, 730127, 730128, 730129, 730130, 730131, 730201, 730203, 730204, 730205, 730206, 730207, 730208, 730210, 730211, 730212, 730728, 730729, 730730, 730731, 730801, 730802, 730804, 730805, 730806, 730807, 730808, 730809

Haines 670126

Haines, Miss 670124

Hall, Charles Irving 720715, 720716, 720719, 720722, 720723

Hallin 710320, 710321, 710322, 710323, 710324

Hambleton, Miss 660608, 661105, 661110

Hambleton, W.D.   660608, 660611, 660612, 660615, 661105, 661109, 661110

Hamblin 741102, 741103

Hammerton, Mrs 671028

Hampton 720115, 720116, 720117, 720118, 720119, 720120

Hampton, Henry 721111, 721112, 721113

Hampton, Miss 720115, 720116, 720117, 720118, 720119, 720120

Handley, J.W. 770707, 770710, 770711, 770712, 770713, 770714

Hannan, Philip 690524, 690525, 700314, 700315, 700318, 700319, 710117, 710118, 710119

Hannan, Mrs Philip   680908, 690524, 690525, 690527, 700314, 700315, 700318, 700319, 710116, 710117, 710118, 710119, 710120

Hannon, Mrs 670507, 670511

Hannon, P. 680302, 680303

Hannon, Mrs P. 680302, 680303

Harcourt 680929

Harcourt, Miss C. 690710, 690712, 690713, 690714, 690715, 690716

Harcourt, Miss 690828, 690830, 690831, 690901, 690902, 690903, 690904, 690906, 690907, 690908, 690909, 690910, 690911

Harcourt, Miss Lottie 730101, 730109, 730110, 730122, 730131, 710320, 710321, 710323, 730204

Hardman 670121

Hargraves 680831

Harker, G. 670211, 670212, 670213, 670214, 670215

Hannan, Mrs 670506, 670508, 670509, 670510

Harrington 671023, 671024

Harrington, J.C. 681026, 681028, 681029, 681030, 681031

Harrold 671028

Hartley 671118, 671119

Hartley 760103

Haynes, H.S. 690710, 690712, 690713, 690714, 690715, 690716

Healey 680328

Heber, Mrs 690710

Hellier, E. 670121, 670123, 670124, 670415, 670416

Hemdesee 670211, 670213, 670214, 670215

Henderson, Miss Marie 751011, 751016, 751018, 751019, 751021, 751022, 770707, 770710, 770711, 770712, 770713, 770714

Henley, Charles 721230, 721231, 730101, 730102, 730103, 730104, 730107, 730108, 730109, 730110, 730111, 730120, 730121, 730122, 730124, 730125, 730127, 730128, 730130, 730131, 730201, 730203, 730204, 730205, 730206, 730207, 730208, 730211, 730212

Henrique, Miss Emilie 741102, 741103

Henry 671023, 671024

Henry, E. Bayle 670121, 670123, 670124, 670126

Henry, Miss Polly 670123, 670124, 670125

Herbert 670123

Herbert, Lister 670826

Herbert, Miss Ettie 660611

Herbert, Miss Patty 680526

Herberte, Miss Minnie 691213, 691214

Herwyn 670128, 670129

Heyden, Miss 691206, 691207, 691208, 691209, 691210

Hilley, A. 730519, 730520, 730521, 730522, 730523, 730524

Hilton, A.T. 720308

Holland 760103

Hollingsworth, Miss Kate 721230, 721231, 730101, 730102, 730103, 730104, 730106, 730107, 730108, 730109, 730110, 730111, 730113, 730114, 730115, 730116, 730117, 730122, 730123, 730125, 730127, 730128, 730129, 730130, 730131, 730201, 730203, 730204, 730205, 730206, 730208, 730212, 730728, 730729, 730730, 730731, 730801, 730802, 730804, 730805, 730806, 730807, 730808, 730809

Holman, William 691213, 691214, 691215, 691216, 730519, 730520, 730521, 730522, 730523, 730524

Holmes 680914

Holmes, W.G. 691011, 691012, 691013, 691015

Hood 690201

Horsman, Charles 660825, 660827, 660828, 660829, 660830, 660831, 660904, 660906, 660912, 660913, 660914, 660919

Howard, Walter 710123, 710124, 710125, 710126, 710127, 710204

Howard, Mrs Walter 710123, 710124, 710125, 710126, 710127, 710204

Howard, Mrs 670213

Howitt, T.C. 671216, 760324

Hudspeth, F. 670918, 670919, 670920

Hurst, W. 691206, 691207, 691208, 691209, 691210, 691211

Hyde, Harry F. 790616, 790617, 790618, 790619, 790620

Irving, Miss 751011

Jackson, J. 730728, 730729, 730730, 730731, 730801, 730802, 730804, 730805, 730806, 730807, 730808, 730809

James 721230, 730101, 730102, 730110, 730111, 730121, 730123, 730127, 730131, 730204, 730208

James, Miss 721230, 730103, 730106, 730127, 730129, 730210

James, Maurice 670415, 670416

Jennings 760103

Johnson 730519, 730520, 730521, 730522, 730524

Johnson, Miss 730101

Johnstone, Miss Clara 691002, 691004, 691005, 691006, 691007, 691011, 691012, 691013

Johnstone, J. 740926, 740928, 741003, 741005, 741006, 741008

Johnstone, James 680627, 680629, 680630, 680701, 680702, 680703

Johnstone, W. 691015

Jones 681029, 681031

Jones 690710. 690712, 690713, 690714, 690715, 690716

Jones 6912306, 691207, 691208, 691209

Jones 740926, 740928

Jones, C. 670211, 670212, 670213, 670216

Jones, Mrs 670213

Joyce, Walter 660825, 660827, 660828, 660829, 660830, 660831, 660904, 660906, 660910, 660911, 660912, 660913, 660914, 660919, 751022

Julien 700112

Kane, Miss 710321

Kearney, Miss Julia 691213, 691214

Kelly 680225, 680226, 680229

Kempster, George 730121

King, Charles 670211, 670212, 670213, 670214, 670215

King, Miss Bessie 730918, 730919

Kinghorne, M. 730517, 730519, 730520, 730521, 730522, 730523, 730524

Kinley, W. 690201

Kinley, Mrs W. 690201

Knight 690906. 690907, 690908, 690909, 701003

Lacy, W. 740926, 740928, 741003, 741005, 741006, 741008, 751011, 770707, 770710, 770711, 770712, 770713, 770714

Laing, W. 741109, 741110, 741117, 741118, 74119, 741120, 741121

Lane, W.E. 680526

Laurie, W.P. 700221, 700222, 700223, 700224, 700228, 700301, 700303

Lauriston 730517

Lawson, Charles 661210

Lawson, Master 691210, 691211

Lavine, Miss 670919, 670920, 670921

Lavis, Miss 730517, 730519, 730520, 730521, 730522, 730524

Lea, Miss Sophia 720308

Lee, Miss Carrie 670215

Lee, Henry 691213, 691214, 691215, 691216

Leete, Miss Amy 741109, 741110

Leicester, Miss 670909, 670910, 670911, 670913

Leigh 751115, 751116

Leigh, Miss Kate 670801

Leigh, Miss Rose 671028, 671106

Lerigo, C. 680225, 680226, 680227, 680228, 280229

Leroy, C.V. 710322, 710324

Lester, F. 680831

Lester, Mrs. L 680831

Lever, E. 670415, 670416

Levey 741102, 741103

Levey, Chas 700411

Lewis 680526

Lewis, Miss Sarah 680224, 680225, 680226, 680227, 680228, 280229

Lewis, Walter 680113, 680114, 680115, 741109, 741110, 741116, 741117, 741118, 74119, 741120, 741121

Lewis, Mrs Walter 680113, 680114, 680115, 741109, 741111, 741117, 741118, 741119, 741120, 741121

Linley, Miss 730517

Litchfield, E.C. 801101

Loome, J.H. 720715, 720722

Lomax, Mrs 670121, 670124, 670125, 670126

Longrove, Mrs 700404, 700405, 700406, 700409

Loome, T.H. 720715, 720722

Lorrick, H. 691210, 691211

Louther, Henry 720304, 720305, 720306, 720307, 720308, 720309

Lyle, Miss 680309

Lyons, E.D. 670128, 670209

Lyons, Mrs E.D. 670128, 670129, 670201, 670206, 670208, 671203. 671204

Macdonald, Miss L. 730630, 730701, 730703, 730705

Mackay, Miss 670209

Mackney, Mrs 661110

Mackenzie 670211, 670212, 670213, 670214, 670215, 670216, 671209, 671210, 680225, 680226, 680227, 680228, 280229

Maclean 660825, 660827, 660828, 660829, 660830, 660831, 660904, 660906

Maclean, John 751022

Maitland, Charles 680309, 680310, 700411

Maitland, Mrs 680309, 680310

Maitland, Miss 680316

Mallilieu 671106

Mansfield, Miss Alice 680302, 680303

Marshall 790616, 790617, 790618, 790619, 790620

Masters, T. 681030

Mayhew 670909, 751115, 751116

McCabe, E. 691213, 691214, 691215, 691216

McEwen, Miss Nellie 680526

McNeill, A. McLean 691001, 691015

Medway, Miss 661022, 661023

Mellon, Miss Victoria 700411, 701003, 701015, 710320, 710321, 710322, 710323, 710324, 710325

Mellor, Mrs 690710, 690712, 690713, 690714, 690715, 690716

Melville 670211, 670213

Merton, Mrs A. 690710, 690712, 690713, 690714, 690715, 690716

M'Pherson 741102, 741103

Miller, Mrs G.H. 671023, 671024, 710320, 710323, 710325

Millward, Mrs 671204, 671209, 671210, 720420, 720722, 720723

Minshull 741102, 741103

Mitchell 670202, 670205, 670209

Moncries 670123

Monkhouse, H. 770707, 770710, 770711, 770712, 770713, 770714

Montague, A. 680627, 680629, 680630, 680701, 680702, 680703

Montague, James 730109, 730110, 730111, 730113, 730114, 730115, 730116, 730117, 730120, 730121, 730122, 730123, 730124, 730125, 730127, 730128, 730129, 730130, 730131, 730201, 730203, 730204, 730205, 730206, 730207, 730208, 730210, 730211, 730212

Montague, William 681207, 730926, 731001

Montague, Mrs. William 731001

Monte, H. 691011, 691012, 691013, 691015

Montford, Miss Grace 670909

Moorhouse 670215

Morgan 681028, 681029, 681030, 681031, 691011, 691012, 691013

Morgan, Mrs 681028, 681029

Morgan, C. 691011, 691015

Morgan, Mrs C. 691015

Morgan Smith, Mrs. Harriet 690915, 690916, 691015, 691112, 691113, 691122, 691210, 700117, 700507, 700525, 701015, 701020, 701021, 701114, 710203, 710217, 710324, 710410, 710411, 710412, 710413, 710414, 710415, 710721, 720108, 720109, 720110, 720111, 720112, 720113, 720422, 720719, 721230, 721231, 730101, 730102, 730103, 730104, 730106, 730107, 730108, 730109, 730110, 730111, 730120, 730121, 730122, 730123, 730124, 730125, 730127, 730128, 730129, 730130, 730131, 730201, 730203, 730204, 730205, 730206, 730207, 730208, 730210, 730211, 730212, 730213, 730404, 730523, 730704, 730728, 730729, 730730, 730731, 730801, 730802, 730804, 730805, 730806, 730807, 730808, 730809, 730926, 740518, 740520, 740601, 740629, 740701, 740907, 740908, 741106, 741120, 751112, 751119, 751203, 760324, 760520, 760522, 760608, 760609, 760612, 770302, 780316, 780318,780325, 780406, 780408, 780429, 780430, 781025, 781029, 790922, 790923, 790924, 790925, 790926, 790927,

790929, 790930, 791001, 791002, 791003, 791004, 800816, 800817, 800818, 800819, 800820, 800821

Mortimer, Miss Bella 700129

Munro 670124

Munro, J.C. 721230, 721231, 730101, 730102, 730103, 730104, 730106, 730107

Munro, Lewis Mourdaunt 710320, 710321, 710322, 710323, 710324

Murphy, J.A. 670514, 670518

Murray, Miss 701015

Myers, Edgar J. 730404

Nash, Miss 680420, 680421, 681207

Nash, Miss Clara 700411

Neil, Miss 690524, 690525

Nelson, Alfred 751022

Nelson, George 700411

Nelson, Robert 681026, 681027, 681028, 681029, 681030, 681031, 691101, 691102, 691103, 691106

Nerney 670910

Newbound. E. 730623, 730624, 730626, 730627, 730628, 730630, 730701, 730703, 730705

Newham, Miss 730623, 730624, 730626, 730627, 730628

Newton, Mrs George 660608, 660611

Nillson, Miss 730109, 730110, 730122, 730130, 730131

Noakes 760103

Norman 660919

Norris 671118, 671119, 690201

O'Lacy, Mrs 690201

Oliphant 690710, 690712, 690713, 690714, 690715, 690716

Osborne 661105, 751011

Pakenham   670211, 670212, 670213, 670214, 730331, 730401, 730402

Parke, C. 680831

Parker 671216

Parker, H.   751011, 770707, 770710, 770711, 770712, 770713, 770714

Parker, Miss 691015

Parry, Alfred 701003, 701017

Parry, J. 730630, 730701, 730703, 730705, 730926, 731001

Paulton, Joseph 700124

Peeton 730128

Percival 670211, 670212, 670213, 670214, 670215, 670217

Percival, T.   730728, 730729, 730730, 730731, 730801, 730802, 730804, 730805, 730806, 730807, 730808, 730809

Percy 690828, 690830, 690831, 690901, 690902, 690903, 690904, 690906, 690907, 690908, 690909, 690910, 690911, 700404, 700405, 700406, 700409

Percy, Miss   730623, 730624, 730626, 730627, 730628

Perry, W. 670909, 670913

Phague 710323

Pickard, J. 720226, 720227, 720228, 720229, 720302

Pitt, Charles 691213, 691214, 691215, 691216, 730630, 730701, 730703, 730705

Pitt, W. 730623, 730624, 730626, 730627, 730628, 730630, 730701, 730703, 730705

Pitt, W.H. 670415

Pollock, W.H. 730804

Poole 661022, 661023

Poole, J.P. 671118, 671119

Potter, T.H. 680921, 680922, 700502, 700503, 700504, 700505

Poynter, Mrs 660919

Price, Edward 691112, 691113

Price, Master 670514, 670518

Proctor 670121

Quinton, Miss Kate 670202, 670205, 670209

Rainbow 661022, 661023

Raye, Weston P. 710320, 710321, 710322, 710323, 710325

Raymond, Mat 691206, 691207, 691208, 691209, 691210, 691211

Raynham, Walter 730517, 730519, 730520, 730521, 730522, 730523, 730524

Reardon 680421, 691101, 691102, 691103, 691106

Reed, Miss 680914, 680916

Reeve 740926, 740928

Reeves 660910, 660911, 660912, 660913, 660914, 751115, 751116

Reeves, Charles 670729, 670801

Reid 730517

Reid, Miss M. 670415

Reynold, E.R. 691122

Reynolds 670121, 670129, 670201, 670208, 670209, 680225, 680226, 680229, 680421, 730623, 730624, 730626, 730627, 730628

Rhoyds 751115, 751116

Richards, G. 670211, 670212, 670213, 670214, 670215

Richards, J. 681028, 681029, 681031

Richardson 751011

Richardson, A. 680302, 680303

Richmond, Miss Emma 790616, 790617, 790618, 790619, 790620

Righton 710325

Rimmell, Miss 710323

Rivers, B. 680225, 680226, 680228, 280229

Rivers, H. 660825, 660827, 660828, 660829, 660830, 660831, 660904, 660906, 660910, 660911, 660912, 660913, 660914

Robberds, Emma 670408, 680302, 680303

Roberts 661105, 670123, 671118

Roberts, D. 670121, 670124, 670415, 670416

Roberts, David 670801

Roberts, Mrs Emma 770227, 770228, 770303

Roberts, G. 721230, 721231, 730101, 730102, 730103, 730104, 730106, 730107, 730108, 730109, 730110, 730111, 730113, 730114, 730115, 730116, 730117, 730122, 730123, 730124, 730125, 730127, 730128, 730129, 730130, 730131, 730201, 730203, 730205, 730206, 730207, 730208, 730210, 730211, 730212, 730519, 730520, 730521, 730522, 730523, 730524

Roberts, Mrs G. 721230, 730101, 730103, 730104, 730106, 730107, 730108, 730110, 730111, 730124, 730125, 730127, 730128, 730129, 730131, 730201, 730203, 730204, 730205, 730207, 730208, 730210, 730211

Roberts, Miss Kate 720415, 730210

Robertson 671216, 700404, 700405, 700406, 700409

Robinson, G. 691011, 691012, 691013, 691015

Robinson, Miss C. 691206, 691207, 691208, 691209, 691210, 691211

Robinson, Miss Georgina 700217, 700218, 700219

Robson, Mat 720308

Rochford, M. 730519, 730520, 730521, 730522, 730524

Rokeby 790616, 790617, 790618, 790619, 790620

Rooke 680526

Rosalind, Miss Ida 691011, 691012, 691013, 770205, 770207

Rose, Miss 680227, 680228, 680229

Rose, Miss J. 670216

Roselle, Miss Ada   680627, 680629, 680630, 680701, 680702, 680703, 681026, 681028, 681030

Roselle, Miss Amy 681026, 681027, 681028, 681030, 681031

Rosette 680421

Ross, Miss Adelaide 660806, 660807, 670322, 670323

Rousby 751115, 751116

Rudge, J.F. 701015, 701114

Rusette 680421

Russell, T. 671028

Russell, Mrs 680627, 680629, 680630, 680701, 680702, 680703

Ryder, John 751022

Sanders, Miss Mary   691206, 691207, 691208, 691209, 691210, 691211

Sandford 760103

Sault 690828, 690830, 690831, 690901, 690902, 690903, 690904, 690906, 690907, 690908, 690909, 690910, 690911

Saunders 690710, 690712, 690713, 690714, 690715, 690716

Saunders, Miss Maud 700406, 700409

Saunders, S. 671118, 671119

Saville, Mrs 660904, 660906

Schavey, Miss 660919

Scott 670124, 701003, 701015

Scott, J.F. 701021

Scottie, Miss Cecilia 680921, 680922, 680923, 680924

Seaman, Alice 691213, 691214, 691215, 670216

Searle 670121

Selton, Miss Laura 690106, 690122, 691210, 691211

Sennet, Charles 670916, 670917, 670918, 670919, 670921, 690710,

690712, 690713, 690714, 690715, 690716, 770707, 770710, 770711, 770712, 770713, 770714

Sennett, Edwin 670121, 670123, 670124, 670125, 670126, 670415, 670416

Seymour 670128, 670209, 671209, 671210

Seymour, Charles 660521, 660523, 660608, 660612, 660613, 660615

Seymour, Frank 751011

Seymour, Miss 680908

Seymour, Miss T. 690201

Sharpe, Miss 670209

Shepherd 690710, 690712, 690713, 690714, 690715, 690716

Sheridan, Brinsley 720722

Siddons 720308

Siddons, Harry 710320, 710321, 710322, 710323, 710324, 710325

Sidney 670121

Sidney, Miss Emma 710320, 710321, 710322, 710323, 710324, 710325, 721231, 730103, 730106, 730107, 730108, 730109, 730111, 730120, 730121, 730122, 730125, 730127, 730129, 730130, 730203, 730205, 730206, 730208, 730210, 730728, 730729, 730730, 730731, 730801, 730802, 730804, 730805, 730806, 730807, 730808, 730809

Simeon 680225, 680226, 680227, 680228, 280229

Simkins, W. 670801

Simmonds, H. 681028, 681029, 681031

Simpson, Charles 741109, 741110, 741117, 741118, 74119

Simpson, W.T. 730804

Sinclair 670910, 670913

Sinclair, Miss Annie 670729, 670801

Sinclair, E.V. 670909, 670910, 670913, 700124

Sinclair, Lewis 691206, 691207, 691208, 691209, 691210, 691211

Smith 670121, 730128, 730207

Smith, J.C. 681026

Smith, S. 730519

Smith, Miss Annie 670729

Smith, Miss Mary 680624

Smythe 700112

Soutar, R. 660825, 660827, 660828, 660829, 660830, 660831, 660904, 660906, 660912, 660913, 660914, 660919

Spencer, George 741102, 741103

St. Clair, Miss Jessy 671118, 671119, 680921, 680922, 680923, 680924, 680925, 680928, 680929, 680930, 681001, 681002, 681003

St. Cross, Mrs M. 680831

St. Maur 690710, 690712, 690713, 690714, 690715, 690716

Stacey 680831

Stafford, Miss Maude 730519, 730520, 730521, 730522, 730524

Stanhope, Butler 730331, 730402, 730404

Stanley, E.T. 751011

Stanley, G.H. 680627, 680629, 680630, 680701, 680702, 680703

Stanley, Miss 701015, 730926, 731001

Stanley, Miss Laura 751011, 751022

Stanley, Miss Harriet 671118, 671119

Steele, Chas.

Steele, R.P. 691015

Stephens 700404, 700405, 700406, 700409

Stephenson, Mrs C.H. 690710, 690712, 690713, 690714, 690715, 690716

Stevens 690710, 690712, 690713, 690714, 690715, 690716

Appendix D: Supporting Performers

Stevens 751011

Stevens, Miss L. 680526

Stilt, A. 680526

Stinton, John 670121, 670123, 670124, 670126, 670415, 670416

Stinton, Mrs John 670415, 670416, 680203

Stoddart, B. 720715, 720722

Stoddart, H. 670610, 670611, 670612, 670613, 670614, 670615, 700523, 790922, 790923, 790924, 790925, 790926, 790927, 790929, 790930, 791001, 791002, 791003, 790104

Stoddart, Mrs H. 700523, 790922, 790923, 790924, 790925, 790926, 790927, 790929, 790930, 791001, 791002, 791003, 790104

Stuart 670213

Stuart, Barry 790616, 790617, 790618, 790619, 790620

Summerfield 721230, 730127

Summerville 681028, 681029, 681030, 681031

Swan 741102, 741103

Swanton 670910, 670913

Tannett, C.S. 670920

Taylor, Miss A. 670214, 670216, 680228, 680229

Temple, W. Clarence 690804

Temple, Miss H. 701017

Terry, F.A. 691213, 691214, 691215, 691216, 701003, 701015

Thompson 681030, 681031, 730523

Thompson, Harry D. 660521, 660523, 660529, 660608, 660609, 660611, 660613, 660615, 660616

Thompson, J.H. 691206, 691207, 691208, 691209, 691210, 691211

Thorne, Miss M. 671118, 671119, 691002, 691004, 691005, 691006, 691007, 691011, 691012, 691013, 691015

Thorne, Miss Marguerite 760324

Thorne, Miss Sarah 670826, 670827

Thorne, R. 670826

Thornton, Mrs 671209, 671210

Tostivan 691213, 691214, 691215, 691216

Towler 740926, 740928, 741003, 741005, 741006, 741008

Travers, Miss Annie 740926, 740928, 741003, 741005, 741006, 741008

Tullock, W. 670617

Tully, Miss 760103

Turvey, Bella 690906. 690907, 690908, 690909

Tyler 681030

Tyrrell 671028, 671106

Vaughan, H. 740926, 740928, 741003, 741005, 741006, 741008, 751011

Vaughan, Phillip 790616, 790617, 790618, 790619, 790620

Victor, Miss 730517

Vincent, George 680627, 680629, 680630, 680701, 680702, 680703

Vincent, Miss Annette 680526

Vivash, Miss Sarah E. 670121, 670123, 670124, 670125, 670126, 670916, 670917, 670918

Vollaire 700502, 700503, 700504, 700505

Waite, Master 730123

Waldron, Miss Eliza 671023, 671224

Waldron, W.R. 671023, 671024

Walkon 710323, 710325

Wallace 670916, 670917, 670918, 670919, 670920, 670921

Wallace, W.H. 680225, 680226, 680227, 680228, 280229

Walters, J. 660825, 660827, 660828, 660829, 660830, 660831, 660904, 660906

Appendix D: Supporting Performers

Walters, L. 741109

Warburton 740926, 740928, 741003, 741005, 741006, 741008

Ward, Miss 661023

Warden, J.F. 670909, 670911, 670912, 670914, 700129

Warden, Mrs J.F. 700124, 700125, 700128

Waterfield 700404, 700405, 700406, 700409

Watkins 700221, 700222, 700223, 700224

Watkins, John 690524, 690525

Watkins, Mrs 670209

Watson 670415, 671203

Watson, J.B. 691011, 691012, 691013, 691015

Watts, F.J. 680526

Weathersby, Miss B. 670213, 670216

Weldone 710322, 710323, 710324

West 670211, 670215

Weston, Miss Clara 670211, 670212, 670213, 670214, 670215, 670216

Weston, Miss Corbett 700112

Weston, J.P. 670619

Wetherill 691206, 691207, 691208, 691209, 691210, 691211

Weymark 660615, 671216

Whitbread 790616, 790617, 790618, 790619, 790620

Whitby, Augustus 690804

White 680421

White, Master Willie 730128, 730204

Wilkinson 680225, 680226, 680227, 680228, 280229

Williams 660919, 721230, 730102, 730106, 730121, 730123, 730127, 730129, 730204, 751115, 751116

Williams, Arthur 670211, 670212, 670213, 670214, 670215, 670216

Appendix E:
Lessees, Managers, Staff

Chronology

1866

London, Gravesend 660521-616   Samuel Morgan Smith
     Stage Manager and Director: H.D. Thompson
Birmingham, Prince of Wales 660806-11   Mrs. Macready
London, Olympic 660825-919   Edward Hastings
Leicester 661022-27   G. Owen
     Stage Manager: J. Hudspeth
     Prompter: H. Mayhew
Rochester 661105-10   C.A. Clarke
Northampton 661112-17   H. Nicholson
Kilmarnock 661119-1201   John Wylsone
Paisley 661203-08   T.C. Howitt
Coatbridge 661210-15   W.H. Sennett
Carlisle 661221-29   James Macdonald

1867

Worcester 670114-19   ?
Hartlepool 670121-26   Charles King

Stage Manager E. Bayle Henry

Dundee 670128-209 E.D. Lyons

Bradford 670211-16 F.B. Egan and Harry Read

Aberdeen 670219-23 A. McLein McNeill

Hanley 670225-302 John Windley

Tredegar 670304-16 ?

Cardiff 670318-23 George Melville

Darlington 670401-06 Macdonald

North Shields 670408-13 George Grant

Hartlepool 670415-16 W.H. Pitt and G.F. Charles

Middlesborough 670417

Wrexham 670506-11 H.S. Ashton

Kendal 670513-18 ?

Wigan 670603-08 but theatre was closed by the manager, Mr. Baldie, on June 1st.

Barrow-in-Furness 670610-15 A. Malcolmson

Bolton 670617-22 J.P. Weston

Aberystwyth 670624-29 H.S. Ashton

Lancaster 670701-06 ?

Stockport 670715-20 ?

Great Grimsby 670729-803 W. Raymond

Margate 670826-27 Miss Thorne

Belfast 670909-14 J.F. Warden

Dublin 670916-21 George Owen

Arbroath 670924-28 ?

Rochdale 671007-12? (cancelled due to death of wife on October 6th)

Barnstaple 671021-26 F. Belton (may have been cancelled too)

Rochdale 671028-1102, 671107-11 S.A. Pickuls

Birkenhead 671112-20 Miss M. Thorne

Great Yarmouth 671125-30 C.A. Clarke

Dundee 671202-14 Mrs. E.D. Lyons

Dunfermline 671216-21 ?

1868

Kidderminster 670113-18 Mr. Mellon and Mr. Maitland

Cheltenham 680203-08 S. Onley

Leeds 680224-29 Arthur and Charles Leclercq
Dewsbury 680302-07 Job Joy
Kidderminster 680309-14 A. Stooke
Sunderland 680327-28 Hudspeth and Loome
Wakefield 680330-404 C.H. Duval
Newcastle-on-Tyne 680407-08 G. Stanley
Wishaw 680413-18 ?
Blackburn 680420-25 C.H. Duval
Stockport 680427 ?
Wishaw 680506-16 ?
London, Marylebone 680526 Clifford Lacy
     Acting Manager: T. Austin Stack
Preston 680622-26 C.H. Duval
London, Pavilion 680627-703 Edward Hastings
Margate 680820-22 R. Thorne
Ipswich 680831-905 Miss Ada Dowsing and Ernest Siddons
Aberystwith 680907-08 H.S. Ashton
Wrexham 680914-16 H.S. Ashton
Oswestry 680917-18 H.S. Ashton
Wrexham 680919 H.S. Ashton
Dublin 680921-1003 George Owen
Wrexham 681010 H.S. Ashton
Swansea 681012-24 Mrs. C. Pitt
Cardiff 681026-31 W.H. Rosella
     Stage manager: J.C. Smith; Prompter: Richards
Tunbridge Wells 681109-14 ?
Hastings 681207-19 William Montague

1869
Port Glasgow 690201-06 ?
Hanley 690215-20 John Windley
Northampton 690329-403 C.A. Clarke
Wrexham 690524-29 Philip Hannan
Stockton-on-Tees 290531-606 Mr. Stoddart
London, Royal Alfred 690710 W. Worboys
     Acting Manager: Charles Harcourt
London, Sadler's Wells 690804 Mr. Edgar

Glasgow 690828-911 Charles Cooke
     Stage Manager: George Blythe
Arbroath 690914-16 Mr. Kilpack
Edinburgh, Princess's 690918-1001 ?
Dundee 691002-15 A. McLean McNeill
Aberdeen 691101-13 Edward Price
Perth 691115-16 ?
Longton 691122-27 M. Wardhaugh
Hull 691206-11 C.H. Duval
     Acting Manager: T.M. White
Exeter 691213-18 Frederick Neebe

1870

Maidstone 700112-18 George Ellerton
     Stage Manager: Mr. Julien
Belfast 700124-29 J.F. Warden
Dublin 700201-08 George Owen
Whitehaven 700214-19 Mr. Paumier
Dublin 700221-312 George Owen
Wrexham 700314-19 Philip Hannan
Birmingham 700328-409 James Rodgers
Wolverhampton 700411-12 Harry Simms
Northampton 700425-29 Walter Edwin
Rochdale 700502-07 S.A. Pickuls
Lancaster 700516-19, 700523-25 Richard Stoddart
Bolton 700620-21 J.P. Weston
Douglas, Isle of Man 700728-29 Mercer H. Simpson
Bilston 700925 Mr. Parry
Shrewsbury 701003-17 David Lewis
     Acting Manager: Alfred Parry
Ludlow 701021 Alfred Parry
Ross-on-Wye 701114 ?

1871

Shrewsbury 710109-14 David Lewis
     Acting Manager: Alfred Parry
Wrexham 710116-20 Philip Hannan

Landport 710123-204 William Montague
Leicester 710211-18 John Windley
West Hartlepool 710320-25 J. Batist
     Acting Manager: C.V. Leroy; Prompter: Hallin
Earlston 710410-15 Forrest Knowles
Dundee 710717-22 Miss Annie Manners
Glasgow 711111-18 W. Sidney

1872
Brighouse 720108-13 ?
Macclesfield 720115-27 Henry Hampton
Carmarthen 720129-203 John Russell
Sheffield 720226-309 Thomas Youdan
Macclesfield 720412-22 Brinsley Sheridan
     Acting Manager: T.H. Loome
Warrington 720715-23 Brinsley Sheridan
     Acting Manager: T.H. Loome
Mexborough ca. 720903-ca. 1208 (14 weeks)
Runcorn 721111-16 Henry Hampton
West Hartlepool 721230-31 W.H. Wright
     Acting Manager: William Chadwick Dews

1873
West Hartlepool 730101-11 W.H. Wright
     Acting Manager: William Chadwick Dews
Hartlepool 730120-215 William Chadwick Dews
Coventry 730317-22 F.G. Venimore
Southport 730331-405 Thomas Harris
Neath 730421-26 ?
London, Surrey 730517-24 Miss Virginia Blackwood
     Acting Manager: Murray Wood
London, Britannia 730623-705 Mrs. S. Lane
West Hartlepool 730728-805 William Chadwick Dews
Grantham 730918-19 Miss Jenny Floyd
Barnstaple 730922-1004 William Montague
Newton Abbot 731013-16, 731103-08 William Montague

1874

Fowey 740518-20 ?
Grampound 740601 ?
Roche 740629-701 ?
Truro 740907-08 ?
London, Elephant and Castle 740926-1009 R.E. Freeborne
Oldham 741102-07 G. Spencer
Coxhoe 741109-21 William Chadwick Dews
Sutton-in-Ashfield 741123-28 T. Hughes
Tunstall 741130-1212 ?
Gloucester 741214-19 Auguste Creamer

1875

Chesterfield 750426-507 B. Kelly
London, Elephant & Castle 751011-23 Marie Henderson
        Acting Manager: J. Aubrey
London, New Albion 751108-13 W. Lovegrove
Greenwich 751115-20 Jones Finch
        Stage Manager: Herbert Rhoyds
        Scenic Artist: W. Laffer
Cardiff 751129-1204 Louis Esmonde

1876

Aberdare 760103-06 ?
Dowlais 760110 ?
Merthyr Tydfil 760117 ?
South Wales 760124-29 ?
Macclesfield 760131-202 E. Bell
Paisley 760318-25 W. Williams
        Stage Manager: T.C. Howitt
Perth 760417-22 ?
Hawick 760424-29 ?
Earlston 760520, 760522 ?
Stow 760608-09, 760612 ?

1877

Glasgow 770205-10 Auguste Creamer

Belfast 770226-303 J.F. Warren
Musselburgh 770402-14 ?
Crook 770514-19 ?
Croydon 770609 ?
London, Elephant and Castle 770630-714 J. Aubrey
   Directress: Miss Marie Henderson
   Stage Manager: Frank Fuller
   Musical Director: H. Day
Rochester 771008-13, 771118 ?

1878
Coventry 780316, 780318 E. Bell
Atherstone 780325 ?
Hinckley 780406, 780408 ?
Lutterworth 780429-30 ?
Billingborough 781025, 781029 ?
Spalding 781220 ?

1879
Scarborough 790616-20 J. Eldred and T.D. Yorke
Barnsley 790922-1004 Ben Walker
Keigley 791110-15 ?

1880
Leeds 800809-21 J. Hobson
   Acting Manager: Henry Leslie
Ashton-under-Lyne 801101-06 E.C. Litchfield

1881
Barnsley 811007, 81110, 811222 ?

Personnel
Ashton, H.S.: Wrexham 670506-11; Aberystwyth 670624-29,
 680907-08; Wrexham 680914-16; Oswestry 680917-18;
 Wrexham 680919, 681010
Aubrey, J.: London, Elephant & Castle 751011-23, 770630-714
Baldie: Wigan 670603-08

Batist, J. West Hartlepool 710320-25

Bell, E.: Macclesfield 760131-202; Coventry 780316, 780318

Belton, F.: Barnstaple 671021-26

Blackwood, Miss Virginia: London, Surrey 730517-24

Blythe, George: Glasgow 690828-911

Branston, W.S.: Tunstall 741130-1212

Charles, G.F.: Hartlepool 670415-16

Clarke, C.A.: Rochester 661105-10; Great Yarmouth 671125-30; Northampton 690329-403

Cooke, Charles: Glasgow 690828-911

Creamer, Auguste: Gloucester 741214-19; Glasgow 770205-10

Dews, William Chadwick: West Hartlepool 721230-31, 730101-11; Hartlepool 730120-215; West Hartlepool 730728-805; Coxhoe 741109-21

Dowsing, Miss Ada: Ipswich 680831-905

Duval, C.H.: Wakefield 680330-404; Blackburn 680420-25; Preston 680622-26; Hull 691206-11

Edgar: London, Sadler's Wells 690804

Edwin, Walter: Northampton 700425-29

Egan, F.B.: Bradford 670211-16

Eldred, J.: Scarborough 790616-20 and T.D. Yorke

Ellerton, George: Maidstone 700112-18

Esmonde, Louis: Cardiff 751129-1204

Finch, Jones: Greenwich 751115-20

Floyd, Miss Jenny: Grantham 730918-19

Freeborne, R.E.: London, Elephant and Castle 740926-1009

Fuller, Frank: London, Elephant and Castle 770630-714

Grant, George: North Shields 670408-13

Hampton, Henry: Macclesfield 720115-27; Runcorn 721111-16

Hannan, Philip: Wrexham 690524-29, 700314-19, 710116-20

Harcourt, Charles: London, Royal Alfred 690710

Harris, Thomas: Southport 730331-405

Hastings, Edward: London, Olympic 660825-919; London, Pavilion 680627-703

Heffernon, E.: Londonderry 690104-22

Henderson, Marie: London, Elephant & Castle 751009-23, 770630-714

Henry, E. Bayle: Hartlepool 670121-26
Hobson, J.: Leeds 800809-21
Howitt, T.C.: Paisley 661203-08, 760318-25
Hudspeth, J.: Leicester 661022-27; Sunderland 680327-28
Hughes, T.: Sutton-in-Ashfield 741123-28
Joy, Job: Dewsbury 680302-07
Julien: Maidstone 700112-18
Kelly, B.: Chesterfield 750426-507
Kilpack: Arbroath 690914-16
King, Charles: Hartlepool 670121-26
Knowles, Forrest: Earlston 710410-15
Lacy, Clifford: London, Marylebone 680526
Lane, Mrs S.: London, Britannia 730623-705
Leclercq, Arthur: Leeds 680224-29
Leclercq, Charles: Leeds 680224-29
Leroy, C.V.: West Hartlepool 710320-25
Leslie, Henry: Leeds 800809-21
Lewis, David: Shrewsbury 701003-17, 710109-14
Litchfield, E.C.: Ashton-under-Lyne 801101-06
Loome, T.H.: Sunderland 680327-28; Macclesfield 720412-22;
    Warrington 720715-23
Lovegrove, W.: London, New Albion 751108-13
Lyons, E.D.: Dundee 670128-209
Lyons, Mrs E.D.: Dundee 671202-14
Macdonald: Darlington 670401-06
Macdonald, James: Carlisle 661221-29
Macready, Mrs: Birmingham, Prince of Wales 660806-11
Maitland: Kidderminster 670113-18
McNeill, A. McLein: Aberdeen 670219-23; Dundee 691002-15
Manners, Miss Annie: Dundee 710717-22
Mellon: Kidderminster 670113-18
Melville, George: Cardiff 670318-23
Malcolmson, A.: Barrow-in-Furness 670610-15
Montague, William: Hastings 681207-19; Landport 710123-204;
    Barnstaple 730922-1004; Newton Abbot 731013-16, 731103-08
Neebe, Frederick: Exeter 691213-18
Nicholson, H.: Northampton 661112-17

Onley, S.: Cheltenham 680203-08

Owen, G.: Leicester 661022-27

Owen, George: Dublin 670916-21, 680921-1003, 700201-08, 700221-312

Parry, Alfred: Leeds 680224-29; Bilston 70925; Ludlow 701021; Shrewsbury 710109-14

Paumier, Mr.: Whitehaven 700214-19

Pickuls, S.A.: Rochdale 671028-1102, 671107-11, 700502-07

Pitt, Mrs C.: Swansea 681012-24

Pitt, W.H.: Hartlepool 670415-16

Price, Edward: Aberdeen 691101-13

Raymond, W.: Great Grimsby 670729-803

Read, Harry: Bradford 670211-16

Rhoyds, Herbert: Greenwich 751115-20

Rodgers, James: Birmingham 700328-409

Rosella, W.H.: Cardiff 681026-31

Russell, John: Carmarthen 720129-203

Sennett, W.H.: Coatbridge 661210-15

Sheridan, Brinsley: Macclesfield 720412-22; Warrington 720715-23

Siddons, Ernest: Ipswich 680831-905

Sidney, W.: Glasgow 711111-18

Simms, Harry: Wolverhampton 700411-12

Simpson, Mercer H.: Douglas, Isle of Man 700728-29

Smith, J.C.: Cardiff 681026-31

Smith, Samuel Morgan: London, Gravesend 660521-616

Spencer, G.: Oldham 741102-07

Stack, T. Austin: London, Marylebone 680526

Stanley, G.: Newcastle-on-Tyne 680407-08

Stoddart, Mr. Stockton-on-Tees 690531-605

Stoddart, Richard: Lancaster 700516-19, 700523-25

Stooke, A.: Kidderminster 680309-14

Thompson, H.D.: London, Gravesend 660521-616

Thorne, Miss M.: Margate 670826-27; Birkenhead 671112-20

Thorne, R.: Margate 680820-22

Venimore, F.G.: Coventry 730317-22

Waldron, W.R.: Barnstaple 671021-26

Walker, Ben: Barnsley 790922-1004
Warden, J.F.: Belfast 670909-14, 700124-29
Wardhaugh, M.: Longton 691122-27
Warren, J.F.: Belfast 770226-303
Weston, J.P.: Bolton 670617-22, 700620-21
White, T.M.: Hull 691206-11
Williams, W.: Paisley 760320-25
Windley, John: Hanley 670225-302, 690215-20; Leicester 710211-18
Wood, Murray: London, Surrey 730517-24
Worboys, W.: London, Royal Alfred 690710
Wright, W.H.: West Hartlepool 721230-31, 730101-11
Wylsone, John: Kilmarnock 661119-1201
Yorke, T.D.: Scarborough 790616-20
Youdan, Thomas: Sheffield 720226-309

Unknowns
Aberdare 760103-06
Arbroath 670924-28
Atherstone 780325
Barnsley 811007, 81110, 811222
Billingborough 781025, 781029
Brighouse 720108-13
Crook 770514-19
Croydon 770609
Dowlais 760110
Dunfermline 671216-21
Earlston 760520, 760522
Edinburgh, Princess's 690918-1001
Fowey 740518-20
Grampound 740601
Hawick 760424-29
Hinckley 780406, 780408
Keigley 791110-15
Kendal 670513-18
Lancaster 670701-06
Lutterworth 780429-30

Merthyr Tydfil 760117
Mexborough   ca. 720903-ca. 1208 (14 weeks)
Middlesborough 670417
Musselburgh 770402-14
Neath 730421-26
Perth 691115-16, 760417-22
Port Glasgow 690201-06
Roche 740629-701
Rochester 771008-13, 771118
Ross-on-Wye 701114
South Wales 760124-29
Spalding 781220
Stockport 670715-20, 680427
Stow 760608-09, 760612
Tredegar 670304-16
Truro 740907-08
Tunbridge Wells 681109-14
Wishaw 680413-18; 680506-16
Worcester 670114-19

Index

305

B

C

F

G

Harvard University, 31, 35-36, 45n98

Hastings, 136, 247, 254, 295, 301

Hastings, Edward, 293, 295, 300

Hastings, Warren, 126

Hawick, 225, 250, 254, 298, 303

Hawick Theatre, 225

Haymarket Theatre, London, 19, 195

Haynes, H.S., 274

Healey, Mr., 274

Hebden Bridge, 192n36, 249, 254

Heber, Mrs., 274

Heffernon, E., 300

Hellier, E., 274

Hemdesee, Mr., 274

Henderson, Miss Marie, 274

Henley, Charles, 274

Henrique, Miss Emilie, 274

Henry, E. Bayle, 275

Henry, Miss Polly, 275

Henry, Mr., 274

Henry IV (Shakespeare), 216n11

Henty, G.A., *The March to Magdala*, 164

Herbert, Lister, 275

Herbert, Miss Ettie, 275

Herbert, Miss Patty, 275

Herbert, Mr., 275

Herberte, Miss Minnie, 275

Hereford, 172

Herwyn, Mr., 275

Hewlett, Aaron Molyneaux, 36-37

Heyden, Miss, 275

high school, 1, 13

Hilley, A., 275

Hilton, A.T., 275

Hinckley, 236, 250, 254, 299, 303

Hindoo, 224

Historical Society of Pennsylvania, 3, 10-12

hoax, 135

Hobson, J., 299, 301

Holland, Mr., 275

Hollingsworth, Miss Kate, 275

Holman, William, 275

Holmes, Mr., 275

Holmes, Oliver Wendell, 23

Holmes, W.G., 275

Honey Moon, The (John Tobin), 195, 213, 215, 232, 259

Hood, Mr., 275

Hood, Thomas, 26, 275

Horbling School-room, Billingborough, 236

Horsman, Charles, 275

Houghton Library, 31, 35

House of Blois, 188

House of Commons, 126, 139n59

Howard, Morgan, 135, 139n59

Howard, Mrs., 275

Howard, Mrs. Walter, 275

M

S